Incident Response
Evidence Preservation and Collection

By Information Warfare Center

Incident Response
Evidence Preservation and Collection
Cyber Secrets 6

First Edition First Published: January 1, 2021

Authors: Jeremy Martin, Richard Medlin, Nitin Sharma, LaShanda Edwards, Kevin John Hermosa, Mossaraf Zaman Khan, Vishal Belbase, Frederico Ferreira, Carlyle Collins, Tajamul Sheeraz, Steve "Butchy" Bartimote, Ambadi MP

Editors: Jeremy Martin, Daniel Traci, Joshua Martin

The writer and publisher of this article do not condone the misuse of Tor for illegal activity. This is purely instructional for the purposes of anonymous surfing on the internet for legal usage and for testing Tor traffic monitoring in a subsequent article. **To access .onion sites, you must have access to the Tor network. To access i2p sites, you must have access to the I2P network. To access any Surface Web site, you must have access to the Internet.**

Cataloging-in-Publication Data:
ISBN: 9798586992826
ASIN:

Disclaimer: Do NOT break the law!

About the Team

Jeremy Martin, CISSP-ISSAP/ISSMP, LPT (CSI Linux Developer)
linkedin.com/in/infosecwriter

A Security Researcher that has focused his work on Red Team penetration testing, Computer Forensics, and Cyber Warfare. He is also a qualified expert witness with cyber/digital forensics. He has been teaching classes such as OSINT, Advanced Ethical Hacking, Computer Forensics, Data Recovery, AND SCADA/ICS security since 2003.

Richard Medlin (CSI Linux Developer)
linkedin.com/in/richard-medlin1

An Information Security researcher with 20 years of information security experience. He is currently focused on writing about bug hunting, vulnerability research, exploitation, and digital forensic investigations. Richard is an author and one of the original developers on the first all-inclusive digital forensic investigations operating systems, CSI Linux.

Nitin Sharma (CSI Linux Developer)
linkedin.com/in/nitinsharma87

A cyber and cloud enthusiast who can help you in starting your Infosec journey and automating your manual security burden with his tech skillset and articles related to IT world. He found his first love, Linux while working on Embedded Systems during college projects along with his second love, Python for automation and security.

LaShanda Edwards CECS-A, MSN, BS
linkedin.com/in/lashanda-edwards-cecs-a-msn-bs-221282140
facebook.com/AbstractionsPrintingandDesigns

As a Cyber Defense Infrastructure Support Specialist and a Freelance Graphic Artist, her background is not traditional but extensive. Capable of facing challenges head on, offering diverse experiences, and I am an agile learner. 11+ years of military service, as well as healthcare experience.

Mossaraf Zaman Khan
linkedin.com/in/mossaraf

Mossaraf is a Cyber Forensic Enthusiast. His areas of interest are Digital Forensics, Malware Analysis & Cyber Security. He is passionate and works hard to put his knowledge practically into the field of Cyber.

Steve "Butchy" Bartimote
linkedin.com/in/stephenbartimote

Steve or Butchy as he is known, has a long-held interest and fascination in security and defense. He originally trained as a locksmith, however for the last 25 years he has worked within the IT Industry. As with many in this industry Butchy initially followed the pathways of Web Development and IT Support. He has provided Server Administration (Windows and Linux) before developing greater skills in programming and software development. More recently, Butchy has developed his skill set as a 'solution architect' as well as his interest in cyber security. He continues to work with technology, including electronics, from one end of the spectrum to the other and has developed a passion for the 'Raspberry Pi platform'. In his away from technology time Butchy is an avid martial artist and instructor.

Carlyle Collins
linkedin.com/in/carlyle-c-cyber

Carlyle is currently pursuing an MSc. Cyber Security Engineering while serving as an intern at the Information Warfare Center. For over three years he has served as a Forensic Chemist and is now interested in applying his analytical skills and critical thinking to the Digital Forensics arena.

Kevin John O. Hermosa

An aspiring cybersecurity professional who once was stuck in web and systems development. But his world turning upside-down one day has suddenly changed everything about his life and led him to newly found passions in Linux, Computer Networking, Electronics, and Cybersecurity. Kevin strongly holds unto the importance of a strong stance towards cybersecurity in order to keep not only businesses and organizations safe but also to help the common citizen uphold their personal cyber safety for the sake of the greater good of the community. With this in mind, Kevin continues to grow his knowledge and skill on cybersecurity.

Vishal Belbase
in.linkedin.com/in/vishal-belbase-0396b313a

He is a young security enthusiast who loves to know the inner working, how do things happen how are they working this curiosity led to make him pursue diploma in computer science and then undergrad in cybersecurity and forensics. Area of interest malware analysis, red teaming, and digital forensics.

Frederico Ferreira
linkedin.com/in/frederico-l-ferreira

He is a Cyber Security Enthusiast, currently working as a Senior IT Analyst. Experience and broad knowledge in a wide range of IT fields. Skilled in IT and OT systems with a demonstrated history of working in the oil & energy industry. Frederico is passionate about new technologies and world history.

Ambadi MP
linkedin.com/in/ambadi-m-p-16a95217b

A Cyber Security Researcher primarily focused on Red Teaming and Penetration Testing. Experience within web application and network penetration testing and Vulnerability Assessment. Passion towards IT Industry led to choose career in IT Sector. With a short period of experience in Cyber Security domain got several achievements and Acknowledged by Top Reputed Companies and Governmental Organizations for Securing their CyberSpace.

Tajamul Sheeraz
https://www.linkedin.com/in/tajamulsheeraz/

A DFIR who works for Fortune 500 companies and government organizations defending them from adversaries. He has worked on some notable critical incidents. Tajamul does consulting, performs point of view for security devices, defines process workflows and provides advice for fine-tuning the security device policies and rules.

Table of Contents

What is inside?

Cyber Secrets is a cybersecurity publication focusing on an array of subjects ranging from Exploitations, Advanced Persistent Threats (APT)s, National Infrastructure, (ICS/SCADA), *Darknet/Dark Web*, Digital Forensics & Incident Response (DIFR), Malware Analysis, and the gambit of digital dangers.

Cyber Secrets rotates between odd issues focusing on DFIR / Blue Team / Defense and even issues on Hacking / Red Team / Offense.

Cyber WAR *(Weekly Awareness Report)*

We have another publication *(Free)* called the Cyber WAR. It is an OSINT resource to keep you up to date with what is going on in the Cyber Security Realm. You can download or subscribe at:

InformationWarfareCenter.com/CIR

Digital Evidence

"Digital evidence or electronic evidence is any probative information stored or transmitted in digital form that a party to a court case may use at trial. Before accepting digital evidence, a court will determine if the evidence is relevant, whether it is authentic, if it is hearsay and whether a copy is acceptable, or the original is required." - Wikipedia

What happens if the evidence you need is located on someone else's network or device?

Each country has their own set of laws when it comes to this. In the US, this ties into the preservation of evidence under penalty of law or Legal Hold. On the next page, is a sample preservation letter that sent to the other side to in order to ensure the evidence is not destroyed on accident or intentionally. This is procedural and hopefully the other side will comply. There are no guarantees.

If the evidence is in another country, this may have to be escalated to the use of a mutual legal assistance treaty (MLAT). An MLAT is an agreement between two or more countries for the purpose of gathering and exchanging information in an effort to enforce public or criminal laws. Unfortunately, if the source of an attack is in a country that is not friendly with the one you are in, the likelihood of getting the evidence, let alone a successful conviction of the suspect, is very low. Just look at the US federal grand jury indictments of State sponsored foreign hackers from China, Russia, Iran, and North Korea. A big gesture, but there will be no remedy of the victims of these criminal actions. We will cover what you can do to capture evidence on your network.

Sample Preservation letter

[attorney/org/agency]
[date/address]

Re: Notice to Preserve Electronic Evidence [Legal Matter]

Dear _____:

Our law firm represents [name] in the above legal matter in which you [your business] are [is] [will be] named as a defendant. This letter requests your immediate action to preserve electronically stored information that may contain evidence important to the above legal matter. Briefly, the matter involves [short statement of facts in case].

This notice applies to your [company's] on- and off-site computer systems and removable electronic media plus all computer systems, services, and devices (including all remote access and wireless devices) used for your [company's] overall operation. This includes, but is not limited to, e-mail and other electronic communications; electronically stored documents, records, images, graphics, recordings, spreadsheets, databases; calendars, system usage logs, contact manager information, telephone logs, internet usage files, deleted files, cache files, user information, and other data. Further, this notice applies to archives, backup and disaster recovery tapes, discs, drives, cartridges, voicemail and other data. All operating systems, software, applications, hardware, operating manuals, codes, keys and other support information needed to fully search, use, and access the electronically stored information must also be preserved.

The importance of immediate action cannot be overstated. Electronically stored information is easily corrupted, altered, and deleted in normal daily operations. Even booting a drive, running an application, or reviewing a document can permanently alter evidence. An important method for preserving data in its original state is to have a forensic image (mirror image or clone image) made of pertinent hard drives of both office and home computers used for business and of network servers. This image captures all current data, including the background or metadata about each document. Simply copying data to a CD-ROM or other common backup medium is not adequate. For each captured image file, record and identify the person creating the image and the date of creation. Secure the file to prevent subsequent alteration or corruption and create a chain of custody log. Once the forensic data image file is created, the pertinent computer or other device can be placed back into operation.

[If known, identify any key persons', officers', supervisors', and employees' computers to which special attention for forensic imaging must be directed.]

This preservation notice covers the above items and information between the following dates: [state dates]. Follow the above procedures to preserve electronic information created after this notice.

Current law and rules of civil procedure clearly apply to the discovery of electronically stored information just as they apply to other evidence and confirm the duty to preserve such information for discovery. You [company] and your officers, employees, agents, and affiliated organizations must take all reasonable steps to preserve this information until this legal matter is finally resolved. Failure to take the necessary steps to preserve the information addressed in this letter or other pertinent information in your possession or control may result in serious sanctions or penalties.

In order to avoid spoliation, you will need to provide the data requested on the original media. Do not reuse any media to provide this data.

Although we may bring a motion for an order preserving documents and things from destruction or alteration, your client's obligation to preserve documents and things for discovery in this case arises in law and equity independently from any order on any such motion.

Further, to properly fulfill your preservation obligation, stop all scheduled data destruction, electronic shredding, rotation of backup tapes, and the sale, gift, or destruction of hardware. Notify all individuals and affiliated organizations of the need and duty to take the necessary affirmatives steps to comply with the duty to preserve evidence.

This request also applies to all data, whether in hard copy or electronic, that is created or modified after your receipt of this letter.

To assure that you or your client's obligation to preserve documents and things will be met, please forward a copy of this letter to all persons and entities with custodial responsibility for the items referred to in this letter.

Sincerely,
[attorney/org/agency]
[address]

"Spoliation of evidence is the intentional, reckless, or negligent withholding, hiding, altering, fabricating, or destroying of evidence relevant to a legal proceeding. Spoliation has three possible consequences: in jurisdictions where the (intentional) act is criminal by statute, it may result in fines and incarceration (if convicted in a separate criminal proceeding) for the parties who engaged in the spoliation; in jurisdictions where relevant case law precedent has been established, proceedings possibly altered by spoliation may be interpreted under a spoliation inference, or by other corrective measures, depending on the jurisdiction; in some jurisdictions the act of spoliation can itself be an actionable tort." - **Wikipedia**

Note: In the US, this ties directly to **Rule 37**. *"Failure to Make Disclosures or to Cooperate in Discovery; Sanctions"*

Dark Web Corner

Cryptocurrency

Terms

Emergency BTC Address: An address to be held on record to send all funds to in case of a market shut down. This would ideally be a cold storage address with no information that could be used to connect the owner to their identity. This address would only be checked after a market was shut down to recover outstanding funds.

Escrow: With market transactions, the use of a neutral third party to ensure that a transaction payment will be made to a seller on completion of items sent to a buyer. Sometimes, after a purchase is made, the funds are held 'in escrow' to be released when the buyer states the seller has met the terms of the purchase. Generally, the third party will also offer arbitration in case of a dispute between the two parties.

LocalBitcoins: A site designed to allow over-the counter trading of Bitcoins. Famed for its anonymous nature, people who sell on the site have been under constant pressure to avoid being prosecuted as unlicensed money traders. This extra risk and the extra work generally cause a significant price difference between the site and a more open (and regulated) exchange

Tumble: A method to anonymize the source of your Bitcoins.

Tx ID: Bitcoin transaction ID.

Bitcoin Tumblers on Tor

BitcoinMixer
mixerbtnvqktfsvo.onion

ChipMixer
chipmixdi3tqpx6p.onion

CryptoMixer.io
cryptomixns23scr.onion

VulcanMix
vulkanh2tjj4ls4c.onion

Tracking Cryptocurrencies

The number of users using cryptocurrencies has increased to over 35 million in 2020. This rise in has also led to an increase in this vector being used to black market sales, illegal purchases, and money laundering.

In April 2019, New York prosecutors got their first conviction for money laundering involving cryptocurrency worth $2.8 million.

"Between 2013 and 2018, the two men sold steroids and other drugs including Viagra across the U.S. via their website 'NextDayGear' and on the dark web. They sold over 10,000 packages and accepted payments in cryptocurrency" - Coindesk.com

"FBI Supervisory Special Agent Kyle Armstrong told the Crypto Evolved conference in New York that the agency currently has around 130 different investigations involving cryptocurrencies being used in a variety of crimes, including human trafficking, drug transactions, kidnapping, and ransomware." - Bloomberg

How can these transactions be tracked? Blockchain is an open, decentralized ledger that records transactions between two parties. This means the ledger is public for most cryptocurrencies.

Take Bitcoin for example. Bitcoin is pseudonymous. A bitcoin pseudonym is the address where users receive bitcoin. Every transaction involving that address is stored in the blockchain.

If a user's address is ever linked to their identity, every transaction will be linked to that user. Here are some OSINT tools that allow investigators to search by block number, address, block hash, or transaction hash to find out more about bitcoin transactions.

- blockexplorer.com
- blockchain.info
- chainalysis.com
- bitcoinwhoswho.com

Due to the pseudonymous nature of bitcoin and transactions being tracked by investigators, money launderers are starting to use a system known as cryptocurrency tumblers. Cryptocurrency tumblers mix potentially identifiable currency with untraceable currency to make it harder to track.

Some addresses can be grouped by their ownership, using behavior patterns and publicly available information from off-chain sources. The challenge for forensic investigators, as usual, is to identify the person behind the keyboard, which may be accomplished through a mixture of traditional investigative and digital forensic techniques.

Raid Forums: The Hacker Repo of Your Data

"A data breach is the intentional or unintentional release of secure or private/confidential information to an untrusted environment. Other terms for this phenomenon include unintentional information disclosure, data leak, information leakage and also data spill." - Wikipedia

Raid Forums is a site dedicated to selling and trading breach (hacked) databases, tools, and user account information commonly used in credential stuffing and unauthorized access. The site is active, and for around $8, you can download or gain access to almost any database on their site. This includes a wide range of plundered information including voter registration databases all the way to the largest compilation of username and passwords known to the public called Collection #1-5 set that was released in January 2019.

If you have ever received an email claiming that a hacker now has your password with a password listed in the email while trying to extort money from you, data sets like this are where they probably got the password. Especially if it is an older, non-active password. Many people fall for this trick and sent the scammers the money anyway.

From a purely defensive standpoint, this data is very useful to see of accounts owned by you, your organization, or clients have been leaked. From an offensive perspective, many people do not change their passwords or reuse them over long periods of time.

Some organizations have a policy in place that says to NOT use your organization email for online accounts outside the org. This is one of the reasons why. That makes the user a much bigger target for scammers, hackers, and other criminals.

Due to all these breaches, it has become common policy to test the current passwords in an organization against the leaked data to force users to use "less common" passwords. This minimizes risk against dictionary attacks

Below is a screenshot of https://raidforums.com/ verified hacked databases.

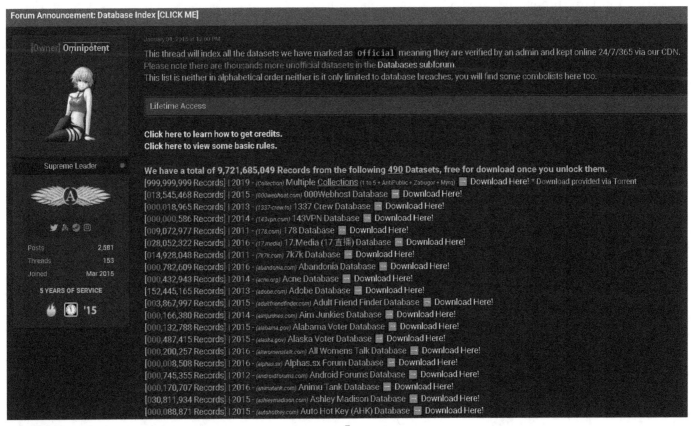

Raspberry Pi Zero Tor Gateway

By: Steve (Butchy) Bartimote

Over the last 2 years I have been taking part in the Trace Labs' National Missing Person Hackathon, a hackathon using OSINT techniques to look for new leads on missing people. It looked like a good way to use my cyber security skills for Good!

You earn points based on the leads you submit and there are varying point levels. From friends and family contacts, to emails and social media accounts, locations and breach data. One of the big point earners in the hackathon is "Dark Web" leads, a huge 500 points each. Usually, the highest next to an actual location within the last 24 hours. My team and I have always been able to find the smaller leads and some more interesting ones leaked financial records but never a dark web reference or a location.

So, of recent months I have been delving into the world of the dark web, tor and the tor browser. I've also looked into what mistakes people make when using the dark web (see the "Warnings") and where the technology has limits or shortcomings and how I can mitigate them.

Tor has one outstanding purpose "Anonymity" and some secondary features like hidden services. However, there are things you can do (the mistakes) that remove that anonymity. It is important to read the Warnings section…seriously **do not** skip it!

The standard mechanism for accessing Tor, is the Tor browser, it connects to the Tor network, the sites you browse with it are routed through Tor and anonymized and it is preconfigured to block JavaScript and to use HTTPS. All very important things when protecting your anonymity.

People ask "Well, then why are you looking at the mistakes people make with it?"

Well for my purpose we are looking for missing people, some of them might not be missing by choice! And someone may not want people looking into finding them! So, protecting my anonymity is important, I also have loved ones so best to be anonymous and avoid mistakes that could put them at risk.

Now the Tor browser probably the most common way to access the Tor network is awesome and I do highly recommend using it, however the Tor browser only does the traffic going through it alone… not anything else on your system is routed through Tor. Over confidence in a single layer of protection is a mistake, so that's why I add extra layers.

OSINT

"Open-source intelligence (OSINT) is a multi-methods (qualitative, quantitative) methodology for collecting, analyzing, and making decisions about data accessible in publicly available sources to be used in an intelligence context. In the intelligence community, the term "open" refers to overt, publicly available sources (as opposed to covert or clandestine sources). It is not related to open-source software or collective intelligence.

OSINT under one name or another has been around for hundreds of years. With the advent of instant communications and rapid information transfer, a great deal of actionable and predictive intelligence can now be obtained from public, unclassified sources." – Wikipedia

When tying this in with an investigation, especially if it is an ongoing attack, divorcing your activity from what the attacker knows about you or their target can be extremely useful. If the attacker knows their victim is investigating and getting close, then they may change what they are doing or even worse, start to destroy what they have.

This means that the more anonymous or separated your traffic, signatures, and persona is, the less likely the attacker or suspect will either move to destroy the data or change their attacks or become more aggressive.

One method to do this is to go through proxies or VPNs. Another cheap or free method is to use Tor or other Dark Web networks to mask your original identity. This also gives you the added benefit of accessing resources on those networks.

The anonymity factor is a major benefit when doing research or investigating any kind of crime or incident. The end goal is to get actionable intelligence or information that can help you achieve the goals of the mission.

Whether you are investigating a hacking case, intellectual property theft, terrorism, or human trafficking, you want to minimize the destruction of evidence and gain more if you can while at the same time, building your case.

Enter a Tor Gateway!

Your laptop/pc connects to it (the Gateway) and all traffic from your laptop is then routed through Tor by default. This helps with some technical limitations, like using a second browser... It's not the Tor browser, it doesn't route its traffic through Tor and Bam! Just like that you are no longer anonymous. I always have more than one browser installed it's a common thing for a programmer and an Info Sec guy to do

Connecting through a Gateway removes this technological limitation or mistake because even when I accidentally start up my second browser, it's going through the gateway by default. So, we have addressed that limitation and it isn't the user's fault for just simply doing our learned behavior. I would highly recommend researching browser privacy settings for your other browsers on your laptop, I could write an entire article on that alone just with Firefox.

For that matter do you know what other applications you are using, running in the background? And what information are they sending?

This is where I say... Read the damn Warnings section!

Warnings:

As fantastic as technology is, it is fallible, it has weaknesses, vulnerabilities but it can be made worse by incorrect usage (those pesky mistakes we make). Tor, a Tor gateway, and any other anonymization mechanism is not going to keep you anonymous if you use them to then say.... Log into your Facebook account! Your internet banking! Your Gmail accounts! Or anything else that specifically identifies you the person using it... The moment you do your anonymity is gone!

Add to this list. Going into a forum and telling people your name, the city you live in, your hometown, your partner's name... Now you think these things would make commonsense and well they do. However, anyone who has ever been caught when using Tor has not been caught because a failure of Tor to encrypt their traffic and hide their IP address, it's by their lack of Operation Security or OpSec.

There are several books and articles on how hackers have been caught even though they were using the "Dark Web" but when you investigate these cases a good 99% are the slipups, the mistakes and well the bragging hackers have done that gave them away. Sharing too much information about themselves, their habits from concerts they went to, to previous arrests, to habits like connecting to Tor from the same coffee shop 100m from their house at the same time every day...

Yes, I too am shaking my head in disbelief but alas many a famous hacker got pwned this way.

To add to this, I guess is a little bit of what Tor is and is not!

- Tor is anonymity not privacy.
- Tor is right thing for you or Tor by itself is not enough for your particular use case.
- Tor is not for Windows.
- Tor is not a VPN.
- Tor is something that requires technical skill to setup and use correctly.
- Tor is completely useless if you don't know, if you have bad or absolutely zero OpSec.

This last point is important, no technology, no device in the world will fix this... Period!

That all being said, let's start building our Pi!

About Our Pi Gateway

So, what are we building? And why use a Pi Zero?

Let us start with the Raspberry Pi Zero...

Raspberry Pi computers are such handy little devices in the Cyber Security world from dropboxes, to a pwnagotchi and of course network implants all very useful. The Raspberry Pi Zero is the smallest of the Raspberry Pi family is to me the most useful.

Here is mine!

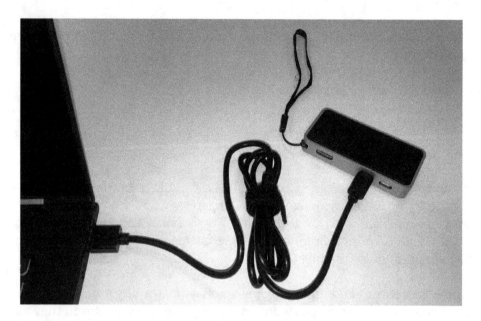

It is in a "Flirc" case that acts as a heat sync, but that wasn't the reason I chose it. I chose it because when it is plugged into my ultrabook, it looks a USB hub or Dock completely inconspicuous, nothing unusual about it at all. If you've ever own an ultrabook you know it has limited ports and that is common to have a hub or dock. I did look at a raspberry pi 3 or 4 but seeing them on a table in a café, can look a little out of place but a USB hub plugged into my ultrabook... not so much!

So, what are we building?

This build is a single user Tor gateway using a Raspberry Pi Zero (Wireless), which is connecting to our laptop via USB. The Raspberry Pi Zero has the ability to be connected via USB as a "USB gadget" or "Serial" device. So, our laptop connects to the Pi via USB, but the Pi Zero Wireless model has its own WiFi card, we will be using that to connect to the internet and Tor.

The traffic will go Laptop -> USB -> Pi Zero -> Tor -> WiFi -> Internet. The Pi routes everything through Tor to the internet. Your laptop without the Pi does not connect to the internet at all.

You will be able to access the Pi via SSH and VNC from your laptop.

SSH is used to control, update and shutdown the Pi from your laptop. It is important to always patch or update your system to protect against vulnerabilities and Tor is no exception.

VNC is used for 1 very handy purpose, when connecting to Free WiFi, if it has a captive portal. You can VNC onto the Pi from your laptop, open the Pi's browser and accept the terms and conditions of the Free WiFi. You will not be able accept these terms and conditions on your laptop's browser.

It takes a slightly different setup to work as a USB gadget, but it does help with the OpSec of being inconspicuous. I have coupled together a few different tutorials I found online and added some extra things to mitigate some of those technological limitations. All credit is due to those original authors, their work, helped my work and they deserve recognition.

Equipment:

- 1 x Raspberry Pi Zero Wireless (https://core-electronics.com.au/raspberry-pi-zero-w-wireless.html)
- 1 x 16GB MicroSD card (https://core-electronics.com.au/16gb-microsd-card-with-noobs-for-all-raspberry-pi-boards.html)
- 1 x Flirc Raspberry Pi Zero Case (https://core-electronics.com.au/flirc-raspberry-pi-zero-case.html)
- 1 x Micro USB cable (https://core-electronics.com.au/micro-usb-cable.html)

Software:

- Raspberry Pi OS Lite (https://www.raspberrypi.org/software/operating-systems/)
- Balena Etcher (https://www.balena.io/etcher/)

Preparation:

I am using my Kali Linux laptop; this build is easier with a Linux machine than a Windows machine (pesky drivers) not only that but going back to our OpSec talk... Do not use Windows on Tor!

Now to flash the SD card with Raspberry Pi OS.

1. Insert your SD into your laptop
2. Open Etcher and select the Raspberry Pi OS Lite image
3. Select your SD card (if it has already auto detected it)
4. Click Flash!

Before we boot the Pi for the first time, we need to enable the "USB Gadget", Wifi and SSH functionality, with your Micro SD card still in your laptop.

1. Open your file manager and navigate to the SD card's boot partition, there edit the following files
   a. config.txt at the end of the file add the following **dtoverlay=dwc2** save and close the file.
   b. cmdline.txt find "rootwait" then add a space after it and then type **modules-load=dwc2,g_ether** save and close the file
2. Now SSH, in the root partition create an empty file called "ssh" nothing in it and no extension just ssh.
3. Now WiFi, in the root partition create a file called wpa_supplicant.conf add your wifi details to it like below.

```
1.  country=US
2.  ctrl_interface=DIR=/var/run/wpa_supplicant GROUP=netdev
3.  update_config=1
4.  network={
5.      ssid="MyWiFiNetwork"
6.      psk="aVeryStrongPassword"
7.      key_mgmt=WPA-PSK
8.  }
```

Be sure to change the details to match your Wi-Fi network and country.

Build:

For the moment don't put your Pi in your Flirc case, we will do that after we've tested it works. Boot your Pi then open a terminal, SSH into your Pi and run these commands in order… alternatively you can copy these into a bash file and then execute it!

```
1.  # First become root
2.  sudo su
3.
4.  # Updating OS and installing other components
5.  apt update -y &&  apt-get dist-upgrade -y
6.  apt install tor vim dnsmasq iptables-persistent macchanger monit -y

7.  # Disable IPv6
8.  echo "net.ipv6.conf.all.disable_ipv6=1" >> /etc/sysctl.conf
9.  echo "net.ipv6.conf.default.disable_ipv6=1" >> /etc/sysctl.conf
10. echo "net.ipv6.conf.lo.disable_ipv6=1" >> /etc/sysctl.conf
11. echo "net.ipv6.conf.eth0.disable_ipv6 = 1" >> /etc/sysctl.conf
12. echo "net.ipv6.conf.wlan0.disable_ipv6 = 1" >> /etc/sysctl.conf

13. # Configuring DHCP for the USB0 connection
14. echo "interface usb0" >> /etc/dhcpcd.conf
15. echo "static ip_address=192.168.1.1/24" >> /etc/dhcpcd.conf
16. echo "static domain_name_servers=208.67.222.222 208.67.220.220" >> /etc/dhcpcd.conf

17. # Configure DNSMasq for the USB0 connection
18. echo "interface=usb0" >> /etc/dnsmasq.conf
19. echo "dhcp-range=192.168.1.11,192.168.1.30,255.255.255.0,24h" >> /etc/dnsmasq.conf

20. # Configuring Tor
21. echo "VirtualAddrNetwork 10.192.0.0/10" > /etc/tor/torrc
22. echo "AutomapHostsSuffixes .onion,.exit" >> /etc/tor/torrc
23. echo "AutomapHostsOnResolve 1" >> /etc/tor/torrc
24. echo "TransPort 192.168.1.1:9040" >> /etc/tor/torrc
25. echo "DNSPort 192.168.1.1:53" >> /etc/tor/torrc
26. echo "RunAsDaemon 1" >> /etc/tor/torrc
27. echo "CircuitBuildTimeout 10" >> /etc/tor/torrc
28. echo "LearnCircuitBuildTimeout 0" >> /etc/tor/torrc
29. echo "MaxCircuitDirtiness 10" >> /etc/tor/torrc
30. sudo sed -i "s/NoNewPrivileges=yes/NoNewPrivileges=no/g" /lib/systemd/system/tor@default.service
31. sudo sed -i "s/NoNewPrivileges=yes/NoNewPrivileges=no/g" /lib/systemd/system/tor@.service
```

```
32. # Adding Tor to start automatically on Boot
33. update-rc.d tor enable
34. systemctl start tor.service
35. systemctl enable tor.service

36. # Configuring monit to start Tor if it doesn't start on boot
37. echo "check process gdm with pidfile /var/run/tor/tor.pid" >> /etc/monit/monitrc
38. echo "  start program = \"/etc/init.d/tor start\"" >> /etc/monit/monitrc
39. echo "  stop program = \"/etc/init.d/tor stop\"" >> /etc/monit/monitrc
40. systemctl restart monit
41. systemctl enable monit

42. # Creating a script to randomize MAC addresses for WLAN0 and USB0 on startup
43. echo '#!/bin/bash' > /etc/init.d/macchangerstartup
44. echo "ifconfig wlan0 down" >> /etc/init.d/macchangerstartup
45. echo "ifconfig usb0 down" >> /etc/init.d/macchangerstartup
46. echo "macchanger -r wlan0" >> /etc/init.d/macchangerstartup
47. echo "macchanger -r usb0" >> /etc/init.d/macchangerstartup
48. echo "ifconfig wlan0 up" >> /etc/init.d/macchangerstartup
49. echo "ifconfig usb0 up" >> /etc/init.d/macchangerstartup
50. chmod +x /etc/init.d/macchangerstartup

51. # Configure or create /etc/rc.local to run macchangerstartup script on boot
52. echo '#!/bin/sh -e' > /etc/rc.local
53. echo "/etc/init.d/macchangerstartup" >> /etc/rc.local
54. Echo "service procps reload" >> /etc/rc.local
55. echo "exit 0" >> /etc/rc.local
56. chmod 755 /etc/rc.local

57. # Configure /var/log as tmpfs kill logs after on reboot
58. rm -R /var/log/*
59. echo "tmpfs /var/log tmpfs nodev,nosuid,size=40M 0 0" >> /etc/fstab
60. mount -a
```

Now we do some iptables commands, you will find your SSH connection over the WiFi we be blocked... funny that, at this point hopefully the Pi should be shutdown. We switch the Micro USB cable from the power socket on the Pi, to the Data socket and plug the other end into your laptop. Once it boots you should notice on your laptop that it is connecting to a new network connection. Once it is connected, in a terminal window type the following

```
1. ip a
```

This should list an Interface (hopefully called USB0) with an IP address of 192.168.1.11, you can now SSH into your Pi by typing. The Pi's IP address is 192.168.1.1.

```
1. sh pi@192.168.1.1
```

```
1. # Switch to root again
2.   sudo su
3.
4.   # Configure IPTables to route all traffic through Tor, enabling NAT
5.   iptables -F
6.   iptables -t nat -F
7.   iptables -t nat -A POSTROUTING -o wlan0 -j MASQUERADE
8.   iptables -A FORWARD -i wlan0 -o usb0 -m state --state RELATED,ESTABLISHED -j ACCEPT
9.   iptables -A FORWARD -i usb0 -o wlan0 -j ACCEPT
10.  iptables -A INPUT -i wlan0 -p tcp --dport 5900 -j DROP
11.  iptables -A INPUT -i wlan0 -p tcp --dport 22 -j DROP
12.  iptables -t nat -A PREROUTING -i usb0 -p tcp --dport 5900 -j REDIRECT --to-ports 5900
13.  iptables -t nat -A PREROUTING -i usb0 -p tcp --dport 22 -j REDIRECT --to-ports 22
14.  iptables -t nat -A PREROUTING -i usb0 -p udp --dport 53 -j REDIRECT --to-ports 53
15.  iptables -t nat -A PREROUTING -i usb0 -p tcp --syn -j REDIRECT --to-ports 9040
16.  sh -c "iptables-save > /etc/iptables/rules.v4"
17.  sh -c "iptables-save > /etc/iptables.ipv4.nat"
18.  echo "net.ipv4.ip_forward=1" > /etc/sysctl.conf
```

```
19.  sudo reboot
```

The raspberry pi has a utility called raspi-config. You can use this in future for doing OS and package updates, I would strongly advise changing the Pi's default password and this is also how you connect to new WiFi network by running the command below and configuring the network settings and you can enable VNC.

```
1.  sudo raspi-config
```

Now that we've configured and rebooted our PI lets test it is routing through Tor
On your laptop open your standard browser and go to https://check.torproject.org and you should hopefully see a "Congratulations. This browser is configured to use Tor."

Now that we've tested it and everything works, it's time to put your Pi in the Flirc case. It was best to do this after everything was setup and working, so we didn't have to pull it all apart to flash the card if we messed it up.

The Final Word:

Having a Tor Gateway that is portable and inconspicuous is fantastic for Dark Web research, security engagements, red teaming and of course hacking. Like any tool of the trade, you must be skilled in its use/execution and know its purpose and limitations. Other things you need to look at or research are things like encryption (end-to-end and at-rest), burners, communications (secure emailing, messaging), anonymous finances, your personal threat matrix and for the love of god people OpSec!!!

APT: The Ultimate Threat

By: Ambadi MP

What is an APT?

In order to mine highly sensitive data, an advanced persistent threat (APT) is used to describe an attack campaign in which an attacker or team of intruders develops an illegal, long-term presence on a network.

Usually, the targets of these attacks, which are very carefully selected and investigated, involve large corporations or government networks. There are vast implications of such intrusions and they include:

- Theft of Intellectual Property (e.g., trade secrets or patents)
- Compromised information that is sensitive (e.g., employee and user private data)
- Sabotaging the essential infrastructures of organizations (e.g., database deletion)
- Full takeovers of sites

It takes more time to perform an APT attack than a typical web application attack. The perpetrators are typically teams with considerable financial support from seasoned cybercriminals. Some attacks by the APT are government-funded and used as tools of cyber warfare.

APT attacks are distinct from conventional threats to web applications in that:

- They are considerably more nuanced.
- When a network is compromised, the attacker stays to collect as much data as possible. This is also an Intelligence Operations, not simple hit and run assaults.
- They are executed (not automated) manually against a particular mark and fired indiscriminately against a wide pool of goals.
- In contrast to one particular aspect, they also attempt to penetrate an entire network.

Famous APT Groups

China

The APT landscape in China is operated in a 'whole country' approach, integrating skills from universities, individuals, and private and public sectors, according to security researcher Timo Steffens

- PLA Unit 61398 (also known as APT1)
- PLA Unit 61486 (also known as APT2)
- Buckeye (also known as APT3)
- Red Apollo (also known as APT10)
- Numbered Panda (also known as APT12)
- Codoso Team (also known as APT19)
- Wocao (also known as APT20)
- PLA Unit 78020 (also known as APT30 and Naikon)
- Zirconium [39] (also known as APT31)
- Periscope Group (also known as APT40)
- Double Dragon (hacking organization) (also known as APT41, Winnti Group, Barium, or Axiom)
- Tropic Trooper

Israel

- Unit 8200

United States

- Equation Group

Russia

- Fancy Bear (also known as APT28)
- Cozy Bear (also known as APT29)
- Sandworm, Berserk Bear, Venomous Bear

Iran

- Elfin Team (also known as APT33)
- Helix Kitten (also known as APT34)
- Charming Kitten (also known as APT35)
- APT39
- Pioneer Kitten

North Korea

- Ricochet Chollima (also known as APT37)
- Lazarus Group (also known as APT38)

Uzbekistan

- SandCat (associated with the National Security Service (Uzbekistan))

Vietnam

- OceanLotus (also known as APT32)

Hacker Groups and APT Groups Differences

These groups differ from other cybercriminals in that they appear to adapt to defenses and can for months or even years maintain their presence in a system.

Most hacking attacks carry out a fast, damaging attack, but APTs take a different approach that is more strategic and stealthier. The attackers come in through traditional malware such as trojans or phishing, but then cover their tracks as they secretly move around and plant their attack instruments in the network. APT groups' attacks are more subtle and nuanced than the normal hacking. These groups are made up of highly trained, competent, and enigmatic participants with vast technical backgrounds. Some of the motivation behind hacker groups is economic or political, although most of the time the motivation behind the APT groups is strategic. APT organizations are usually a nation-state or state-sponsored organization that has much more and more modern equipment and is already financially secured.

Why are the APT attacks so dangerous?

Since APT varies a lot. An APT intruder is highly skilled and broad understanding with latest technologies, well-funded and has a long-term objective. GhostNet, ShadowNet, and Operation Aurora were some of the examples of APT attacks. Those organizations were targeted by APT groups who used sophisticated techniques to infect and penetrate their networks. The attackers lost nothing. Without worrying anybody, they only gathered as much information as they could.

When a target is chosen by the intruder, it analyses its security and uses advanced techniques, tools and strategies. In the APT cyber world, most of the tools are custom-built and explicitly designed for the target company or entity that makes these kinds of attacks much more threatening.

APT Life Cycle

By pursuing a continuous mechanism or kill chain, actors behind advanced persistent threats establish an increasing and evolving danger to the financial assets, intellectual property, and credibility of organizations:

1. Via an email, network, file, or application vulnerability, the cybercriminal, or threat actor, gains entry and inserts malware into the network of an entity. The network is regarded as compromised, but not violated.
2. Advanced malware checks or communicates with command-and-control (C&C) servers to receive extra instructions and/or malicious code for additional network access and vulnerabilities.
3. Usually, the malware creates additional points of vulnerability to ensure that if one point is closed, the cyber-attack will continue.
4. They collect target data, such as account names and passwords, once a threat actor decides that they have gained secure network access. Encryption can be broken, even though passwords are frequently encrypted. The threat actor will identify and access data until that happens.
5. The malware collects data on a staging server, then exfiltrates the data off the network and under the full control of the threat actor. At this point, the network is considered to have been compromised.
6. Once after the network is compromised, the proofs of the attack will be wiped, at any time, the cybercriminal will return to resume the breach of data.

You may have heard that an APT attack happened against the Cyber Security Firm FireEye. FireEye is the first call for government agencies and businesses across the globe who have been compromised, or suspect they may be, by the most advanced attackers. FireEye has built its credibility on protecting hacker clients from high-stakes customers. Now it was the target of a breach itself, and with some of its offensive tools, the attackers made off. It is an impressive revelation, but almost certainly not as devastating as it may sound at first. The F.B.I. announced that the hack was done by state sponsored Hackers, but it would not tell which one, either. Matt Gorham, F.B.I. Cyber Division assistant director, said, "The F.B.I. is investigating the incident and preliminary indications show an actor with a high level of sophistication consistent with a nation-state." .Even a top reputed cybersecurity firm who protects other companies and Organizations had become a victim ,so think how dangerous these APT's are.

How do you know if your business is the target of APTs?

It is likely that a combination of warning signs will alert you to an APT. However, working with an expert cyber protection company, using purpose-built anti-APT software, or using Threat Hunting for detecting and preventing covert threats is also crucial. The following include common warning signs:

Emails are also used by hackers as their entry points. They choose subjects that are likely to draw the attention of the staff they target, based on the recognition they carry out before the attack. An infected attachment or a connection that installs a program providing access to your device may be included in the messages. Owing to their highly targeted nature, these are called spear-phishing scams. They differ from traditional phishing scams that are indiscriminately distributed, are not personalized, and attempt to trick large numbers of individuals into sharing personal data or information. Spear-phishing targets specific individuals in specific industries, and spear-phishers use the personal details of their targets to appear more trustworthy and give their messages credibility. Red flags are any emails sent to high-level company executives with attachments from unknown persons. It is necessary to make staff aware of the dangers of phishing and the risks associated with opening attachments and clicking on links in unsolicited messages.

To retain access to computers, hackers also deploy backdoor Trojans. These are software programs that allow hackers to remotely link and send or receive commands to computers on compromised networks. They're like leaving a back door open, because even if user credentials change, there is still a way in.

Often watch the network logins. If there are lots of logins that take place after work hours, or there are other unusual login activities, it is a cause for concern. This is especially true if these logins are individuals with high-level access to your network in executive positions. Hackers may be on the other side of the planet in foreign countries, which could account for the odd timing. They also try to work when they know that few, if any, people are in your office to catch and deter suspicious activity.

Check for huge files that aren't where they need to be. Often, in one location, hackers' group, and compress data before exporting it out of your network. This approach makes transferring greater volumes of information at a time simpler for them. Another indication that hackers are planning to sell data packages is that the compressed data usually does not use the company's archive format. Pay careful attention to bundled data extensions of the file.

For a cause, hackers are in your system: they are after particular data. Watch for big batches of moving content. Files may have been transmitted or data transferred from server to server. Look for data moving on the same internal networks between computers and data moving to external computers. Keep an eye out for unusual links, like external resource ties.

How to protect From APT Attacks?

There isn't a 100 percent solution when it comes to defending the company from APTs. Because of their sophisticated and persistent nature, the only way to even identify their vulnerabilities is by using a combination of malware detection and protection technologies capable of triangulating logs and out-of-norm operation inside corporate networks.

- Identify and take appropriate steps to safeguard the organization's most important and confidential data from any possible point. Using multiple security layers to make it more difficult for attackers to gain entry.
- Put tight access management protocols in place to ensure that workers only have access to the information they need to perform their jobs efficiently, nothing more.
- Monitor and Review logins and access requests on a regular basis, thereby allowing suspicious patterns, actions and requests to be easily identified.

- Deploy cybersecurity best practices and policies and educate staff on the latent and imminent dangers of APTs, especially those with access to admin level.
- Often use whitelisting for applications where practicable. This guarantees the installation of only trustworthy (i.e., whitelisted) software. The forced installation of malicious programs would trigger an alert/event, allowing for easier and faster detection.
- With the network of your company, recognize and address holes. Organizations may use modern hardware and software solutions, especially outward-facing ones such as web browsers and email programs, to protect and monitor programs. Some of these methods include:
- Remote browser isolation (RBI) technology
- SIEMs
- Intrusion prevention systems
- Next-generation firewalls
- AV solutions
- EDR solutions

What Steps to take if you are compromised by APT?

The following steps are important for organizations which have already been hacked via APTs:

- Determine the extent of exposure and what knowledge the hackers are already accessing.
- Learn as much about the APT as possible, as well as the hackers' methodologies and goals.

Following these measures will help you to gain insight into how to tackle the APT and how to handle and neutralize it. You can create a simple and practical strategy to eliminate the presence of the hacker by using that data. You should remember, however, that this will take a great deal of time, experience, and both human and financial capital.

When you've measured the extent of the attack and set up a recovery plan:

- Isolate all endpoints which are compromised.
- Do a reset of user passwords organization wide.

Regardless of the size of the organization, protecting sensitive information and even the credibility of the company should be a top priority. A negative reputation or lack of company data may have a significant effect on your client base and potentially a loss of faith in the services you offer. APT's are not going anywhere soon at any moment. To avoid loss of credibility, knowledge and monetary loss, businesses should continue to have the various mitigation strategies listed previously.

References

- (n.d.). Retrieved from www.nytimes.com/2020/12/08/technology/fireeye-hacked-russians.html
- (n.d.). Retrieved from www.wired.com/story/russia-fireeye-hack-statement-not-catastrophe/
- (n.d.). Retrieved from www.bleepingcomputer.com/news/security/fireeye-reveals-that-it-was-hacked-by-a-nation-state-apt-group/
- (n.d.). Retrieved from www.kaspersky.com/resource-center/threats/advanced-persistent-threat
- (n.d.). Retrieved from en.wikipedia.org: https://en.wikipedia.org/wiki/Advanced_persistent_threat
- (n.d.). Retrieved from www.imperva.com/learn/application-security/apt-advanced-persistent-threat/
- (n.d.). Retrieved from www.varonis.com/blog/apt-groups/
- Seker, E. (n.d.). Retrieved from medium.com/datadriveninvestor/top-famous-and-active-apt-groups-who-can-turn-life-to-a-nightmare-5d130168f43

INCIDENT RESPONSE in a Nutshell

By: Tajamul Sheeraz S

In this chapter, we will try to cover as much as possible about Incident Response on a high level. Incident Response is an ocean within itself, as it requires knowledge of multiple technologies, different skills and to keep yourself up to date on the ongoing Cyber-attacks in the industry.

We will look into the CIA triad, Incident Response framework and its types, Playbooks, Cyber kill chain, DATA Classification and followed by skills, knowledge required to be an IR analyst. Before jumping into the topics let me give you a brief on how to understand the IR workflow and how-to framework and stuff comes into play during an incident.

- Once an alert is triggered from the security devices in the environment, the IR analyst needs to validate the incident within a short period of time.
- During this time, we need to follow the IR framework (NIST/SANS) for handling the incident.
- We have to understand how the incident needs to be handled while considering the phase of attack and its severity by correlating the incident with Cyber kill chain to get a clear picture. We need to identify what the adversary is trying to accomplish (i.e., Tactic's) and how did the adversary accomplish the goal (i.e., Techniques), this is where Mitre tactic is used.

Note: This is not a limitation, organizations in the industry have their own Framework for handling Cyber Security incidents. Few organizations have customized NIST and SANS frameworks depending upon their needs. It is also applicable for the Cyber Kill Chain.

CIA Triad

What is the CIA Triad?

Information security, sometimes shortened to infosec, is the practice of protecting information by mitigating information risks. It is part of information risk management. It typically involves preventing or at least reducing the probability of unauthorized/inappropriate access to data, or the unlawful use, disclosure, disruption, deletion, corruption, modification, inspection, recording or devaluation of information.[1] It also involves actions intended to reduce the adverse impacts of such incidents. Protected information may take any form, e.g., electronic or physical, tangible (e.g., paperwork) or intangible (e.g., knowledge). Information security's primary focus is the balanced protection of the confidentiality, integrity and availability of data (also known as the CIA triad) while maintaining a focus on efficient policy implementation, all without hampering organization productivity. This is largely achieved through a structured risk management process that involves:

- Identifying information and related assets, plus potential threats, vulnerabilities and impacts.
- Evaluating the risks.
- Deciding how to address or treat the risks i.e., to avoid, mitigate, share or accept them.
- Where risk mitigation is required, selecting or designing appropriate security controls and implementing them.
- Monitoring the activities, making adjustments as necessary to address any issues, changes and improvement opportunities.

"To standardize this discipline, academics and professionals collaborate to offer guidance, policies, and industry standards on password, antivirus software, firewall, encryption software, legal liability, security awareness and training, and so forth. This standardization may be further driven by a wide variety of laws and regulations that affect how data is accessed, processed, stored, transferred, and destroyed. However, the implementation of any standards and guidance within an entity may have limited effect if a culture of continual improvement isn't adopted." - Wikipedia

Incident Response Frameworks

There are two well-known frameworks in the industry for incident response.

1.   NIST Framework
2.   SANS Framework

What is NIST and Who are they?

"The National Institute of Standards and Technology (NIST) is a physical sciences laboratory and a non-regulatory agency of the United States Department of Commerce. Its mission is to promote innovation and industrial competitiveness. NIST's activities are organized into laboratory programs that include nanoscale science and technology, engineering, information technology, neutron research, material measurement, and physical measurement. From 1901–1988, the agency was named the National Bureau of Standards." - Wikipedia

What is SANS and Who are they?

"The SANS Institute (officially the Escal Institute of Advanced Technologies) is a private U.S. for-profit company founded in 1989 that specializes in information security, cybersecurity training, and selling certificates. Topics available for training include cyber and network defenses, penetration testing, incident response, digital forensics, and auditing. The information security courses are developed through a consensus process involving administrators, security managers, and information security professionals. The courses cover security fundamentals and technical aspects of information security. The institute has been recognized for its training programs and certification programs. SANS stands for SysAdmin, Audit, Network, and Security." - **Wikipedia**

NIST Framework

1.   Preparation
2.   Detection & Analysis
3.   Containment Eradication and Recovery
4.   Post-Incident Activity

Source: https://nvlpubs.nist.gov/nistpubs/SpecialPublications/NIST.SP.800-61r2.pdf

SANS Framework

1.   Preparation
2.   Identification
3.   Containment
4.   Eradication
5.   Recovery
6.   Lessons Learned

Source: https://www.sans.org/reading-room/whitepapers/incident/incident-handlers-handbook-33901

Incident Response Playbooks

Playbooks are nothing but the set of instructions which are defined based on the framework which the organization uses. The instructions are predefined considering the teams and process followed in the environment and it differs from one organization to organization though they follow the same framework.

The playbooks have a set of instructions for analyzing the incident based upon the type of incident. Few types of playbooks like phishing, malware, vulnerability, etc...,

Data Classification

In the field of data management, data classification as a part of the Information Lifecycle Management (ILM) process can be defined as a tool for categorization of data to enable/help organizations to effectively answer the following questions:

- What data types are available?
- Where are certain data located?
- What access levels are implemented?
- What protection level is implemented, and does it adhere to compliance regulations?

When implemented it provides a bridge between IT professionals and process or application owners. IT staff are informed about the data value and management (usually application owners) understands better which part of the data centre needs to be invested in to keep operations running effectively. This can be of particular importance in risk management, legal discovery, and compliance with government regulations. Data classification is typically a manual process; however, there are many tools from different vendors that can help gather information about the data.

Data classification needs to take into account the following:

- Regulatory requirements
- Strategic or proprietary worth
- Organization specific policies
- Ethical and privacy considerations
- Contractual agreements

Skills and Knowledge required

- Security and Networking Devices
- Scripting
- Networking
- Red Teaming
- Threat Hunting
- Forensics
- Operating System
- Malware Analysis
- Log Analysis
- Threat Intel

The IR should have a deep understanding of the organization's network, the Pro's, and Con's.

The IR must be up to date of the new attacks occurring in the industry. This means Threat Intelligence...

Now we will look into a kind of real-life scenario and how to handle the Cyber Security Incident following the guidelines which we have come across.

Imagine there is a malware incident in the organization and the organization follows NIST framework and MITRE Tactics for Mapping the technique and tactic used to perform the attack.

Let's Begin Analyzing the Incident.

We could see that there is no proper detection observed in the security devices besides huge amounts of data being transferred to an external source.

The IP is found to be legitimate and not much information is available in the OSINT. We have found the source machine to be a server which acts as an internal FTP server.

There are no traces of malicious software or suspicious activities being observed apart from the outbound traffic.

Sounds like time for memory forensics, after performing forensics we have identified that there is a living off the land binary which is transferring the data with the help of BITS admin.

After collecting the artifacts and tracking down the timeline of events we could see that the endpoint has some suspicious connection to the FTP server.

On further investigation, we have observed the HR has received resume emails with malicious Zipped attachment in the email inbox. The HR has unzipped the malicious attachment and opened it. we found that the attachment has a file less malware which is being executed in the background without the user's knowledge. This is also known as living off the land binary.

Let's put this incident into the NIST framework.

1.   Preparation - In this phase, we will cover the rating of the severity for the incident and to create a communication plan.
2.   Detection & Analysis - This was where we had identified the suspicious outbound connection of the data being transferred following which the analysis which we had performed.
3.   Containment, Eradication and Recovery - This is the phase where we block(containment) the IOC's which were collected during the analysis and remove(eradication) the malware from the environment and recover the infected systems.
4.   Post-Incident Activity - Here we will be analyzing the flaws, patching the vulnerabilities and fine tuning the directions on the security devices.

Remember whom to reach and how to reach the point of contact and when and how to perform the analysis under the guidelines of the organization will be captured in the playbook of the incident.

Mapping the incident to the Mitre Attack framework.

Mitre Tactic: Initial access, Execution, Persistence, Defense Evasion, Lateral Movement, Exfiltration.
Mitre Technique: Spear phishing(T1566.001), powershell(T1059.001), BITS jobs(T1197), Exploitation of remote services(T1210), Exfiltration over web service(T1567).

Note: Kindly consider this example to get a clear picture, the analysis could change from IR analyst perspective and the organization's procedures. Mitre Attack mapping also slightly differs from analyst to analyst in the same organization.

Reactive Incident Response Handling

By: Jeremy Martin

To give a little more focus on this, we are going to look at three specific documents from NIST, US-CERT, and MITRE and how they can add strength to your Computer Security Incident Response Team (CSIRT).

The NIST 800 Series is a set of documents that describe United States Federal government computer security policies, procedures, and guidelines. The publications can be useful as guidelines for enforcement of security rules and as legal references in case of litigation involving security issues even if you are not covered within the US Federal jurisdiction.

The NIST SP800-61 r2 has been around for a while and was published August 2012. You can find the full document here: https://csrc.nist.gov/publications/detail/sp/800-61/rev-2/final

Communications

One of the issues that a lot of incident response teams to not take into consideration is the communications chain or who contacts who. Some companies even refuse to admit they were hacked in the fear that it will negatively affect their reputation profit. Figure 2-1 shows the different third-party resources you may need to work with during and after an event.

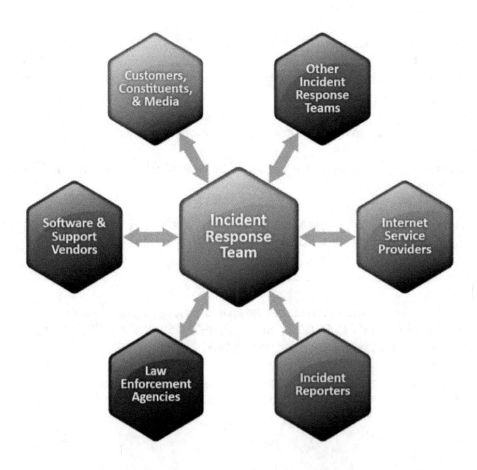

Figure 2-1. Communications with Outside Parties

Impact Category Descriptions

US-CERT has developed a good list related to types of incidents, taken from here: https://us-cert.cisa.gov/incident-notification-guidelines

Impact Category	Category Severity Levels
Functional Impact: A measure of the impact to business functionality or ability to provide services	NO IMPACT – Event has no impact.
	NO IMPACT TO SERVICES – Event has no impact to any business or Industrial Control Systems (ICS) services or delivery to entity customers.
	MINIMAL IMPACT TO NON-CRITICAL SERVICES – Some small level of impact to non-critical systems and services.
	MINIMAL IMPACT TO CRITICAL SERVICES –Minimal impact but to a critical system or service, such as email or active directory.
	SIGNIFICANT IMPACT TO NON-CRITICAL SERVICES – A non-critical service or system has a significant impact.
	DENIAL OF NON-CRITICAL SERVICES – A non-critical system is denied or destroyed.
	SIGNIFICANT IMPACT TO CRITICAL SERVICES – A critical system has a significant impact, such as local administrative account compromise.
	DENIAL OF CRITICAL SERVICES/LOSS OF CONTROL – A critical system has been rendered unavailable.
Information Impact: Describes the type of information lost, compromised, or corrupted.	NO IMPACT – No known data impact.
	SUSPECTED BUT NOT IDENTIFIED – A data loss or impact to availability is suspected, but no direct confirmation exists.
	PRIVACY DATA BREACH – The confidentiality of personally identifiable information (PII) [6] or personal health information (PHI) was compromised.
	PROPRIETARY INFORMATION BREACH – The confidentiality of unclassified proprietary information [7], such as protected critical infrastructure information (PCII), intellectual property, or trade secrets was compromised.
	DESTRUCTION OF NON-CRITICAL SYSTEMS – Destructive techniques, such as master boot record (MBR) overwrites; have been used against a non-critical system.
	CRITICAL SYSTEMS DATA BREACH - Data pertaining to a critical system has been exfiltrated.
	CORE CREDENTIAL COMPROMISE – Core system credentials (such as domain or enterprise administrative credentials) or credentials for critical systems have been exfiltrated.
	DESTRUCTION OF CRITICAL SYSTEM – Destructive techniques, such as MBR overwrite; have been used against a critical system.

Impact Category	Category Severity Levels
Recoverability: Identifies the scope of resources needed to recover from the incident	REGULAR – Time to recovery is predictable with existing resources.
	SUPPLEMENTED – Time to recovery is predictable with additional resources.
	EXTENDED – Time to recovery is unpredictable; additional resources and outside help are needed.
	NOT RECOVERABLE – Recovery from the incident is not possible (e.g., sensitive data exfiltrated and posted publicly).

The US-Cert resource also covers Attack Vectors Taxonomy and Incident Attributes.

"MITRE ATT&CK® is a globally-accessible knowledge base of adversary tactics and techniques based on real-world observations. The ATT&CK knowledge base is used as a foundation for the development of specific threat models and methodologies in the private sector, in government, and in the cybersecurity product and service community." - https://attack.mitre.org

This framework contains 14 distinct subsections

1. Reconnaissance (10 techniques)
2. Resource Development (6 techniques)
3. Initial Access (9 techniques)
4. Execution (10 techniques)
5. Persistence (18 techniques)
6. Privilege Escalation (12 techniques)
7. Defense Evasion (37 techniques)
8. Credential Access (14 techniques)
9. Discovery (25 techniques)
10. Lateral Movement (9 techniques)
11. Collection (17 techniques)
12. Command and Control (16 techniques)
13. Exfiltration (9 techniques)
14. Impact (13 techniques)

The NIST SP800-61 r2 breaks down the response process into 4 steps. We are going to paraphrase each one. If you would like more in-depth information, please download and read the NIST SP800-61 r2 document.

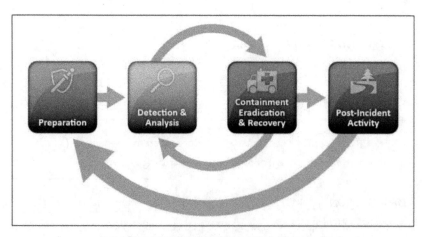

Figure 3-1. Incident Response Life Cycle

Preparation

This is **THE MOST IMPORTAN**T step out of the 4. Without it, you will not be able to detect incidents. This means you must have policies and procedures in place, your call list, the ability to track and manage the activities, the employees on staff trained to handle incidents, and the controls in place and configured to identify threats.

IT is hard to identify a hacker inside your network if you don't have an IDS/IPS alerting on the traffic or an employee looking at the logs. One big failure that is common is that the controls are in place, but the organization doesn't have the trained people analyzing the logs or findings. The systems may light up like a Christmas tree, but if no one is there to see it, did it really happen?

Detection & Analysis

Once an event has been identified, the very next step is to validate the finding. False positives do happen and when they do, many organizations waste a LOT of resources investigating something that never happened. Once it has been verified, figure out what, where, when, how, and why. This will allow you to move to the next phase. You start your notification process here.

Containment, Eradication, & Recovery

If computer forensics is needed, this is the step it comes into play. In many cases, this is not needed, or the organization makes a business decision not to pursue this route due to time, cost, and resources. If the event is larger than you originally thought, you may need to go back a step and re-evaluate the event

Post-Incident Activity

Your after-action reports and lessons learned starts here. You have already recovered from the event and now you need to do a gap analysis to see where you can do better. This may mean react faster, prevent from occurring, or use resources more effectively. In turn, this directly drives changes in the preparation phase. This can be something as simple as information security/awareness training for employees or tuning/modifying your security appliances. It could also mean you need an entirely different solution.

Final words

Simple fact of the matter is that you cannot prevent all risk to an organization. You can only minimize it. It is management's responsibility to decide what is an acceptable risk and move from there. The Incident Response team is just another factor in minimizing risk, even unknown risk.

Proactive measures such as employing threat intelligence and threat hunting can minimize your detection delta (time of an event to the time to identify said event), but there will always be issue that were unforeseen. Hacking and state sponsored espionage is on the rise and they often employ zero-day attacks. Having a solid response team actively searching out these threats and monitoring the environment for malicious activity is now part of an organizations due care and due diligence. Not doing so is a critical liability.

Using all three of the resources from NIST, US-CERT, and MITRE adds a complex set of things to look for during your Digital Forensics and Incident Response (DFIR) activities and can add more business justification for potential preventative tactics and techniques you may employ when choosing a security strategy.

Proactive Threat Hunting

By Jeremy Martin

Threat Hunting attempts combat advanced threats including APT with staff called "Threat Hunters" by attempting to identify ongoing threats that the Incident Response team has missed. There are many reasons for this, with many not pointing to inadequacies of the CERT/CSIRT. The Dunning-Kruger effect suggests that when we don't know something, we aren't aware of our own lack of knowledge. In other words, we don't know what we don't know. The more you know, the more you understand the landscape of risk is very large.

Because there remains a delta between detection and compromise, attribution combined with Threat Hunting, can drastically reduce that detection delta and to minimize the effects of a targeted attack. This can help reduce overall risk, even when considering an attack that no one has seen before. Threat Hunters are focusing to resolve a few items.

Minimize the Detection Delta

"Detecting threats and adversaries on networks continues to be a problem for many organizations. In the 2017 M-Trends report by FireEye, "the global median time from compromise to discovery has dropped significantly from 146 days in 2015 to 99 days in 2016" ("M-Trends," 2017). This disparity is known as the detection delta. Although positive, the number still indicates that it takes over three months before an organization realizes they have been breached. Significant damage and data exfiltration can happen in 99 days. Put another way, 99 days is equal to 8.554e+6 seconds. At dial-up speeds of 56Kbps, that means an attacker could transfer approximately 59.87GB of data, assuming a constant bandwidth and connection. If an average customer record is 2KB in size, the total records lost would equate to 29,935,000—even at low and slow speeds. Adding bandwidth or multiple avenues for the attacker to exfiltrate the data only exacerbates the loss to the organization. These numbers are daunting and almost impossible to comprehend. Traditional alerting further adds to the exhausting task of reactive detection techniques." - **csiac.org**

Alert Fatigue

Simply put, the analyst sees too many alerts, does not have to tools needed for their job, or the tools are not configured properly. Some attackers will use the to their advantage in a "fog of war" or "sleight of hand" type of attack and send millions of false positives to redirect the attention of the analyst to one thing while the attacker does something else. Especially when it comes to redundant activities that take time and resources. You can attempt to automate some of this to get a better quality of monitoring.

Human Adversaries

There are times where certain adversarial movements are missed because it does not follow a "heartbeat" of activity. For example, a botnet that calls home every thirty seconds is easier to notice than traffic that looks like normal web traffic without a consistent pattern. Port scans are easy to catch if they are using the defaults of the scanner and should trip sensors. If the foe is scanning at an interval of once per 90-600 seconds, the traffic may not get picked up by your security solutions and would not be obvious when looking at the visual representation of the data.

Consistency in Know Attack Patterns

Techniques, Tactics, and Procedures (TTPs) of known groups or the MITRE Adversarial Tactics, Techniques & Common Knowledge (ATT&CK) matrix are very helpful in deciding what you search for. You will be using mostly the same data the CSIRT team has but targeting your searches for very specific data set or content that may not have tripped the security sensors. For example, a fragmented attack that bypassed the IDS/IPS or what looks like regular user accounts not tied to a real employee accessing sensitive data.

Indicators of Compromise (IOC)

An IOC is an artifact left behind by an attack. This could be malware (trojans, rootkits, etc.), user accounts, or other trace evidence. These are known indicator. That tie directly into the **TTPs**.

TTPs

Are the abstract descriptions of adversary behavior that IOCs indicate, so are the "known unknowns", as the methodology is understood, but any subsequent IOCs are not known prior to the attack. Zero-day exploits2 would therefore be the "unknown unknowns".

"The behavior of an actor. A tactic is the highest-level description of this behavior, while techniques give a more detailed description of behavior in the context of a tactic, and procedures an even lower-level, highly detailed description in the context of a technique." - csrc.nist.gov

Pyramid of Pain

"As popularized by David Bianco's Pyramid of Pain, adversaries can easily change hash values, IP addresses, domains, and other indicators produced by their activities. This means that these indicator types are only useful to detect adversaries for a fleeting time. The Pyramid of Pain encourages us to focus on actor tactics, techniques, and procedures (TTPs), which cause the most pain (or hassle) for an adversary to change. While the community largely accepts that we need to move to TTPs, analysts struggle with how to track them in a way that facilitates actionable detection and mitigation." - mitre.org

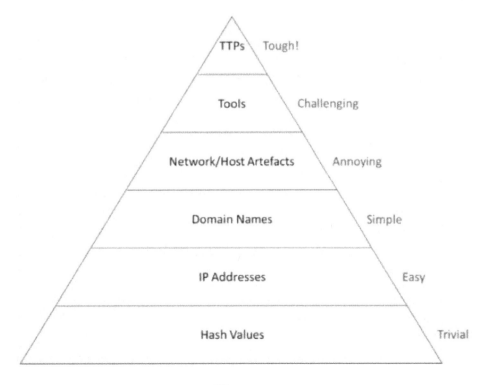

Prioritization of Adversaries

Identify what threat is a bigger threat. Is it an APT going after your Industrial Control System (ICS) access or a competitor trying to steal your flagship product? Industrial Espionage has been around for a long time and is not going anywhere anytime soon.

A more common threat that gets missed for too long is the insider threat or disgruntled employee. Many of them know the rules and what would flag the internal security sensors along with potential ways around those controls. Even worse if they are system admins or developers where they may already have elevated privileges.

Crown Jewels Analysis (CJA)

This means identify the critical assets in the organization and identify all of the dependencies to that asset or process. The organization should already have a list of critical assets after completing and continually reassessing a Business Impact Analysis (BIA). If they don't, this needs to be done first. For example, their customer database may be a Crown Jewel. The organization makes residual profit from the customers by selling services and marketing new products. Some of the dependencies that are tied to the customer database may include the payment processing system, email server, customer portal, and anything else that helps make the organization accomplish their mission with the customer. Now that you have these listed out, identify possible break points or weaknesses that could cause the dependency chain to break.

Threat Hunting with a Hypothesis

The process of threat hunting can be broken down into three steps:

> Creating an actionable hypothesis
> Executing the hypothesis
> Testing the hypothesis to completion.

What a threat hunter does is creates a theory based of a perceived threat, analyses logs, and attempts to prove or disprove that the theory was correct. Take for instance the APT attack that compromised the SolarWinds supply chains. A threat hunter would gather as much identifying information as possible about the attackers, IP addresses, tools, and techniques used, write up a hypothesis and hunt for the evidence.

If the theory is proven correct, the incident gets kicked over to the Incident Response team for action and investigation. IF there was no evidence found of that attack or group, the hypothesis is deemed unprovable and shelved for possible review at a later date. A new hunt then starts. If you go on several hunts and don't find anything, verify your data is good, tools are working, and go to the next. Not "tagging your prey" is a good thing. If you do get something, you just helped minimize the detection delta and potentially saved the organization a lot of money and resources. It is key for the hypotheses to be built on observations, intelligence, and experience and should be actionable, as well as testable, and tuned constantly.

Note: It is important that you leverage both internal and external threat intelligence

The hunting Loop

Like the Incident Response, this is the hunt brought full circle in 4 steps. Assuming you uncover what you were looking for, you then communicate with the CSIRT to start the "Containment, Eradication, & Recovery" process and finish with the ""Post-Incident Activity" before you move on to the next hypothesis.

This helps to improve both the reactive and proactive teams.

If not, go back to step 1 and try again

Note: It is suggested to Rotate SOC analysts into the Threat Hunting team for learning and development.

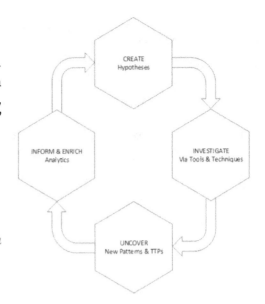

Image from: hodigital.blog.gov.uk

Threat Hunting Capability Maturity Model (TH-CMM)

Like other CMM processes, the TH-CMM ranges from level 1-5, with 1 being the lowest level of maturity and 5 being the greatest. What is missing is 0 which effectively is there is no capability.

Threat Hunting Capability Maturity Model	Level 1 INITIAL	Level 2 MANAGED	Level 3 DEFINED	Level 4 QUANTITATIVELY MANAGED	Level 5 OPTIMISING
People	• Existing SOC analysts • Resourcing needs not known • Training needs not known • Performance not managed • Lack of career development plan • Normal systems behaviour not sufficiently understood	• Threat Hunting lead • Informal view of resourcing • Informal view of training • Performance is qualitatively managed • Career development informally managed • Normal systems behaviour is moderately understood	• Dedicated threat hunters • Formal recruitment plan • Formal training plan • Performance expectations defined with role profiles • Formalised career development plan • Normal systems behaviour is fully understood	• SOC analysts rotated for L&D • Succession plans in place • Training completion tracked • Metrics utilised for team performance • Mission critical systems identified	• Teams integrated across SOC • Resourcing needs integrated • Training needs integrated • Improvement plans to address underperformance • Situational awareness
Process	• Hypothesis generation is unstructured • *Hunts occur ad-hoc, if at all* • *Little or no data collected* • Little understanding of anomalies indicative of malicious activity • Abnormalities not routinely searched for	• CTI and Domain Expertise used to generate hypotheses and prioritisation by lead • Hunts occur occasionally • *Moderate data collection from key areas* • *Basic threat feeds with IOCs utilised* • Targeting of IOCs at bottom of POP	• Formal hunting process • Hunts occur regularly • *High data collection from key areas* • CTI and previous experience used to detect malicious activity • Targeting of IOCs in middle of POP	• Manual risk scoring e.g. Crown Jewels • Hunts occur frequently • *Moderate data collection from most of estate* • *CTI tailored to organisation* • Targeting of IOCs at top of POP	• Automated risk scoring e.g. machine learning • Hunts occur continuously • *High data collection from full estate* • Hunt analytics and IOCs shared across community • Automated TTP and campaign tracking
Tools	• *Reactive SOC tools* • Little or no automation • Little or no documentation produced	• Basic searching via text or SQL-like queries • *Automatic matching of IOCs* • Documentation using basic office suites	• Statistical analysis techniques • Library of hunt procedures automated on regular schedule • Central workflow and knowledge repository tools • Lab environments used to aid hypothesis generation and testing	• Visualisation tools utilised, and analytics tested for effectiveness • Library of hunt procedures automated on frequent schedule • Dashboards utilised	• Machine learning is leveraged, with horizon scanning maintained • Library of hunt procedures automated continuously • Central workflow and knowledge repository are integrated and shared

Note: Items in *italics* are not strictly part of a Threat Hunting capability, but are essential prerequisites and enablers.

Table from: hodigital.blog.gov.uk

Now we have the basics covered, happy hunting!

Incident Response Cheat Sheet for Windows

By LaShanda Edwards

For some of those that use their computer systems, their systems may appear normal to them, but they could never realize there may well be something really abnormal going on or perhaps that proven fact that their systems could be compromised. Making use of Incident Response an outsized number of attacks at the main level can be detected. Investigations are often administered to get any digital evidence.

This article primary focus is on Incident response for Windows systems. So, let us begin with this clue card to give you a jumpstart.

Table of Contents

- What is Incident Response?
- User Accounts
- Processes
- Services
- Task Scheduler
- Startup
- Registry Entries
- Active TCP & UDP ports
- File Shares
- Files
- Firewall Settings
- Sessions with other Systems
- Open Sessions
- Log Entries

What is Incident Response?

Incident response may be a term utilized to describe the method by which a company handles an information breach or cyberattack, including the way the organization attempts to manage the results of the attack or breach. The goal is to effectively manage the incident, so that the damage is restricted and both recovery time and costs, likewise as damaged collateral like brand reputation, are kept at a modicum.

10 possible security events that could occur:

- Unusual behavior from privileged user accounts. Any anomalies within the behavior of a privileged user account can indicate that somebody is using it to achieve a footing into a company's network.
- Unauthorized insiders trying to access servers and data. Many insiders will test the waters to see exactly what systems and data they will access. Warning signs include unauthorized users attempting to access servers and data, requesting access to data that are not associated with their jobs, logging in at very abnormal times from unusual locations or logging in from multiple locations in a short timeframe.
- Anomalies in outbound network traffic. It is not just traffic that comes into a network that organizations should worry about. Organizations should monitor for traffic leaving their perimeters in addition. This might include insiders uploading large files to private cloud applications; downloading large files to secondary storage devices, like USB flash drives; or sending large numbers of email messages with attachments outside the corporate.
- Traffic sent to or from unknown locations. For an organization that only operates in one country, any traffic sent to other countries could indicate malicious activity. Administrators should investigate any traffic to unknown networks to confirm it is legitimate.
- Excessive consumption. A rise within the performance of server memory or hard drives may mean an attacker is accessing them illegally.
- Changes in configuration. Changes that have not been approved, including reconfiguration of services, installation of startup programs or firewall changes, are an indication of possible malicious activity. The identical is true of scheduled tasks that are added.
- Hidden files. These are often considered suspicious thanks at their file names, sizes, or locations, which indicate the information, or logs may be leaked.
- Unexpected changes. These include user account lockouts, password changes or sudden changes in group memberships.
- Abnormal browsing behavior. This might be unexpected redirects, changes within the browser configuration or repeated pop-ups.
- Suspicious registry entries. This happens mostly when malware infects Windows systems. It is one among the most ways malware ensures it remains within the infected system.

User Accounts

In incident response it is very necessary to research the user activity. The research goal is to find if there is any suspicious user account present or any restricted permissions are assigned to a user. By checking the user account, one can get answers to the questions like which user is currently logged in, and how reasonable a user account is.

The following are some of the ways to view user accounts:

To view the local user accounts in GUI:

1. Press, 'Windows+R'
2. type **lusrmgr.msc** to open [Local Users and Groups (Local)]:

Now click on '**ok**', and you will be ready to see the user accounts, and their descriptions.

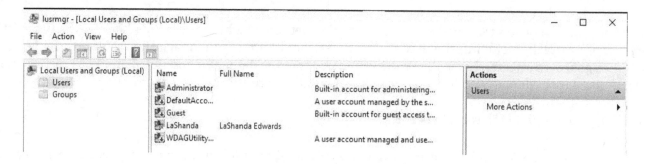

To view the system user accounts and the kind of account it is:

Run command prompt as administrator and type command **net user**:

To view and manage local user groups on a system:

Net localgroup group name is employed to manage local user groups on a system. By using this command, an administrator can add the local or domain users to a particular group, delete users from a group, create new groups, and delete existing groups.

1. Open prompt and run as an administrator
2. type **net localgroup administrators**:

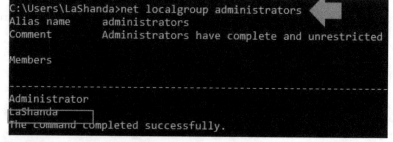

To view local user accounts, with their names, if they are enabled and their description:

Run PowerShell as an administrator, type **Get-LocalUser**:

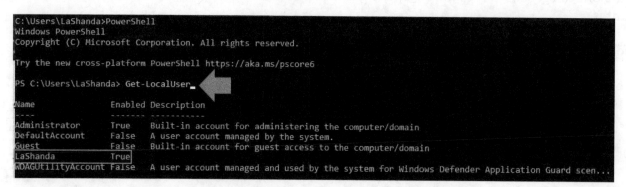

Processes

To view the list of all the processes running on the system, you can use, '**tasklist**' command for this purpose. By making use of this command, you will get a +-a list of the processes the memory space used, period, image file name, services running within the process, etc.

To view the processes, you will use the subsequent methods to look at the running processes:

> Press, '**Windows+R**'
> Type **taskmgr.exe**

Now click on '**OK**' and you can see all the running processes in your system and can be ready to check if there is any unnecessary process running.

To view all the running processes with their Process ID (PID) and their session name and the amount of memory used:

1. Run command prompt as an administrator
2. Type tasklist

To get an inventory of all active processes run on the local computer:

1. Run PowerShell as an administrator
2. Type get-process

Windows systems have an especially powerful tool with the Windows Management Instrumentation Command (wmic). Wmic is extremely useful when it involves incident response. This tool is enough to note some abnormal signs within the system. This command is often utilized in the Command-prompt likewise as PowerShell when running as an administrator. The syntax is **wmic process list full**.

```
PS C:\Users\LaShanda> wmic process list full
```

After you establish which process is performing a weird network activity.

To view more details about the parent process IDs, Name of the method and the process ID:

1. Open PowerShell as an administrator
2. Type wmic process get name,parentprocessid,processed

```
PS C:\Users\LaShanda> wmic process get name,parentprocessid,processid
Name                    ParentProcessId   ProcessId
System Idle Process     0                 0
System                  0                 4
Registry                4                 100
smss.exe                4                 588
csrss.exe               660               672
```

To view the trail of the WMIC process:

1. Open PowerShell
2. type **wmic process where 'ProcessID=PID' get CommandLine**

```
PS C:\Users\LaShanda> wmic process where 'ProcessID=10520' get CommandLine
CommandLine
"C:\WINDOWS\system32\SnippingTool.exe"

PS C:\Users\LaShanda>
```

Services

To identify if there is any **abnormal service** running in your system or some service is not functioning properly, you can view your services.

To view all the services in GUI:

1. Press 'Windows+R'
2. Type services.msc

Now click on '**Ok**' to see the list of processes.

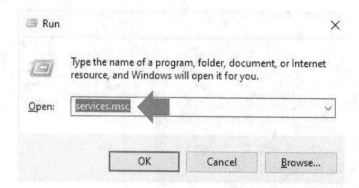

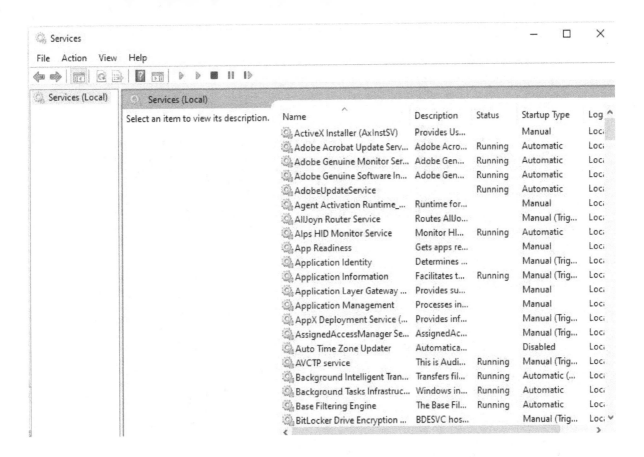

To start and view the list of services that are currently running in your system:

Open command prompt as an administrator

Type net start

To view whether a service is running and to retrieve more details like its service name, display name etc.:

Type sc query | more

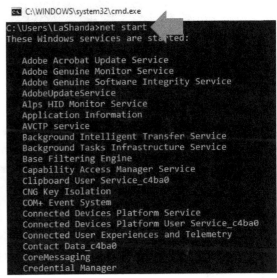

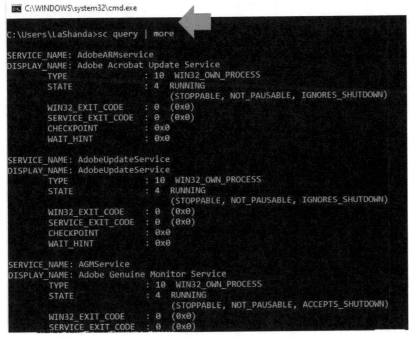

If you liked an inventory of running processes with their associated services within the prompt:

Run cmd as an administrator
Type **tasklist /svc**.

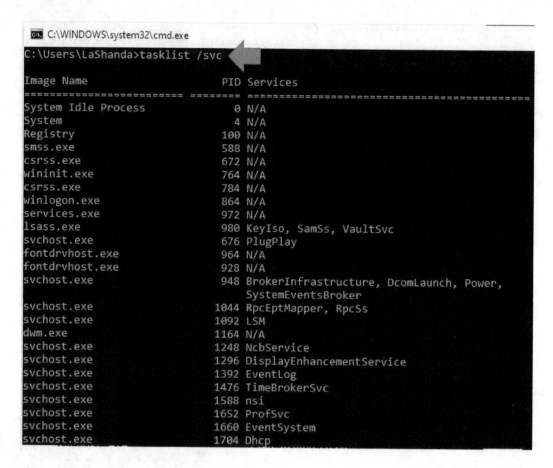

Task Scheduler

Task Scheduler is a component within the Windows which provides the flexibility to schedule the launch of programs or any scripts at a predefined time or after specified time intervals. You can view these scheduled tasks which are of high privileges and appearance suspicious.

To view the task Scheduler in GUI:

Press 'Windows+R'
Type taskschd.msc
Press '**OK**'

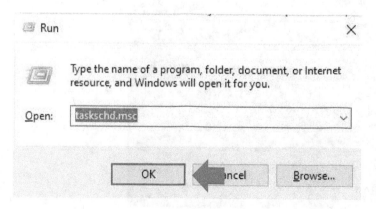

Enter the following path and press enter,
C:\ ProgramData\Microsoft\Windows\Start Menu\Programs\Administrative Tools

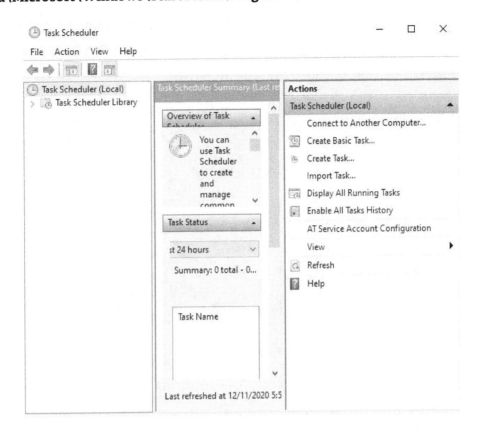

To view the schedule tasks in the command prompt:

Run command prompt as an administrator
Type schtasks

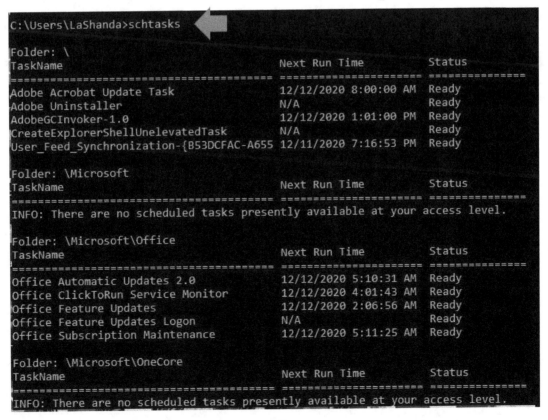

Startup

The *startup* folder in *Windows* automatically runs applications after you go online. So, an incident handler, you would be able observe the applications that auto-start.

To view the applications within the Startup menu within the GUI:

> Press 'Windows+R'
> Type taskmgr
> Press '**OK**'

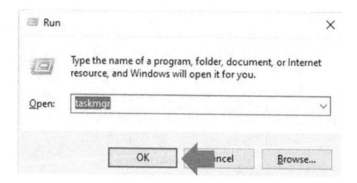

Open the task manager and click on the '**Startup**' menu.

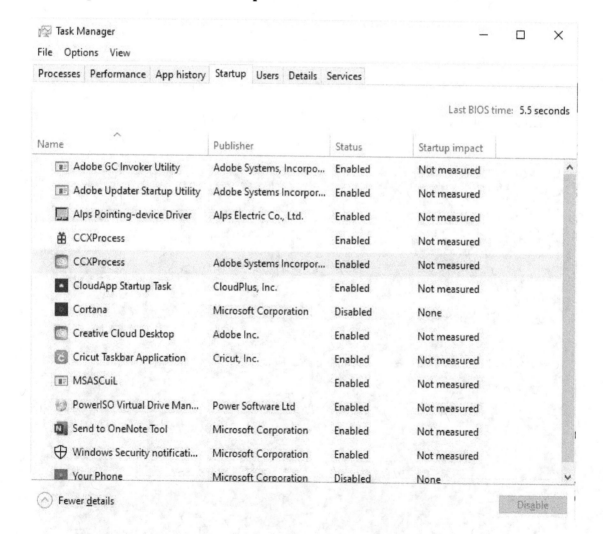

By doing this, you will be able to see which applications are enabled and disabled on startup. On opening the subsequent path, it will offer you the identical option.

To view, the startup applications in the PowerShell run the PowerShell as an administrator:

Type wmic startup get caption,command

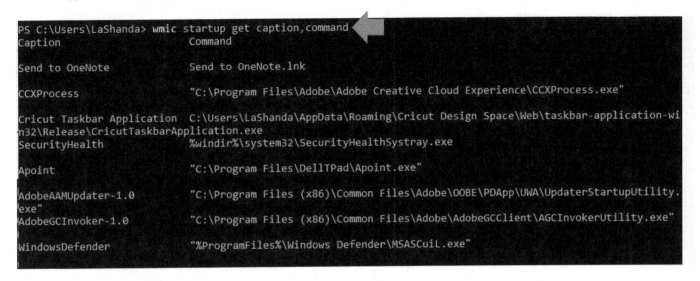

```
PS C:\Users\LaShanda> wmic startup get caption,command
Caption                     Command

Send to OneNote             Send to OneNote.lnk

CCXProcess                      "C:\Program Files\Adobe\Adobe Creative Cloud Experience\CCXProcess.exe"

Cricut Taskbar Application  C:\Users\LaShanda\AppData\Roaming\Cricut Design Space\Web\taskbar-application-wi
n32\Release\CricutTaskbarApplication.exe
SecurityHealth                  %windir%\system32\SecurityHealthSystray.exe

Apoint                          "C:\Program Files\DellTPad\Apoint.exe"

AdobeAAMUpdater-1.0             "C:\Program Files (x86)\Common Files\Adobe\OOBE\PDApp\UWA\UpdaterStartupUtility.
exe"
AdobeGCInvoker-1.0             "C:\Program Files (x86)\Common Files\Adobe\AdobeGCClient\AGCInvokerUtility.exe"

WindowsDefender                "%ProgramFiles%\Windows Defender\MSASCuiL.exe"
```

To view a detailed list of the AutoStart applications in PowerShell, you can run it as an administrator:

Type Get-CimInstance Win32_StartupCommand | Select-Object Name, command, Location, User | Format-List

```
C:\WINDOWS\system32\cmd.exe - PowerShell                                          —    □    ✕

PS C:\Users\LaShanda> Get-CimInstance Win32_StartupCommand | Select-Object Name, command, Location, User | F
ormat-List

Name     : Send to OneNote
command  : Send to OneNote.lnk
Location : Startup
User     : MINE\LaShanda

Name     : CCXProcess
command  : "C:\Program Files\Adobe\Adobe Creative Cloud Experience\CCXProcess.exe"
Location : HKU\S-1-5-21-3641352181-1430935677-600944533-1001\SOFTWARE\Microsoft\Windows\CurrentVersion\Run
User     : MINE\LaShanda

Name     : Cricut Taskbar Application
command  : C:\Users\LaShanda\AppData\Roaming\Cricut Design
           Space\Web\taskbar-application-win32\Release\CricutTaskbarApplication.exe
Location : Common Startup
User     : Public

Name     : SecurityHealth
command  : %windir%\system32\SecurityHealthSystray.exe
Location : HKLM\SOFTWARE\Microsoft\Windows\CurrentVersion\Run
User     : Public

Name     : Apoint
command  : "C:\Program Files\DellTPad\Apoint.exe"
Location : HKLM\SOFTWARE\Microsoft\Windows\CurrentVersion\Run
User     : Public
```

Registry Entries

Sometimes if there is a presence of unsophisticated malware it may be found by taking a glance at the Windows Registry's run key.

To view the GUI of the registry key:

Open **REGEDIT** reach the run key manually.

The Registry Editor can be opened in two of the following ways: In the search box on the taskbar, type **regedit**. Select the top result for **Registry Editor** (Desktop app). It can also be assessed if you press and hold or right-click the **Start** button, then select **Run**. Enter **regedit** in the **Open:** box and select **OK**.

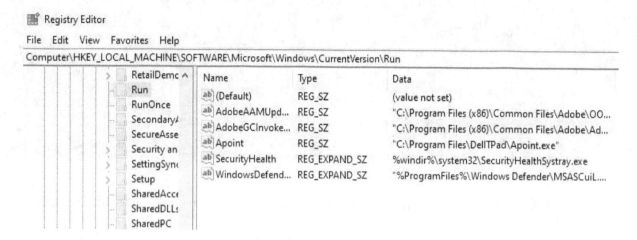

You can also view the registry of the Local Machine of the Run key in the PowerShell, by running it as an administrator:

Type reg query HKLM\SOFTWARE\Microsoft\Windows\CurrentVersion\Run

You can view the registry of the Current User of the Run key in the PowerShell, by running it as an administrator:

2. Type **reg query HKEY_CURRENT_USER\SOFTWARE\Microsoft\Windows\CurrentVersion\Run**

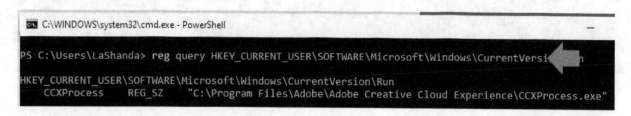

Active TCP & UDP ports

As an Incident Responder, you must carefully listen to the active TCP and UDP ports of your system. The network statistics of a system is employing a tool. The standards tested are incoming and outgoing connections, routing tables, port listening, and usage statistics.

1. Open the command prompt
2. Type netstat -ano

This can also be checked in the PowerShell with a different command to see the IP and the local ports.

Run PowerShell as administrator:

Open command prompt, type **cmd.**

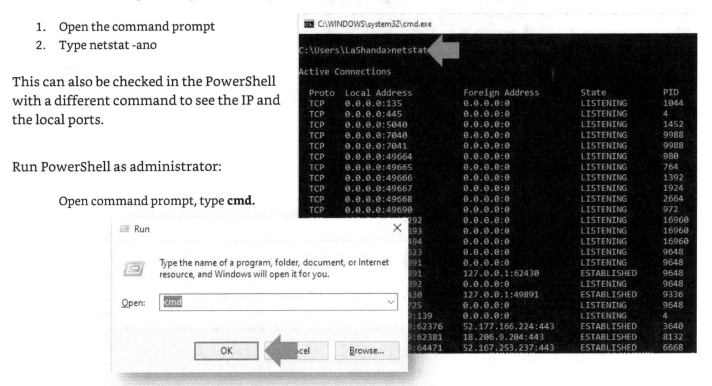

Open PowerShell as administrator, type **start-process PowerShell -verb runas**.

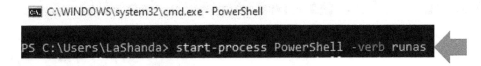

Type Get-NetTCPConnection -LocalAddress 192.168.1.129 | Sort-Object LocalPort

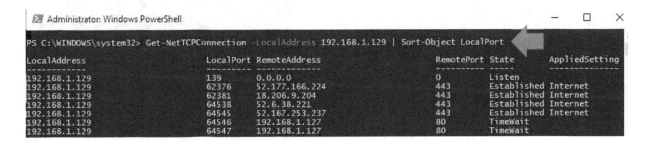

File sharing

As an Incident Responder, you must ensure that each file share is accountable and reasonable, and there is no unnecessary file sharing.

To check the file-sharing options within the prompt:

Type net view **\\<localhost>**
To view the file-sharing in PowerShell, you can type **Get-SMBShare**.

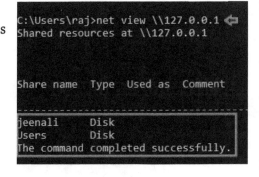

41

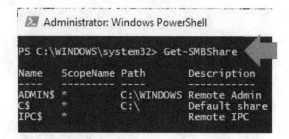

Files

To view the files which can be malicious or end with a selected extension, you can use, 'forfiles' command. Forfiles, a command-line utility software, was shipped with Microsoft Windows Vista. During that point, management of multiples files through the program line was difficult as most of the commands at that point we made to figure on single files.

To view the .exe files with their path to locate them within the command prompt:

Type forfiles /D -10 /S /M *.exe /C "cmd /c echo @path"

```
C:\WINDOWS\system32\cmd.exe - forfiles /D -10 /S /M *.exe /C "cmd /c echo @path"
C:\Users\LaShanda>forfiles /D -10 /S /M *.exe /C "cmd /c echo @path"

"C:\Users\LaShanda\AppData\Local\app-desktop-design-updater\installer.exe"
"C:\Users\LaShanda\AppData\Local\Discord\Update.exe"
```

To View files without its path and more details of the file extension and its modification date:

Type forfiles /D -10 /S /M *.exe /C "cmd /c echo @ext @fname @fdate"

```
C:\Users\LaShanda>forfiles /D -10 /S /M *.exe /C "cmd /c echo @ext @fname @fdate"

"exe" "installer" 5/23/2020
"exe" "Update" 2/24/2020
```

To check for files modified in the last 10 days:

Type forfiles /p c: /S /D -10

To check for file size below 6MB:

Use the file explorer's search box and enter **size:>6M**

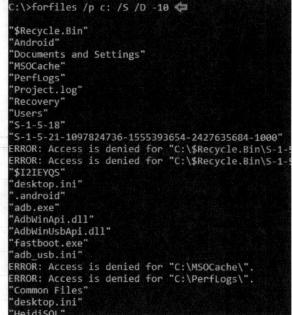

Figure: i2.wp.com/1.bp.blogspot.com

Firewall Settings

The incident responder should focus on the firewall configurations and settings and should maintain it regularly.

To view the firewall configurations and the inbound and outbound traffic in the command prompt:

> Type netsh firewall show config

To view the firewall settings of the current profile in the command prompt:

> Type netsh advfirewall show currentprofile

Sessions with other Systems

To view session details that are established with other systems:

Run command prompt and type **net use**

```
Microsoft Windows [Version 10.0.18362.1016]
(c) 2019 Microsoft Corporation. All rights reserved.

C:\Users\raj>net use
New connections will be remembered.


Status       Local     Remote                  Network

-------------------------------------------------------------------
OK                     \\192.168.0.106\IPC$    Microsoft Windows Network
The command completed successfully.
```

Figure: i1.wp.com/1.bp.blogspot.com

Open Sessions

To view any open sessions of your system, you can get the details about the duration of the session:

Run the command prompt and type **net session**

```
Microsoft Windows [Version 10.0.14393]
(c) 2016 Microsoft Corporation. All rights reserved.

C:\Users\Administrator>net session

Computer            User name        Client Type       Opens Idle time

-------------------------------------------------------------------
\\192.168.0.110     administrator                       0 00:02:31
The command completed successfully.
```

Figure: i2.wp.com/1.bp.blogspot.com

Log Entries

Viewing the log entries in GUI, can all you to open the event viewer and see the logs.

Press 'Windows+ R'
Type eventvwr.msc

To export certain logs of a particular event in command prompt:

Type **wevtutil qe security**

```
C:\Windows\system32>wevtutil qe security ⇦
```

To get the event log list in the PowerShell:

Type Get-EventLog -List

```
PS C:\Users\raj> Get-EventLog -List ⇦

 Max(K) Retain OverflowAction      Entries Log
 ------ ------ --------------      ------- ---
 20,480      0 OverwriteAsNeeded    12,676 Application
 20,480      0 OverwriteAsNeeded         0 HardwareEvents
    512      7 OverwriteOlder            0 Internet Explorer
 20,480      0 OverwriteAsNeeded         0 Key Management Service
    128      0 OverwriteAsNeeded       128 OAlerts
    512      7 OverwriteOlder            2 OneApp_IGCC
                                          Security
 20,480      0 OverwriteAsNeeded     7,887 System
 15,360      0 OverwriteAsNeeded       422 Windows PowerShell


PS C:\Users\raj> Get-EventLog ⇦

cmdlet Get-EventLog at command pipeline position 1
Supply values for the following parameters:
LogName: OAlerts

 Index Time          EntryType  Source                 InstanceID Message
 ----- ----          ---------  ------                 ---------- -------
   128 Aug 16 12:55  Information Microsoft Office ...          300 Microsoft Word...
   127 Aug 16 02:22  Information Microsoft Office ...          300 Microsoft Word...
   126 Aug 16 01:59  Information Microsoft Office ...          300 Microsoft Word...
   125 Aug 15 04:11  Information Microsoft Office ...          300 Microsoft Word...
   124 Aug 14 19:33  Information Microsoft Office ...          300 Microsoft Word...
   123 Aug 14 18:13  Information Microsoft Office ...          300 Microsoft Word...
```

Figure: i1.wp.com/1.bp.blogspot.com

Type the specific event in the supply value and you will get event details of that specific event.

Conclusion

These commands can be used as an Incident Responder to help keep systems safe from threats. Proper preparation and planning are necessary to an effective incident response. This clue sheet provides a clear course of action for using windows, it is often too late to organize effective response efforts after a breach or attack has occurred.

Citation

Chandel, R. (2020). Hacking Articles. Incident Response: Windows Cheatsheet. Retrieved October 25, 2020, from https://www.hackingarticles.in/incident-response-windows-cheatsheet/

Lord, N. (2018). DataGuardian. What is Incident Response? Retrieved October 25, 2020, from https://digitalguardian.com/blog/what-incident-response

Rosencrance, L. (2017). TechTarget. 10 types of security incidents and how to handle them. Retrieved November 10, 2020, from https://searchsecurity.techtarget.com/feature/10-types-of-security-incidents-and-how-to-handle-them

Event Logs

"Many applications record errors and events in proprietary error logs, each with their own format and user interface. Data from different applications can't easily be merged into one complete report, requiring system administrators or support representatives to check a variety of sources to diagnose problems." - Microsoft

Modern Windows systems store logs in the %SystemRoot%\System32\winevt\logs directory by default in the binary XML Windows Event Logging format designated by the .evtx extension. Logs can also be stored remotely using log subscriptions. For remote logging, a remote system running the Windows Event Collector service subscribes to subscriptions of logs produced by other systems. The types of logs to be collected can be specified at a granular level and transport occurs over HTTPS on port 5986 using WinRM. GPO's can be used to configure the remote logging facilities on each computer.

Events can be logged in the Security, System and Application event logs or, on modern Windows systems, they may also appear in several other log files. The Setup event log records activities that occurred during installation of Windows. The Forwarded Logs event log is the default location to record events received from other systems. But there are also many additional logs, listed under Applications and Services Logs in Event Viewer, that record details related to specific types of activities. Since these log files are much more targeted than the Security log, they often retain information about events that occurred well before the current Security log has been overwritten. Always look for multiple sources of log information, and do not forget to look for older log files that may be captured by backup systems or volume shadow copies.

Windows Event Viewer

"Event Viewer is a component of Microsoft's Windows NT operating system that lets administrators and users view the event logs on a local or remote machine." – Wikipedia

Windows Event IDs have several fields in common:

- Log Name: The name of the Event Log where the event is stored. Useful when processing numerous logs pulled from the same system.
- Source: The service, Microsoft component or application that generated the event.
- Event ID: A code assigned to each type of audited activity.
- Level: The severity assigned to the event in question.
- User: The user account involved in triggering the activity or the user context that the source was running as when it logged the event. Note that this field often indicates "System" or a user that is not the cause of the event being recorded.
- OpCode: Assigned by the source generating the log. It's meaning is left to the source.
- Logged: The local system date and time when the event was logged.
- Task Category: Assigned by the source generating the log. It's meaning is left to the source.
- Keywords: Assigned by the source and used to group or sort events.
- Computer: The computer on which the event was logged. This is useful when examining logs collected from multiple systems but should not be considered to be the device that caused an event (such as when a remote logon is initiated, the Computer field will still show the name of the system logging the event, not the source of the connection).
- Description: A text block where additional information specific to the event being logged is recorded. This is often the most significant field for the analyst.

Windows Account Management Events

The following events will be recorded on the system where the account was created or modified, which will be the local system for a local account or a domain controller for a domain account.

Event ID	Description
4720	A user account was created.
4722	A user account was enabled.
4723	A user attempted to change an account's password.
4724	An attempt was made to reset an account's password.
4725	A user account was disabled.
4726	A user account was deleted.
4727	A security-enabled global group was created.
4728	A member was added to a security-enabled global group.
4729	A member was removed from a security-enabled global group.
4730	A security-enabled global group was deleted.
4731	A security-enabled local group was created.
4732	A member was added to a security-enabled local group.
4733	A member was removed from a security-enabled local group.
4734	A security-enabled local group was deleted.
4735	A security-enabled local group was changed.
4737	A security-enabled global group was changed.
4738	A user account was changed.
4741	A computer account was created.
4742	A computer account was changed.
4743	A computer account was deleted.
4754	A security-enabled universal group was created.
4755	A security-enabled universal group was changed.
4756	A member was added to a security-enabled universal group.
4757	A member was removed from a security-enabled universal group.
4758	A security-enabled universal group was deleted.
4798	A user's local group membership was enumerated. Large numbers of these events may be indicative of adversary account enumeration.
4799	A security-enabled local group membership was enumerated. Large numbers of these events may be indicative of adversary group enumeration.

Linux Logs for Accounts

The bulk of useful logs on a Linux system will be located in the **/var/log** directory. When looking for account issues, the following log files will record certain activity on the system where the account was created or modified, which will be the local system for a local account or a domain controller for a domain account.

- **auth.log**: user authentication events are logged here including authentication failures.
- **secure**: the auth.log for RedHat and CentOS
- **utmp**: will give you complete picture of user logins at which terminals, logouts, system events and current status of the system, system boot time (used by uptime) etc.
- **wtmp**: gives historical data of utmp.
- **btmp**: records only failed login attempts.
- **faillog**: records only failed login attempts.

One Step Deeper into LOG Analysis

By: Tajamul Sheeraz S

What is Log Analysis?

Log Analysis is evaluating the actions which were performed on or by the device. Mostly we will be looking for the before and after logs for the event or the action based on its timeline. The analyst should know what he/she is looking for in the logs.

Note: Analysis differs from analyst to analyst, but the end goal will remain the same.

What is an event?

An event is an observable change to the normal behavior of a system, environment, process, workflow, or person (components). There are three basic types of events:

- Normal - a normal event does not affect critical components or require change controls prior to the implementation of a resolution. Normal events do not require the participation of senior personnel or management notification of the event.
- Escalation – an escalated event affects critical production systems or requires that implementation of a resolution that must follow a change control process. Escalated events require the participation of senior personnel and stakeholder notification of the event.
- Emergency – an emergency is an event which may
  - Impact the health or safety of human beings
  - Breach primary controls of critical systems
  - Materially affect component performance or because of impact to component systems prevent activities which protect or may affect the health or safety of individuals
  - Deemed an emergency as a matter of policy or by declaration by the available incident coordinator

"Computer security and information technology personnel must handle emergency events according to well-defined computer security incident response plan." - **Wikipedia**

What is an incident?

"An incident is an event attributable to a human root cause. This distinction is particularly important when the event is the product of malicious intent to do harm. An important note: all incidents are events, but many events are not incidents. A system or application failure due to age or defect may be an emergency event but a random flaw or failure is not an incident." - **Wikipedia**

6 rules for Log Analysis

1. When - Date and Time
2. Where - Hostname/Destination machine
3. Who - Machine/User
4. What - Action being performed
5. Why - Why was the event generated
6. How - locally or remotely performed, inbound or outbound traffic

Types of log Analysis

We will cover SIEM based log analysis and Live log analysis (how to analyze log by taking remote sessions and where to look for logs).

SIEM Based

SIEM based alerts are triggered by the predefined written rules. An alert is nothing, other than the number of events combined for the defined rule.

The rule is written based on the organization's structure that some organizations allow users to make 5 login failure attempts after which the accounts get locked for which the alert will get generated and some have more than 5 login failure attempts allowed, basically it varies.

In these cases, we must understand the rule written for which the alert got triggered based on which we will be analyzing the events in that alert.

Live Log Analysis

Live log analysis is done when the machine is unmanaged by the organization, that is the organization is not obtaining logs from the machine. It could be due to several reasons like a testing machine, proof of concept, troubleshooting purposes or third-party managed machines. In these types of machines, we don't have agents installed on the machine for collecting the logs.

Where to look for logs?

Every technology has a different log storage location and path. We will cover windows and Linux technology, as they are commonly known.

Windows

- o We can obtain logs from Event Viewer

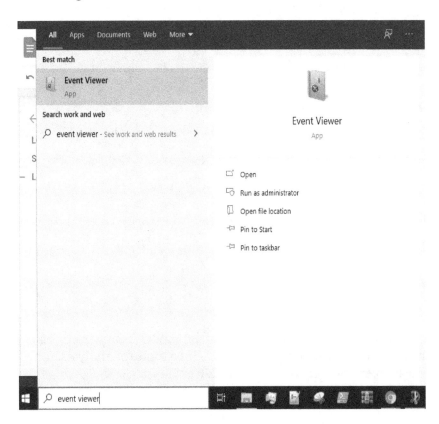

Mostly we will be investigating the System, Security, Application and PowerShell logs in the event viewer. As these obtain the security related events.

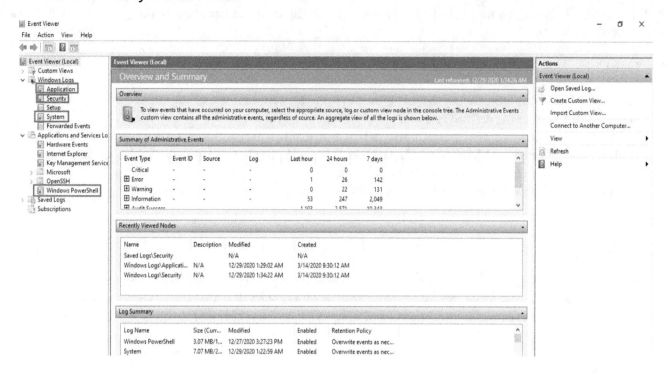

You could also download these logs by clicking save all events as highlighted in the picture.

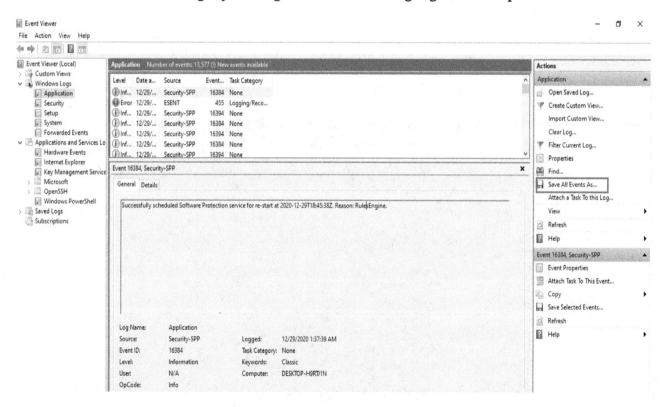

There is also a path in C drive (C:\Windows\System32\winevt\Logs) from where you could obtain the logs. We have faced few issues in the past while exporting these logs into tools for analysis, it had some corruption with the files, but we were able to open them through Event viewer.

Linux

- We could collect the Linux logs from the file path "/var/log". Below are a few examples.
  - /var/log/messages - general messages
  - /var/log/auth.log - Authentication logs
  - /var/log/kern.log - Kernel logs
  - /var/log/maillog - Mail logs
  - /var/log/httpd - Web server logs

Network, Security, Storage (DB) and Cloud devices.

- Mostly these devices will be integrated with the SIEM through Syslog, API, FTP, or DB mechanisms.
- In case if we want recent logs, we could refer to the documentation of the device for the logs storage path and how to collect them.

What to do after collecting the logs?

Once we have collected the logs, we could import them into any tool for analysis which we are familiar with. This makes it easier if you standardize your data into a consistent format There are ways to automate this process, but if you want to look at the logs individually, here are some options.

If you are using a windows machine for analysis.

We could import them in an excel sheet if they are collected in CSV format for analysis.
Specifically, for windows logs we could also use tools like Microsoft log parser, log parser lizard GUI, event viewer, etc., if you are using a windows machine for investigation.

If you are using a Linux machine for investigation.

We could also search for the specific field from the collected logs using the "grep", "sed" or "awk" command which is available in Linux. This makes searching for extremely specific data easier.
Manual (Man page) descriptions
- **Grep:** Searches for PATTERNS in each FILE. PATTERNS is one or more patterns separated by newline characters, and grep prints each line that matches a pattern. Typically, PATTERNS should be quoted when grep is used in a shell command.
  - https://linux.die.net/man/1/grep
- **Sed:** A stream editor is used to perform basic text transformations on an input stream (a file or input from a pipeline). While in some ways similar to an editor which permits scripted edits (such as ed), sed works by making only one pass over the input(s) and is consequently more efficient. But it is sed's ability to filter text in a pipeline which particularly distinguishes it from other types of editors.
  - https://linux.die.net/man/1/sed
- **Awk:** The awk utility shall execute programs written in the awk programming language, which is specialized for textual data manipulation. An awk program is a sequence of patterns and corresponding actions. When input is read that matches a pattern, the action associated with that pattern is carried out.
  - https://linux.die.net/man/1/awk
Of course, you can dump your logs into a SIEM or an environment like Elasticsearch using Logstash and Kibana as web interface to make the searching more visual for the analysts. The possibilities are endless.

Note: Technology and log format doesn't matter, we should be able to understand why the event is generated and what we are looking for in the logs. If you don't know what to look in the logs from a technology which you are not familiar with, it's ok. You Could always refer to the device documentation or search in google.

What to look for in the Logs?

Let's see what to look in the logs after collecting them depending upon the few technologies.

Windows Log

> **Aug 29 15:10:51** test_machine AgentDevice=WindowsLog AgentLogFile=Security PluginVersion=7.6.41 Source=Microsoft-Windows-Security-Auditing **Computer=test_machine.example.com** **OriginatingComputer=1.1.1.1** User= Domain= EventID=4625 **EventIDCode=4625** EventType=16 EventCategory=0 RecordNumber=48535925 TimeGenerated=16086500 TimeWritten=1655500 Level=Log Always **Keywords=Audit Failure** Task=SE_ADT_LOGON_LOGON Opcode=Info **Message=An account failed to log on**. Subject: Security ID: NT AUTHORITY\SYSTEM Account **Name: test_machine**$ Account Domain: **Workgroup Logon ID: 0x3e7 Logon Type: 4** Account for Which Logon Failed: Security ID: NULL SID **Account Name:** *Lorem ipsum* Account Domain: Workgroup Failure Information: **Failure Reason: Unknown username or bad password**. Status: 0xc000006d Sub Status: 0xc000006a Process Information: Caller Process ID: 0x4c4 **Caller Process Name: C:\Windows\System32\test.exe** Network Information: Workstation Name: test_machine Source Network Address: - Source Port: - Detailed Authentication Information: **Logon Process: Advapi** Authentication Package: Negotiate Transited Services: - Package Name (NTLM only): - Key Length: 0 **This event is generated when a logon request fails. It is generated on the computer where access was attempted**. The Subject fields indicate the account on the local system which requested the logon. This is most commonly a service such as the Server service, or a local process such as Winlogon.exe or Services.exe. The Logon Type field indicates the kind of logon that was requested. The most common types are 2 (interactive) and 3 (network). The Process Information fields indicate which account and process on the system requested the logon. The Network Information fields indicate where a remote logon request originated. Workstation name is not always available and may be left blank in some cases. The authentication information fields provide detailed information about this specific logon request. - Transited services indicate which intermediate services have participated in this logon request. - Package name indicates which sub-protocol was used among the NTLM protocols. - Key length indicates the length of the generated session key. This will be 0 if no session key was requested.

- When - Aug 29 15:10:51
- Where - Computer=test_machine.example.com and OriginatingComputer=1.1.1.1
- Who - Account Name: *Lorem ipsum* and Caller Process Name: C:\Windows\System32\test.exe
- What - EventIDCode=4625 and This event is generated when a logon request fails
- Why - Message=An account failed to log on and Failure Reason: Unknown username or bad password
- How - Remotely- It is generated on the computer where access was attempted.

Linux Log

> **Jun 02 09:03:09 test_machine sudo: user1 : user NOT in sudoers** ; TTY=pts/0 ; PWD=/home/admin ; USER=root ; **COMMAND=/usr/sbin/tcpdump -i any -A -w test.pcap**

- When - Jun 02 09:03:09
- Where - test machine
- Who - sudo: user1
- What - COMMAND=/usr/sbin/tcpdump -i any -A -w test.pcap
- Why - user NOT in sudoers
- How - locally on the same machine **test_machine**

Firewall Log

> **abcd**: NetScreen device_id=abcd system-notification-00257(traffic): **start_time="2019-3-9 18:05:20"** duration=34 policy_id=116 service=https proto=6 **src zone=external dst zone=dmz action=Permit sent=47 rcvd=3818 src=2.2.2.2 dst=8.8.8.8** src_port=35182 dst_port=443 src-xlated ip=2.2.2.2 port=35182 dst-xlated ip=8.8.8.8 port=443 session_id=896 **reason=Close - AGE OUT**

- When - 2019-3-9 18:05:20
- Where - dst zone=dmz
- Who - src=2.2.2.2
- What - action=Permit
- Why - reason=Close - AGE OUT
- How - Inbound (src zone=external dst zone=dmz)

More Windows Event Log Analysis

By: Nitin Sharma

In the age of advanced malwares, it is becoming increasingly difficult to detect malicious activities and monitor every action associated with them. These actions could vary from events related to system or may be application. Segregation of events is the key here however, once segregated, it will be hard to correlate the same. Even in the times of enhanced SIEM tools, incident responders sometimes require raw event logs from the operating systems where large amount of event data needs to be organized before analysis. In such cases, it is must that the incident responder must be skilled and aware of what needs to be done.

Photo by Sharon McCutcheon, Unsplash [1]

This article provides some basic insights into different events and the types of events which are important from threat perspective. It will cover some native commands associated with Windows workstation in the CMD as well as Powershell. At the end, searching and storing logs with the EVTX format for Windows Workstation is demonstrated which will also help to find threat patterns online for further analysis.

Important Windows Events

Windows Logs have vast categories of log events related to different actions and processes. To understand and go through them, an individual need to understand these events first. For doing the same, one can create a subscription filter or a collector by using the Event Forwarding Feature of the Windows Collector Service. Let's categorize the important Windows Event IDs and analyze the importance of the same.

General Event Descriptions	General Event IDs
Account and Group Activities	4624, 4625, 4648, 4728, 4732, 4634, 4735,4740, 4756
Application Crashes and Hangs	1000 and 1002
Windows Error Reporting	1001
Blue Screen of Death (BSOD)	1001
Windows Defender Errors	1005, 1006, 1008, 1010, 2001, 2003, 2004, 3002, 5008
Windows Integrity Errors	3001, 3002, 3003, 3004, 3010 and 3023
EMET Crash Logs	1 and 2
Windows Firewall Logs	2004, 2005, 2006, 2009, 2033
MSI Packages Installed	1022 and 1033
Windows Update Installed	2 and 19
Windows Service Manager Errors	7022, 7023, 7024, 7026, 7031, 7032, 7034
Group Policy Errors	1125, 1127, 1129
AppLocker and SRP Logs	865, 866, 867, 868, 882, 8003, 8004, 8006, 8007
Windows Update Errors	20, 24, 25, 31, 34, 35
Hotpatching Error	1009
Kernel Driver and Kernel Driver Signing Errors	5038, 6281, 219
Log Clearing	104 and 1102
Kernel Filter Driver	6
Windows Service Installed	7045
Program Inventory	800, 903, 904, 905, 906, 907, 908
Wireless Activities	8000, 8001, 8002, 8003, 8011, 10000, 10001, 11000, 11001, 11002, 11004, 11005, 11006, 11010, 12011, 12012, 12013
USB Activities	43, 400, 410
Printing Activities	307

Windows Vista and above Events [2]

The above table is taken from NSA Archives TSA-13-1004-SG [2] which describes some of the most important event IDs with small description. There are thousands of events that can be mentioned, but this article won't be enough to cover them all. It is highly recommended to monitor and collect these activities within any Windows workstation from security perspective. To further narrow down, one can create scheduled alerts for 'Log Clearing', 'USB Activities', 'Windows Firewall Logs' and 'Account and Group Activities'.

Note: Please consider the fact that this list is not complete nor should it be the only set of events to be collected for event monitoring. Each environment will most likely focus on specific events and it depends what other events are critically important as above.

Real-Time Windows Log Analysis

We have discussed about categorizing the consumption of Windows events. And now it's time to move forward with some real-time hands on. A Windows 10 Desktop environment has been created in the VM as lab environment to follow along. There are users created as - 'IWC-4hathacker' and 'MNJ' as administrators. One can follow the same actions into a local windows environment as well. Microsoft Windows has a robust logging subsystem that captures a number of system events and activities by default. Event Sources are grouped into log providers with unique event IDs for each event. For querying these logs and all the formatting concerns, Windows addresses this problem by providing APIs and log viewer programs that make querying easy. There are three main ways for user to access event logs within a Windows environment. This includes the GUI Windows Event Viewer ('*eventvwr.msc*' which is explained in the previous article), the Windows Events Command Line Utility ('*wevtutil.exe*') and the Powershell cmdlets like ('*Get-LogEvent*', '*Get-WinEvent*', *Etc.*)

Windows Event Viewer

The Windows Event Viewer is a graphical program that enables users to view and create complex queries against the various Windows event log providers. It allows for the creation and saving of custom views to facilitate easy analysis of repetitive tasks. Let's engage in some interactive hands-on and see how it works.

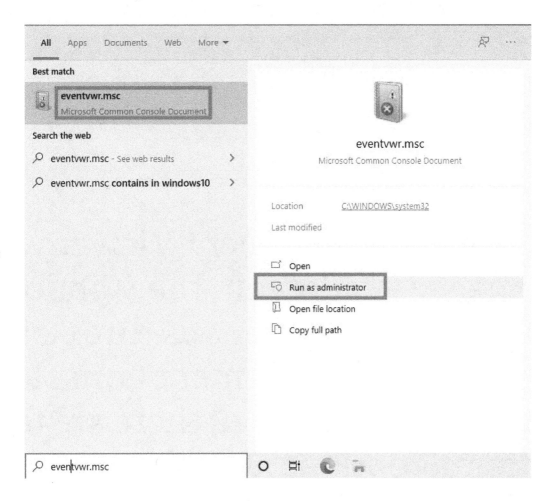

1. Open the Search bar in Windows machine and type 'eventvwr.msc'. Run the app as administrator.

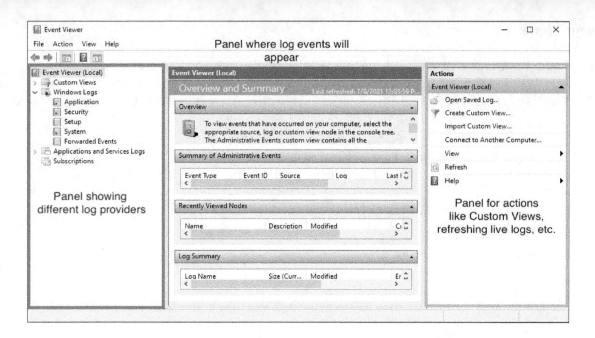

2.   The Windows Event Viewer will be opened. By default, the Windows Event Viewer opens as three-pane Microsoft Management Console. In the left most panel, there are four different options available as Custom Views, Windows Logs, Application and Service Logs, and Subscriptions.

3.   The Windows Logs are significant to understand events related to the complete system. The categories include Application, Security, Setup, System and Forwarded Events.

4.   Let's select 'Security' and a random event from all of the events appearing in the middle pane.

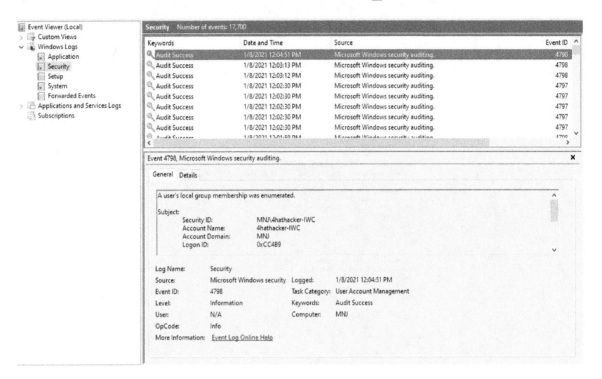

5.   In the middle pane, observe the details and metadata associated with the event. The user '4hathacker-IWC' is the part of 'MNJ' domain. This event is an Audit Success event which implies that user is able to attempt to log on to the system successfully. This could be helpful in getting alerts for malicious users as well. An incident

responder just needs to find all the users associated to the event ID 4798.

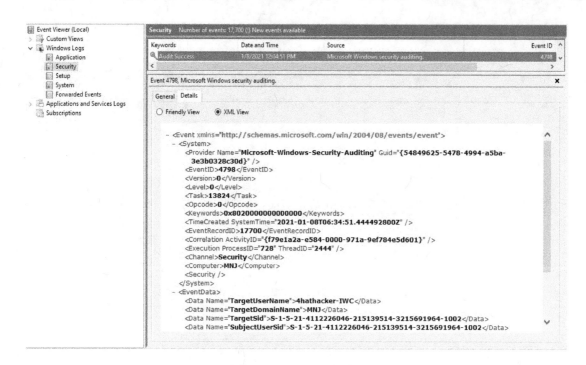

6.   The middle pane's bottom part has one more section aside from 'General' which is 'Details'. Click on the same and expand to see more raw details in XML format about this activity from 'IWC-4hathacker' user. One can see the Log Provider Name, Event ID, Task ID, Timestamp, and a lot more. This is essential for keeping the auditing, accounting and non-repudiation.

The '*wevtutil*' binary can be used to query or numerate logs from a Windows command shell or batch script. This is well suited for automated tasks and log analysis.

7. Open a command prompt with administrator access.

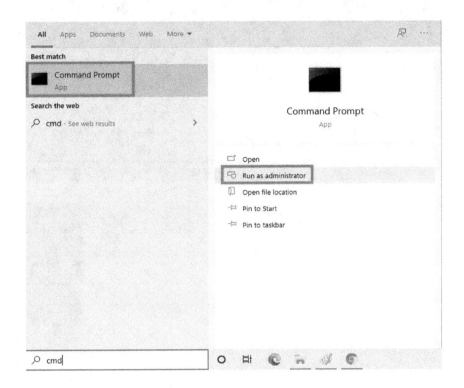

8. Type the help option with 'wevtutil'.

```
wevtutil -help
```

```
Administrator: Command Prompt

C:\WINDOWS\system32>wevtutil -help
Windows Events Command Line Utility.

Enables you to retrieve information about event logs and publishers, install
and uninstall event manifests, run queries, and export, archive, and clear logs.

Usage:

You can use either the short (for example, ep /uni) or long (for example,
enum-publishers /unicode) version of the command and option names. Commands,
options and option values are not case-sensitive.

Variables are noted in all upper-case.

wevtutil COMMAND [ARGUMENT [ARGUMENT] ...] [/OPTION:VALUE [/OPTION:VALUE] ...]

Commands:

el  | enum-logs          List log names.
gl  | get-log            Get log configuration information.
sl  | set-log            Modify configuration of a log.
ep  | enum-publishers    List event publishers.
gp  | get-publisher      Get publisher configuration information.
im  | install-manifest   Install event publishers and logs from manifest.
um  | uninstall-manifest Uninstall event publishers and logs from manifest.
qe  | query-events       Query events from a log or log file.
gli | get-log-info       Get log status information.
epl | export-log         Export a log.
al  | archive-log        Archive an exported log.
```

9. Check the different log names with enumeration.

```
C:\WINDOWS\system32>wevtutil el
AMSI/Debug
Analytic
Application
DebugChannel
DirectShowFilterGraph
DirectShowPluginControl
Els_Hyphenation/Analytic
EndpointMapper
FirstUXPerf-Analytic
ForwardedEvents
HardwareEvents
IHM_DebugChannel
Intel-iaLPSS-GPIO/Analytic
Intel-iaLPSS-I2C/Analytic
Intel-iaLPSS2-GPIO2/Debug
Intel-iaLPSS2-GPIO2/Performance
Intel-iaLPSS2-I2C/Debug
Intel-iaLPSS2-I2C/Performance
Internet Explorer
Key Management Service
MF_MediaFoundationDeviceMFT
MF_MediaFoundationDeviceProxy
MF_MediaFoundationFrameServer
MedaFoundationVideoProc
MedaFoundationVideoProcD3D
MediaFoundationAsyncWrapper
```

```
wevtutil el
```

10. Let's see how to find particular log events. e.g., filtering out log event providers related to 'Windows-Powershell' or 'Windows Security'.

```
wevtutil el | find /I "Windows-Powershell"
```

```
C:\WINDOWS\system32>wevtutil el | find /i "Windows-Powershell"
Microsoft-Windows-PowerShell-DesiredStateConfiguration-FileDownloadManager/Analytic
Microsoft-Windows-PowerShell-DesiredStateConfiguration-FileDownloadManager/Debug
Microsoft-Windows-PowerShell-DesiredStateConfiguration-FileDownloadManager/Operational
Microsoft-Windows-PowerShell/Admin
Microsoft-Windows-PowerShell/Analytic
Microsoft-Windows-PowerShell/Debug
Microsoft-Windows-PowerShell/Operational
```

```
wevtutil el | find /I "Windows-Security"
```

```
C:\WINDOWS\system32>wevtutil el | find /i "Windows-Security"
Microsoft-Windows-Security-Adminless/Operational
Microsoft-Windows-Security-Audit-Configuration-Client/Diagnostic
Microsoft-Windows-Security-Audit-Configuration-Client/Operational
Microsoft-Windows-Security-EnterpriseData-FileRevocationManager/Operational
Microsoft-Windows-Security-ExchangeActiveSyncProvisioning/Operational
Microsoft-Windows-Security-ExchangeActiveSyncProvisioning/Performance
Microsoft-Windows-Security-IdentityListener/Operational
Microsoft-Windows-Security-IdentityStore/Performance
Microsoft-Windows-Security-LessPrivilegedAppContainer/Operational
Microsoft-Windows-Security-Mitigations/KernelMode
Microsoft-Windows-Security-Mitigations/UserMode
Microsoft-Windows-Security-Netlogon/Operational
Microsoft-Windows-Security-SPP-UX-GC/Analytic
Microsoft-Windows-Security-SPP-UX-GenuineCenter-Logging/Operational
Microsoft-Windows-Security-SPP-UX-Notifications/ActionCenter
Microsoft-Windows-Security-SPP-UX/Analytic
Microsoft-Windows-Security-SPP/Perf
Microsoft-Windows-Security-UserConsentVerifier/Audit
Microsoft-Windows-Security-Vault/Performance
Microsoft-Windows-SecurityMitigationsBroker/Admin
Microsoft-Windows-SecurityMitigationsBroker/Operational
Microsoft-Windows-SecurityMitigationsBroker/Perf
```

11. Check how [C:\WINDOWS\system32>wevtutil el | find /c /v "" 1081] many log events are there in total.

```
wevtutil el | find /c /v ""
```

12. Querying different types of logs with defined frequency count of event to show.

```
wevtutil qe Security /c:1
```

```
C:\WINDOWS\system32>wevtutil qe Security /c:1
<Event xmlns='http://schemas.microsoft.com/win/2004/08/events/event'><System><Provider Name='Microsoft-Windows-Security-A
uditing' Guid='{54849625-5478-4994-a5ba-3e3b0328c30d}'/><EventID>4688</EventID><Version>2</Version><Level>0</Level><Task>
13312</Task><Opcode>0</Opcode><Keywords>0x8020000000000000</Keywords><TimeCreated SystemTime='2020-09-27T13:32:19.3786063
00Z'/><EventRecordID>1</EventRecordID><Correlation/><Execution ProcessID='4' ThreadID='32'/><Channel>Security</Channel><C
omputer>MNJ</Computer><Security/></System><EventData><Data Name='SubjectUserSid'>S-1-5-18</Data><Data Name='SubjectUserNa
me'>-</Data><Data Name='SubjectDomainName'>-</Data><Data Name='SubjectLogonId'>0x3e7</Data><Data Name='NewProcessId'>0x60
</Data><Data Name='NewProcessName'>Registry</Data><Data Name='TokenElevationType'>%%1936</Data><Data Name='ProcessId'>0x4
</Data><Data Name='CommandLine'></Data><Data Name='TargetUserSid'>S-1-0-0</Data><Data Name='TargetUserName'>-</Data><Data
 Name='TargetDomainName'>-</Data><Data Name='TargetLogonId'>0x0</Data><Data Name='ParentProcessName'></Data><Data Name='M
andatoryLabel'>S-1-16-16384</Data></EventData></Event>
```

```
wevtutil qe Application /c:1
```

```
C:\WINDOWS\system32>wevtutil qe Application /c:1
<Event xmlns='http://schemas.microsoft.com/win/2004/08/events/event'><System><Provider Name='Microsoft-Windows-WMI' Guid=
'{1edeee53-0afe-4609-b846-d8c0b2075b1f}'/><EventID>5615</EventID><Version>2</Version><Level>4</Level><Task>0</Task><Opcod
e>0</Opcode><Keywords>0x8000000000000000</Keywords><TimeCreated SystemTime='2020-09-27T13:34:36.146606400Z'/><EventRecord
ID>1</EventRecordID><Correlation/><Execution ProcessID='2796' ThreadID='2816'/><Channel>Application</Channel><Computer>MN
J</Computer><Security UserID='S-1-5-18'/></System><EventData></EventData></Event>
```

```
wevtutil qe System /c:1
```

```
C:\WINDOWS\system32>wevtutil qe System /c:1
<Event xmlns='http://schemas.microsoft.com/win/2004/08/events/event'><System><Provider Name='EventLog'/><EventID Qualifie
rs='32768'>6009</EventID><Level>4</Level><Task>0</Task><Keywords>0x8000000000000000</Keywords><TimeCreated SystemTime='2020
-09-27T13:35:58.855338100Z'/><EventRecordID>1</EventRecordID><Channel>System</Channel><Computer>MNJ</Computer><Security/>
</System><EventData><Data>10.00.</Data><Data>18362</Data><Data></Data><Data>Multiprocessor Free</Data><Data>0</Data></Eve
ntData></Event>
```

13. Query the log event with specific event ID say 4624 in the 'Security' logs. '4624' is an event ID for successful logon attempts.

```
wevtutil qe Security /q:*/System/EventID=4624 /c:1
```

```
C:\WINDOWS\system32>wevtutil qe Security /q:*/System/EventID=4624 /c:1
<Event xmlns='http://schemas.microsoft.com/win/2004/08/events/event'><System><Provider Name='Microsoft-Windows-Security-A
uditing' Guid='{54849625-5478-4994-a5ba-3e3b0328c30d}'/><EventID>4624</EventID><Version>2</Version><Level>0</Level><Task>
12544</Task><Opcode>0</Opcode><Keywords>0x8020000000000000</Keywords><TimeCreated SystemTime='2020-09-27T13:32:45.9992481
00Z'/><EventRecordID>16</EventRecordID><Correlation/><Execution ProcessID='692' ThreadID='696'/><Channel>Security</Channe
l><Computer>MNJ</Computer><Security/></System><EventData><Data Name='SubjectUserSid'>S-1-0-0</Data><Data Name='SubjectUse
rName'>-</Data><Data Name='SubjectDomainName'>-</Data><Data Name='SubjectLogonId'>0x0</Data><Data Name='TargetUserSid'>S-
1-5-18</Data><Data Name='TargetUserName'>SYSTEM</Data><Data Name='TargetDomainName'>NT AUTHORITY</Data><Data Name='Target
LogonId'>0x3e7</Data><Data Name='LogonType'>0</Data><Data Name='LogonProcessName'>-</Data><Data Name='AuthenticationPacka
geName'>-</Data><Data Name='WorkstationName'>-</Data><Data Name='LogonGuid'>{00000000-0000-0000-0000-000000000000}</Data>
<Data Name='TransmittedServices'>-</Data><Data Name='LmPackageName'>-</Data><Data Name='KeyLength'>0</Data><Data Name='Pr
ocessId'>0x4</Data><Data Name='ProcessName'></Data><Data Name='IpAddress'>-</Data><Data Name='IpPort'>-</Data><Data Name=
'ImpersonationLevel'>-</Data><Data Name='RestrictedAdminMode'>-</Data><Data Name='TargetOutboundUserName'>-</Data><Data N
ame='TargetOutboundDomainName'>-</Data><Data Name='VirtualAccount'>%%1843</Data><Data Name='TargetLinkedLogonId'>0x0</Dat
a><Data Name='ElevatedToken'>%%1842</Data></EventData></Event>
```

14. To format the above result, one can modify the query results from XML

```
C:\WINDOWS\system32>wevtutil qe Security /q:*/System/EventID=4648 /rd:true /f:text /c:1
Event[0]:
  Log Name: Security
  Source: Microsoft-Windows-Security-Auditing
  Date: 2021-01-06T19:14:05.163
  Event ID: 4648
  Task: Logon
  Level: Information
  Opcode: Info
  Keyword: Audit Success
  User: N/A
  User Name: N/A
  Computer: MNJ
  Description:
A logon was attempted using explicit credentials.

Subject:
        Security ID:             S-1-5-18
        Account Name:            MNJ$
        Account Domain:          WORKGROUP
        Logon ID:                0x3E7
        Logon GUID:              {00000000-0000-0000-0000-000000000000}

Account Whose Credentials Were Used:
        Account Name:            4hathacker-IWC
        Account Domain:          MNJ
        Logon GUID:              {00000000-0000-0000-0000-000000000000}

Target Server:
        Target Server Name:      localhost
        Additional Information:  localhost

Process Information:
        Process ID:              0x6e0
        Process Name:            C:\Windows\System32\svchost.exe

Network Information:
        Network Address:         127.0.0.1
        Port:                    0
```

to text. Let's query the 'Security' logs for event ID 4648 which provides the information around attempted logon using explicit credentials.

```
wevtutil qe Security /q:*/System/EventID=4648 /rd:true /f:text /c:1
```

These are some of the basic commands one needs to be aware of with 'wevtutil' for Windows.

Powershell Cmdlets

Powershell is an essential tool for anyone working with real-time logs in a Windows Workstation. In our Windows 10 lab workstation, Powershell version 5.1 is present by default.

Powershell is built on .NET and everything in Powershell is an object. Powershell native commands are called cmdlets, which consists of a verb and a noun separated by "-". Let's see some important commands related to Windows logs.

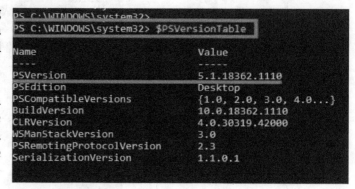

1. Open 'Search' tab and write Powershell. Open Windows Powershell App as Administrator.

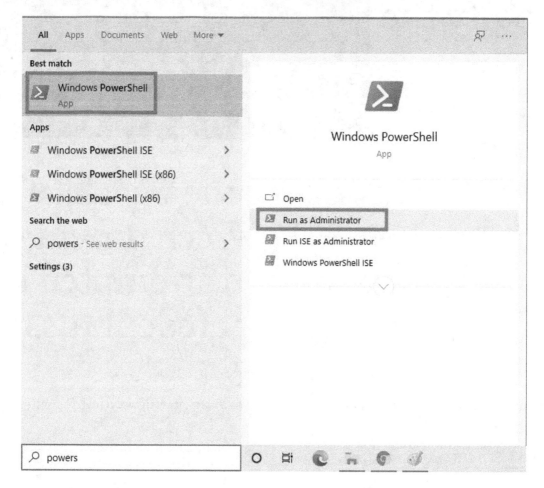

2. The oldest utility to get started with logs in Windows is – **Get-EventLog**. Just provide the log name with '-LogName' option. e.g., Windows Powershell.

```
Get-EventLog -LogName "Windows Powershell"
```

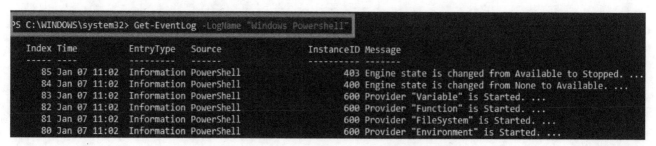

64

3. To access the Powershell object inside the logs, one can utilize '$_'. e.g., Searching for all the events where eventID is equal to 400.

```
Get-EventLog -LogName "Windows Powershell" | where {$_.eventID -eq 400}
```

```
PS C:\WINDOWS\system32> Get-EventLog -LogName "Windows Powershell" | where {$_.eventID -eq 400}

  Index Time          EntryType   Source            InstanceID Message
  ----- ----          ---------   ------            ---------- -------
     84 Jan 07 11:02  Information  PowerShell               400 Engine state is changed from None to Available. ...
     76 Jan 07 11:02  Information  PowerShell               400 Engine state is changed from None to Available. ...
     69 Jan 06 12:22  Information  PowerShell               400 Engine state is changed from None to Available. ...
     62 Jan 06 12:02  Information  PowerShell               400 Engine state is changed from None to Available. ...
     55 Jan 06 11:20  Information  PowerShell               400 Engine state is changed from None to Available. ...
     47 Jan 06 09:42  Information  PowerShell               400 Engine state is changed from None to Available. ...
     39 Jan 06 09:40  Information  PowerShell               400 Engine state is changed from None to Available. ...
     31 Jan 05 22:24  Information  PowerShell               400 Engine state is changed from None to Available. ...
     23 Jan 05 22:23  Information  PowerShell               400 Engine state is changed from None to Available. ...
     15 Dec 18 04:28  Information  PowerShell               400 Engine state is changed from None to Available. ...
      7 Dec 18 04:28  Information  PowerShell               400 Engine state is changed from None to Available. ...
```

4. This is how one can play with different Powershell objects using Get-EventLog cmdlet. Now, to delete the log utilize the Clear-EventLog cmdlet. Below, we will try to delete logs for eventID 400 and 600 and discover an interesting thing. (Event ID 400 provides information about start and stop of Powershell Activity)

```
Clear-EventLog -LogName "Windows Powershell" | where {$_.eventID -eq 400}

Clear-EventLog -LogName "Windows Powershell" | where {$_.eventID -eq 600}
```

```
PS C:\WINDOWS\system32> Clear-EventLog -LogName "Windows Powershell" | where {$_.eventID -eq 400}
PS C:\WINDOWS\system32>
PS C:\WINDOWS\system32> Clear-EventLog -LogName "Windows Powershell" | where {$_.eventID -eq 600}
PS C:\WINDOWS\system32>
```

5. Here, we assume that the specific event ID's will be removed from the Powershell logs. However, this is not the case. Actually 'Clear-EventLog' command clears every other log by the provider log name, which means that complete Windows Powershell logs are removed from the system.

```
Get-EventLog -LogName "Windows Powershell"
```

```
PS C:\WINDOWS\system32> Get-EventLog -LogName "Windows Powershell"
Get-EventLog : No matches found
At line:1 char:1
+ Get-EventLog -LogName "Windows Powershell"
+ ~~~~~~~~~~~~~~~~~~~~~~~~~~~~~~~~~~~~~~~~~~~~
    + CategoryInfo          : ObjectNotFound: (:) [Get-EventLog], ArgumentException
    + FullyQualifiedErrorId : GetEventLogNoEntriesFound,Microsoft.PowerShell.Commands.GetEventLogCommand
```

6. To detect the Event log associated to the Powershell log deletion, the eventID of interest is 104. This is very helpful for incident responders if found to prove any intrusion and will create mess since further investigation will be little difficult without logs.

```
Get-EventLog -LogName "System" | where {$_.eventID -eq 104}
```

```
PS C:\WINDOWS\system32> Get-EventLog -LogName System | where {$_.eventID -eq 104}

  Index Time          EntryType   Source            InstanceID Message
  ----- ----          ---------   ------            ---------- -------
   1730 Jan 07 18:53  Information  Microsoft-Windows...        104 The Windows PowerShell log file was cleared.
   1729 Jan 07 18:52  Information  Microsoft-Windows...        104 The Windows PowerShell log file was cleared.
```

7. Another important utility which is released by Microsoft for Windows Logs is 'Get-WinEvent'. This will get events from event logs and event tracing log files on local and remote computers. This requires Powershell to run as Administrator, otherwise one might see error messages.

Note: To understand the syntax and description of command feel free to use the 'Get-Help' command which comes with options like Online (opens a page about the cmdlet), full (provides complete description) and examples (gives numerous examples about how to run the cmdlet). Here, we will be running it without any such parameter.

```
Get-Help Get-WinEvent
```

8. Let's see how to query 'Security' event logs for auditing successful login events with 'Get-WinEvent' with a limit of max. 10 events. It will retrieve for us the latest 10 events, however for oldest events add "-Oldest" option.

```
Get-WinEvent -LogName Security -FilterXPath '*/System/EventID=4624' -MaxEvents 10
```

```
Get-WinEvent -LogName Security -FilterXPath '*/System/EventID=4648' -MaxEvents 10
```

9. 'Get-WinEvent' is also helpful to analyze the log events from last day, yesterday, till date with the help of mathematical logic. e.g., to view the System logs for last 24 hours, below is the query.

```
Get-WinEvent -LogName System -FilterXPath '*/*/TimeCreated[timediff(@SystemTime)<=
86400000]'
```

```
PS C:\WINDOWS\system32> Get-WinEvent -LogName System -FilterXPath '*/*/TimeCreated[timediff(@SystemTime) <= 86400000]'


   ProviderName: Microsoft-Windows-Power-Troubleshooter

TimeCreated                     Id LevelDisplayName Message
-----------                     -- ---------------- -------
1/7/2021 6:02:35 PM              1 Information      The system has returned from a low power state....


   ProviderName: BTHUSB

TimeCreated                     Id LevelDisplayName Message
-----------                     -- ---------------- -------
1/7/2021 6:02:34 PM             34 Warning          The local adapter does not support an important Low Energy controller
1/7/2021 6:02:34 PM             18 Information      Windows cannot store Bluetooth authentication codes (link keys) on the


   ProviderName: Microsoft-Windows-Kernel-Boot

TimeCreated                     Id LevelDisplayName Message
-----------                     -- ---------------- -------
1/7/2021 6:02:32 PM             32 Information      The bootmgr spent 0 ms waiting for user input.
1/7/2021 6:02:32 PM             18 Information      There are 0x1 boot options on this system.
1/7/2021 6:02:32 PM             27 Information      The boot type was 0x2.
1/7/2021 6:02:32 PM             25 Information      The boot menu policy was 0xFE120.


   ProviderName: Microsoft-Windows-Kernel-General

TimeCreated                     Id LevelDisplayName Message
-----------                     -- ---------------- -------
1/7/2021 6:02:31 PM              1 Information      The system time has changed to [2021[-[01[-[07T12:32:31.500000000Z from
```

EVTX Format and Custom Event Viewer

The Windows XML EventLog (EVTX) format is used by Microsoft Windows to store system log information. This format supersedes the Windows EventLog (EVT) format as used in Window XP. An EVTX file consists of:

- o File header
- o Chunks
- o Trailing Empty Values

Characteristics	Description
Byte order	little-endian
Date and time values	FILETIME in UTC
Character strings	ASCII strings are Single Byte Character (SBC) or Multi Byte Character (MBC) string stored with a codepage. Sometimes referred to as ANSI string representation. Though technically maybe incorrect, this document will use term (extended) ASCII string. Unicode strings are stored in UTF-16 little-endian without the byte order mark (BOM).

Overview of EVTX file [3]

67

The Windows Event Log Software Developer Kit defines channels as streams of events which are used by the OS and applications to publish events to a log.

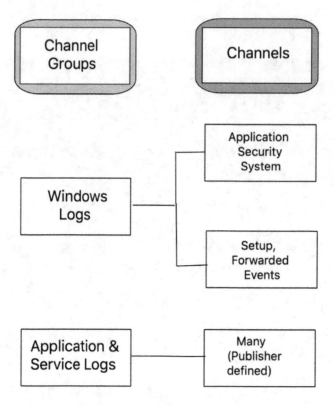

Channel Groups and Channels [4]

Each channel group has two types of channel and each event has an event type. The serviced channel type contains Admin and Operational events. The direct channel type contains Analytic and Debug events. The main difference between the two channel types is that serviced channels can be forwarded and/or collected remotely and direct channels cannot.

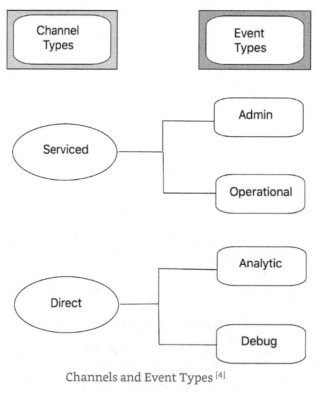

Channels and Event Types [4]

EVTX logs are stored using an XML format. XML was created to provide a format that could be used to share structured data in a format which allows developers to define their own elements. The characteristics of XML make it the ideal language to use for event logs. We have already seen in the previous exercises how windows event viewer arranges the logs in XML view with proper granularity. Now, let's see how to create a custom view to get all the XML views in response to some incident which occurred in last 24 hours.

1. Search for the 'eventvwr.msc' file in the bottom search pane and run it as administrator.

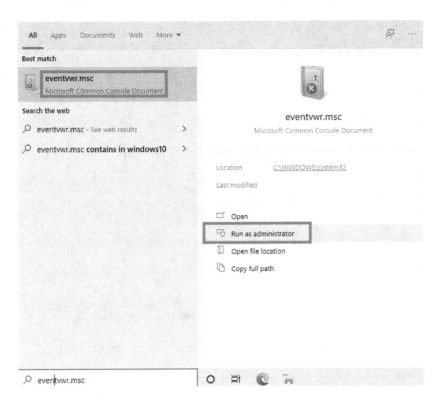

2. Click on "Create custom view" in the Action panel in right. A new GUI pop up will appear.

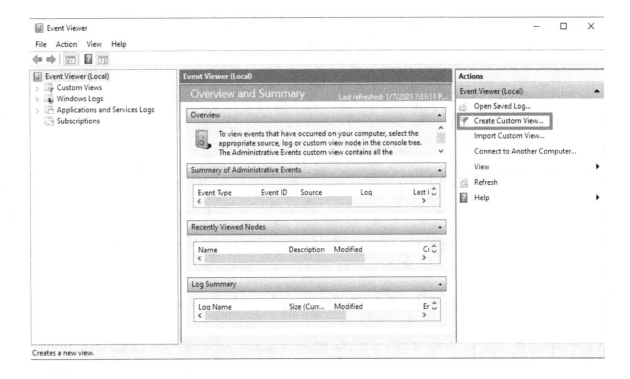

3. In the new panel, select the interval logged as "24 hours", check all the event levels. Set the pointer to "By log" category and select the choice of log providers. Here, Application, Security and System are checked. Let all the things be as is and hit OK.

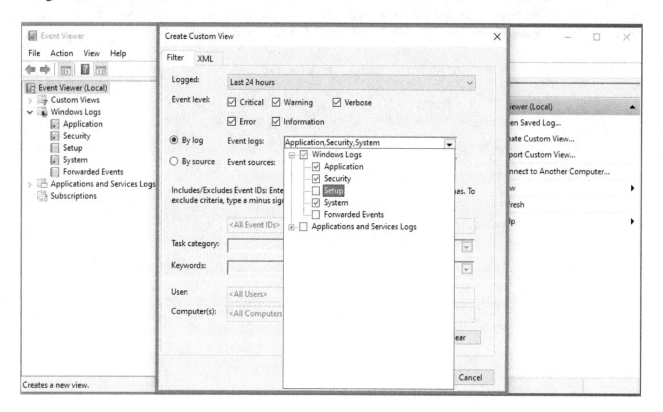

4. A new "Save Filter to Custom View" dialog box will appear. Give the new custom name and hit OK.

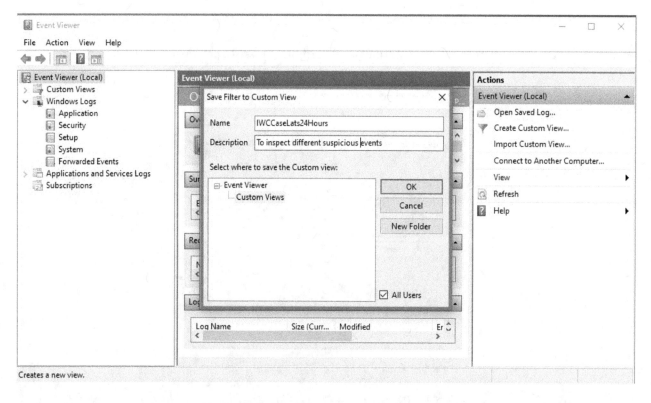

5. Upon saving, the custom view will appear in the left most event viewer pane. Also, it got saved to the location of your choice in the EVTX format. Check how many events occurred in last 24 hours and it will make the work easy for incident analyst. Here it is showing around 616 events occurred during last 24 hours.

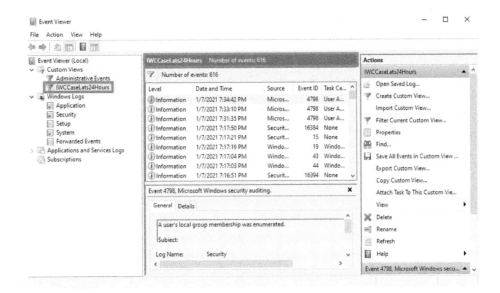

6. By providing the path to EVTX file, event log analysis could be done with Powershell cmdlets. E.g., to check if any log deletion has taken place or not.

```
Get-WinEvent -Path 'C:\Users\4hathacker-IWC\Desktop\IWCCaseLast24Hours.evtx' -FilterXPath
'*/System/eventID=104' -Oldest
```

Lessons Learnt

In this small article, the commands and utilities have been discussed for Windows event log analysis from the scratch. Powershell cmdlets and wevutil helps a lot to dig deep into the logs to search for different event IDs associated with malicious events. The knowledge of both utilities and event IDs are important detect and response during an incident. The most valuable events are more likely from either the Security logs or the System logs. Other important reliable tools which can be utilized along with log analysis include wmic, netstat and tasklist.

References

- Photo by Sharon McCutcheon on Unsplash. Last Accessed on Jan. 8th, 2021.
  Link:unsplash.com/photos/_vkztdUDhvY
- Spotting the Adversary with Windows Event Log Monitoring, Information Assurance Directorate, National Security Agency/Central Security Service, Revision 2, Published on Dec. 16th, 2013. Last Accessed on Jan. 8th, 2021.
- Link: https://apps.nsa.gov/iaarchive/customcf/openAttachment.cfm?FilePath=/iad/library/ia-guidance/security-   configuration/applications/assets/public/upload/Spotting-the-Adversary-with-Windows-Event-Log-Monitoring.pdf&WpKes=aF6woL7fQp3dJiezxQtrtBN5w3KZJyqwH5cQxV
- Windows XML Event Log (EVTX) Format, libyal/libevtx, GitHub. Last Accessed on Jan 12th, 2021.
  Link: github.com/libyal/libevtx
- [4] EVTX and Windows Event Logging, Brandon Charter, SANS Information Security Reading Room, Published on Nov. 13, 2008. Last Accessed on Jan 12th, 2021.
- Link: sans.org/reading-room/whitepapers/logging/paper/32949

Volatility-Memory forensics Framework

By: Vishal M Belbase

Volatility is one of the best open-source software programs for analyzing RAM in 32 bit/64 bit systems. It supports analysis for Linux, Windows, Mac, and Android systems. It is based on Python and can be run on Windows, Linux, and Mac systems. It can analyze raw dumps, crash dumps, VMware dumps (.vmem), virtual box dumps, and many others.

Table of Contents

Memory Acquisition

It is the method of capturing and dumping the contents of a volatile content into a non-volatile storage device to preserve it for further investigation. A ram analysis can only be successfully conducted when the acquisition has been performed accurately without corrupting the image of the volatile memory. In this phase, the investigator has to be careful about his decisions to collect the volatile data as it won't exist after the system undergoes a reboot. The volatile memory can also be prone to alteration of any sort due to the continuous processes running in the background. Any external move made on the suspect system may impact the device's ram adversely.

Importance of Memory Acquisition

When capturing volatile memory (RAM dump), many useful artifacts can be discovered:

- On-going processes and recently terminated processes
- Files mapped in the memory (.exe, .txt, shared files, etc.)
- Any open TCP/UDP ports or any active connections
- Caches (clipboard data, SAM databases, edited files, passwords, web addresses, commands)
- Presence of hidden data, malware, etc.

Here, we have taken a memory dump of a Windows7 system using the Belkasoft RAM Capturer, which can be downloaded from **here**.

Memory Analysis

Once the dump is available, we will begin with the forensic analysis of the memory using the Volatility Memory Forensics Framework which can be downloaded from **here**. The volatility framework support analysis of memory dump from all the versions and services of Windows from XP to Windows 10. It also supports Server 2003 to Server 2016. In this article, we will be analyzing the memory dump in CSI Linux where Volatility comes pre-installed or install volatility via docker and follow instructions in that page if there exist any problem related to the python-libraries. Use the following **link**

Dump Format Supported

- Raw format
- Hibernation File
- VM snapshot
- Microsoft crash dump

Switch on your CSI Linux Machines, and to get a basic list of all the available options, plugins, and flags to use in the analysis, you can type or normally you will use volatility -h but I have configured it to invoke by vol keyword.

```
vol -h
```

Imageinfo

When a Memory dump is taken, it is extremely important to know the information about the operating system that was in use. Volatility will try to read the image and suggest the related profiles for the given memory dump. The image info plugin displays the date and time of the sample that was collected, the number of CPUs present, etc. To obtain the details of the ram, you can type.

```
vol -f Challenge.raw imageinfo
```

A profile is a categorization of specific operating systems, versions and its hardware architecture, A profile generally includes metadata information, system call information, etc. You may notice multiple profiles would be suggested to you.

Kdbgscan

This plugin finds and analyses the profiles based on the Kernel debugger data block. The Kdbgscan thus provides the correct profile related to the raw image. To supply the correct profile for the memory analysis, type

```
vol -f Challenge.raw kdbgscan
```

```
  ┌──(v❀kali)-[~/Documents]
  └─$ vol -f Challenge.raw --profile=Win7SP1x86 kdbgscan
Volatility Foundation Volatility Framework 2.6.1
**************************************************
Instantiating KDBG using: Kernel AS Win7SP1x86 (6.1.7601 32bit)
Offset (V)                 : 0x8273cb78
Offset (P)                 : 0x273cb78
KDBG owner tag check       : True
Profile suggestion (KDBGHeader): Win7SP1x86_23418
Version64                  : 0x8273cb50 (Major: 15, Minor: 7601)
Service Pack (CmNtCSDVersion) : 1
Build string (NtBuildLab)  : 7601.24260.x86fre.win7sp1_ldr.18
PsActiveProcessHead        : 0x82751d70 (34 processes)
PsLoadedModuleList         : 0x82759730 (139 modules)
KernelBase                 : 0x82604000 (Matches MZ: True)
Major (OptionalHeader)     : 6
Minor (OptionalHeader)     : 1
KPCR                       : 0x80b96000 (CPU 0)

**************************************************
Instantiating KDBG using: Kernel AS Win7SP1x86 (6.1.7601 32bit)
Offset (V)                 : 0x8273cb78
Offset (P)                 : 0x273cb78
KDBG owner tag check       : True
Profile suggestion (KDBGHeader): Win7SP1x86_24000
Version64                  : 0x8273cb50 (Major: 15, Minor: 7601)
Service Pack (CmNtCSDVersion) : 1
Build string (NtBuildLab)  : 7601.24260.x86fre.win7sp1_ldr.18
PsActiveProcessHead        : 0x82751d70 (34 processes)
PsLoadedModuleList         : 0x82759730 (139 modules)
KernelBase                 : 0x82604000 (Matches MZ: True)
Major (OptionalHeader)     : 6
Minor (OptionalHeader)     : 1
KPCR                       : 0x80b96000 (CPU 0)
```

Processes

When a system is in an active state it is normal for it to have multiple processes running in the background and can be found in the volatile memory. The presence of any hidden process can also be parsed out of a memory dump. The recently terminated processes before the reboot can also be recorded and analyzed in the memory dump. There are a few plugins that can be used to list down the processes

Pslist

To identify the presence of any rogue processes and to view any high-level running processes, one can use the command written below this paragraph. On executing this command, the list of processes running is displayed, their respective process ID assigned to them and the parent process ID is also displayed along. The details about the threads, sessions, handles are also mentioned. The timestamp according to the start of the process is also displayed. This helps to identify whether an unknown process is running or was running at an unusual time.

```
vol -f Challenge.raw --profile=Win7SP1x86 pslist -P
```

```
┌──(v@kali)-[~/Documents]
└─$ vol -f Challenge.raw --profile=Win7SP1x86 pslist -P
Volatility Foundation Volatility Framework 2.6.1
Offset(P)    Name                PID   PPID   Thds    Hnds   Sess  Wow64 Start
----------   --------------      ----  ----   ----    ----   ----  ----- -----

---
0x3e7b3c58   System              4     0      85      483    ------     0 2018-10-23 08:29:16 UTC+0000
0x3e17db18   smss.exe            260   4      2       29     ------     0 2018-10-23 08:29:16 UTC+0000
0x3d769030   csrss.exe           340   332    8       347    0          0 2018-10-23 08:29:21 UTC+0000
0x3d78d030   csrss.exe           380   372    9       188    1          0 2018-10-23 08:29:23 UTC+0000
0x3d793c68   wininit.exe         388   332    3       79     0          0 2018-10-23 08:29:23 UTC+0000
0x3d7cbd20   winlogon.exe        424   372    6       117    1          0 2018-10-23 08:29:23 UTC+0000
0x3d7ebd20   services.exe        484   388    10      191    0          0 2018-10-23 08:29:25 UTC+0000
0x3d7ef3d8   lsass.exe           492   388    7       480    0          0 2018-10-23 08:29:25 UTC+0000
0x3d7f2378   lsm.exe             500   388    10      146    0          0 2018-10-23 08:29:25 UTC+0000
0x3d423030   svchost.exe         592   484    12      358    0          0 2018-10-23 08:29:30 UTC+0000
0x3d441708   VBoxService.ex      652   484    12      116    0          0 2018-10-23 08:29:31 UTC+0000
0x3d454030   svchost.exe         716   484    9       243    0          0 2018-10-23 08:29:32 UTC+0000
0x3d47ad20   svchost.exe         804   484    19      378    0          0 2018-10-23 08:29:32 UTC+0000
0x3d484898   svchost.exe         848   484    20      400    0          0 2018-10-23 08:29:33 UTC+0000
```

Psscan

This plugin can be used to give a detailed list of processes found in the memory dump. It cannot detect hidden or unlinked processes.

```
volatility -f ram.mem --profile=Win7SP1x64 psscan
```

Pstree

In this plugin, the pslist is represented with a child-parent relationship and shows any unknown or abnormal processes. The child process is represented by indention and periods.

```
volatility -f ram.mem --profile=Win7SP1x64 pstree
```

```
└─$ vol -f Challenge.raw --profile=Win7SP1x86 pstree
Volatility Foundation Volatility Framework 2.6.1
Name                                      Pid    PPid   Thds    Hnds  Time
--------------------------------------    ----   ----   ----    ----  ----
 0x84d93c68:wininit.exe                   388    332    3       79    2018-10-23 08:29:23 UTC+0000
. 0x84debd20:services.exe                 484    388    10      191   2018-10-23 08:29:25 UTC+0000
.. 0x84e8c648:svchost.exe                 896    484    30      809   2018-10-23 08:29:33 UTC+0000
.. 0x84e41708:VBoxService.ex              652    484    12      116   2018-10-23 08:29:31 UTC+0000
.. 0x84e7ad20:svchost.exe                 804    484    19      378   2018-10-23 08:29:32 UTC+0000
... 0x84ea7d20:audiodg.exe                988    804    6       127   2018-10-23 08:29:35 UTC+0000
.. 0x84f7d578:svchost.exe                 1460   484    11      148   2018-10-23 08:29:44 UTC+0000
.. 0x84f323f8:spoolsv.exe                 1336   484    16      295   2018-10-23 08:29:43 UTC+0000
.. 0x850b2538:taskhost.exe                308    484    8       151   2018-10-23 08:29:55 UTC+0000
.. 0x850d0030:sppsvc.exe                  1164   484    6       154   2018-10-23 08:29:57 UTC+0000
.. 0x84e54030:svchost.exe                 716    484    9       243   2018-10-23 08:29:32 UTC+0000
.. 0x84e84898:svchost.exe                 848    484    20      400   2018-10-23 08:29:33 UTC+0000
... 0x85109030:dwm.exe                    1992   848    5       132   2018-10-23 08:30:04 UTC+0000
.. 0x84f4dca0:svchost.exe                 1364   484    19      307   2018-10-23 08:29:43 UTC+0000
.. 0x84f828f8:svchost.exe                 1488   484    8       170   2018-10-23 08:29:44 UTC+0000
.. 0x84e89c68:svchost.exe                 872    484    19      342   2018-10-23 08:29:33 UTC+0000
.. 0x85164030:SearchIndexer.              2032   484    14      614   2018-10-23 08:30:14 UTC+0000
... 0x8515cd20:SearchFilterHo             1292   2032   5       80    2018-10-23 08:30:17 UTC+0000
... 0x8515ad20:SearchProtocol             284    2032   7       235   2018-10-23 08:30:16 UTC+0000
.. 0x84f033c8:svchost.exe                 1192   484    15      365   2018-10-23 08:29:40 UTC+0000
.. 0x84e23030:svchost.exe                 592    484    12      358   2018-10-23 08:29:30 UTC+0000
. 0x84def3d8:lsass.exe                    492    388    7       480   2018-10-23 08:29:25 UTC+0000
. 0x84df2378:lsm.exe                      500    388    10      146   2018-10-23 08:29:25 UTC+0000
0x84d69030:csrss.exe                      340    332    8       347   2018-10-23 08:29:21 UTC+0000
0x83d09c58:System                         4      0      85      483   2018-10-23 08:29:16 UTC+0000
. 0x8437db18:smss.exe                     260    4      2       29    2018-10-23 08:29:16 UTC+0000
0x85097870:explorer.exe                   324    1876   33      827   2018-10-23 08:30:04 UTC+0000
. 0x845a8d20:DumpIt.exe                   2412   324    2       38    2018-10-23 08:30:48 UTC+0000
. 0x851a6610:cmd.exe                      2096   324    1       22    2018-10-23 08:30:18 UTC+0000
. 0x85135af8:VBoxTray.exe                 1000   324    14      159   2018-10-23 08:30:08 UTC+0000
0x84dcbd20:winlogon.exe                   424    372    6       117   2018-10-23 08:29:23 UTC+0000
0x84d8d030:csrss.exe                      380    372    9       188   2018-10-23 08:29:23 UTC+0000
```

DLLs

DLLlist

DLLs stand for Dynamic-link library automatically that is added to this list when a process runs, according to calls the Loading of Library takes and they aren't removed until execution is stopped or finished. To display the DLLs for any particular process instead of all processes use above syntax where 1000 is process id.

```
vol -f Challenge.raw --profile=Win7SP0x86 dlllist -p 1000
```

```
┌──(v❀kali)-[~/Documents]
└─$ vol -f Challenge.raw --profile=Win7SP0x86 dlllist -p 1000
Volatility Foundation Volatility Framework 2.6.1
********************************************************************
VBoxTray.exe pid:   1000
Command line : "C:\Windows\System32\VBoxTray.exe"
Service Pack 1

Base          Size       LoadCount LoadTime                         Path
----------    ---------- --------- ----------------------------     ----
0x010f0000    0x18b000   0xffff    1970-01-01 00:00:00 UTC+0000     C:\Windows\System32\VBoxTray.exe
0x76e50000    0x142000   0xffff    1970-01-01 00:00:00 UTC+0000     C:\Windows\SYSTEM32\ntdll.dll
0x76980000    0xd5000    0xffff    2018-10-23 08:30:08 UTC+0000     C:\Windows\system32\kernel32.dll
0x75050000    0x4b000    0xffff    2018-10-23 08:30:08 UTC+0000     C:\Windows\system32\KERNELBASE.dll
0x74360000    0x12000    0xffff    2018-10-23 08:30:08 UTC+0000     C:\Windows\System32\MPR.dll
0x75430000    0xc9000    0xffff    2018-10-23 08:30:08 UTC+0000     C:\Windows\system32\USER32.dll
0x762d0000    0x4e000    0xffff    2018-10-23 08:30:08 UTC+0000     C:\Windows\system32\GDI32.dll
0x75280000    0xa000     0xffff    2018-10-23 08:30:08 UTC+0000     C:\Windows\system32\LPK.dll
0x76fe0000    0x9d000    0xffff    2018-10-23 08:30:08 UTC+0000     C:\Windows\system32\USP10.dll
0x75290000    0xac000    0xffff    2018-10-23 08:30:08 UTC+0000     C:\Windows\system32\msvcrt.dll
0x76380000    0xa1000    0xffff    2018-10-23 08:30:08 UTC+0000     C:\Windows\system32\ADVAPI32.dll
0x762b0000    0x19000    0xffff    2018-10-23 08:30:08 UTC+0000     C:\Windows\SYSTEM32\sechost.dll
0x76660000    0xa2000    0xffff    2018-10-23 08:30:08 UTC+0000     C:\Windows\system32\RPCRT4.dll
0x75660000    0xc4c000   0xffff    2018-10-23 08:30:08 UTC+0000     C:\Windows\system32\SHELL32.dll
0x76460000    0x57000    0xffff    2018-10-23 08:30:08 UTC+0000     C:\Windows\system32\SHLWAPI.dll
0x76fa0000    0x35000    0xffff    2018-10-23 08:30:08 UTC+0000     C:\Windows\system32\WS2_32.dll
0x76320000    0x6000     0xffff    2018-10-23 08:30:08 UTC+0000     C:\Windows\system32\NSI.dll
0x75500000    0x15d000   0xffff    2018-10-23 08:30:08 UTC+0000     C:\Windows\system32\ole32.dll
0x75340000    0x1f000    0x2       2018-10-23 08:30:08 UTC+0000     C:\Windows\system32\IMM32.DLL
0x75360000    0xcd000    0x1       2018-10-23 08:30:08 UTC+0000     C:\Windows\system32\MSCTF.dll
0x73a10000    0x40000    0x3       2018-10-23 08:30:08 UTC+0000     C:\Windows\system32\uxtheme.dll
0x74430000    0xd000     0x1       2018-10-23 08:30:08 UTC+0000     C:\Windows\system32\WTSAPI32.DLL
0x74f20000    0x29000    0x3       2018-10-23 08:30:08 UTC+0000     C:\Windows\System32\WINSTA.dll
0x73200000    0xf000     0x2       2018-10-23 08:30:08 UTC+0000     C:\Windows\System32\VBoxHook.dll
```

DLLDump

This plugin is used to dump the DLLs from the memory space of the processes into another location to analyze it. To take a dump of the DLLs you can type:

```
volatility -f ram.mem --profile=Win7SP1x64 dlldump --dump-dir /root/ramdump/
```

Handles

This plugin is used to display the open handles that are present in a process. This plugin applies to files, registry keys, events, desktops, threads, and all other types of objects. To see the handles present in the dump, you can type:

```
vol -f Challenge.raw --profile=Win7SP1x86 handles
```

```
┌──(v⊛kali)-[~/Documents]
└─$ vol -f Challenge.raw --profile=Win7SP1x86 handles
Volatility Foundation Volatility Framework 2.6.1
Offset(V)      Pid    Handle   Access Type        Details
---------      ---    ------   ------ ----        -------
0x83d09c58     4      0x4      0x1fffff Process    System(4)
0x87838fd0     4      0x8      0x2001f Key         MACHINE\CONTROLSET001\CONTROL\HIVELIST
0x87806f50     4      0xc      0xf000f Directory   GLOBAL??
0x8780dfd0     4      0x10     0x0 Key
0x8785a360     4      0x14     0x2001f Key         MACHINE\CONTROLSET001\CONTROL\PRODUCTOPTIONS
0x8785b740     4      0x18     0xf003f Key         MACHINE\CONTROLSET001\CONTROL\SESSION MANAGER\MEMORY MANAGEMENT\PREFETCHPARAM
ETERS
0x8785d1e0     4      0x1c     0x2001f Key         MACHINE\SETUP
0x83d84470     4      0x20     0x1f0001 ALPC Port  PowerMonitorPort
0x83d706f8     4      0x24     0x1f0001 ALPC Port  PowerPort
0x8784ef90     4      0x28     0x20019 Key         MACHINE\DESCRIPTION\SYSTEM\MULTIFUNCTIONADAPTER
0x83e41748     4      0x2c     0x1fffff Thread     TID 160 PID 4
0x8784bfd0     4      0x30     0xf003f Key         MACHINE\CONTROLSET001
0x8785ae78     4      0x34     0xf003f Key         MACHINE\CONTROLSET001\ENUM
0x878571b0     4      0x38     0xf003f Key         MACHINE\CONTROLSET001\CONTROL\CLASS
0x8785b900     4      0x3c     0xf003f Key         MACHINE\CONTROLSET001\SERVICES
0x87905840     4      0x40     0x20019 Key         MACHINE\CONTROLSET001\CONTROL\WMI\SECURITY
0x92c68020     4      0x44     0x20019 Key         MACHINE\DESCRIPTION\SYSTEM\BIOS
0x879a8cd0     4      0x48     0xe Token
0x84d5f700     4      0x4c     0x10003 File        \Device\HarddiskVolume2\Windows\System32\config\RegBack\DEFAULT
0x845b0560     4      0x50     0x10003 File        \Device\HarddiskVolume2\Windows\System32\config\RegBack\SYSTEM
0x84cfe020     4      0x54     0x0 Thread          TID 320 PID 4
0x8f4ddef0     4      0x58     0x10 Key            MACHINE\CONTROLSET001\CONTROL\LSA
0x8458b950     4      0x5c     0x12019f File       \Device\HarddiskVolume1\$Extend\$RmMetadata\$TxfLog\$TxfLogContainer000000000
00000000002
0x84d5e288     4      0x60     0x1f0003 Event      UniqueSessionIdEvent
0x84563c30     4      0x64     0x1f0001 ALPC Port  SeRmCommandPort
0x84585678     4      0x68     0x12019f File       \Device\HarddiskVolume1\$Extend\$RmMetadata\$TxfLog\$TxfLog.blf
```

Getsids

This plugin is used to view the SIDs stands for Security Identifiers that are associated with a process. This plugin can help in identifying processes that have maliciously escalated privileges and which processes belong to specific users. To get detail on a particular process id, you can type:

```
vol -f Challenge.raw --profile=Win7SP1x86 getsids -p
```

```
┌──(v⊛kali)-[~/Documents]
└─$ vol -f Challenge.raw --profile=Win7SP1x86 getsids -p  4
Volatility Foundation Volatility Framework 2.6.1
System (4): S-1-5-18 (Local System)
System (4): S-1-5-32-544 (Administrators)
System (4): S-1-1-0 (Everyone)
System (4): S-1-5-11 (Authenticated Users)
System (4): S-1-16-16384 (System Mandatory Level)
```

Netscan

This plugin helps in finding network-related artifacts present in the memory dump. It makes use of pool tag scanning. This plugin finds all the TCP endpoints, TCP listeners, UDP endpoints, and UDP listeners. It provides details about the local and remote IP and also about the local and remote port. To get details on the network artifacts, you can type:

```
vol -f Challenge.raw --profile=Win7SP1x86 netscan
```

```
┌──(v⊛kali)-[~/Documents]
└─$ vol -f Challenge.raw --profile=Win7SP1x86 netscan
Volatility Foundation Volatility Framework 2.6.1
Offset(P)      Proto  Local Address            Foreign Address    State       Pid   Owner          Created
0x3d257308     UDPv4  0.0.0.0:0                *:*                            652   VBoxService.ex 2018-10-23 08
:31:02 UTC+0000
0x3d25d6a8     UDPv4  0.0.0.0:3702             *:*                            1488  svchost.exe    2018-10-23 08
:29:53 UTC+0000
0x3d25d6a8     UDPv6  :::3702                  *:*                            1488  svchost.exe    2018-10-23 08
:29:53 UTC+0000
0x3d25dc30     UDPv4  0.0.0.0:3702             *:*                            1488  svchost.exe    2018-10-23 08
:29:53 UTC+0000
0x3d31c310     UDPv4  0.0.0.0:0                *:*                            652   VBoxService.ex 2018-10-23 08
:31:07 UTC+0000
0x3d38a008     UDPv4  0.0.0.0:0                *:*                            652   VBoxService.ex 2018-10-23 08
:31:13 UTC+0000
0x3d3cf310     UDPv4  0.0.0.0:0                *:*                            652   VBoxService.ex 2018-10-23 08
:31:07 UTC+0000
0x3d23ff58     TCPv4  0.0.0.0:49156            0.0.0.0:0          LISTENING   484   services.exe
0x3d23ff58     TCPv6  :::49156                 :::0               LISTENING   484   services.exe
0x3d435008     UDPv6  fe80::147b:c8fd:e2c6:69de:546  *:*                      804   svchost.exe    2018-10-23 08
:29:41 UTC+0000
```

77

Hivelist

This plugin can be used to locate the virtual addresses present in the registry hives in memory, and their entire paths to hive on the disk. To obtain the details on the hivelist from the memory dump, you can type:

```
volatility -f ram.mem --profile=Win7SP1x64 hivelist
```

```
  ┌──(v⬤kali)-[~/Documents]
  └─$ vol -f Challenge.raw --profile=Win7SP1x86 hivelist
Volatility Foundation Volatility Framework 2.6.1
Virtual     Physical    Name
----------  ----------  ----
0x8780a6a8  0x251a16a8  [no name]
0x87818218  0x251e7218  \REGISTRY\MACHINE\SYSTEM
0x87838008  0x250c7008  \REGISTRY\MACHINE\HARDWARE
0x878c23b0  0x1fc543b0  \SystemRoot\System32\Config\DEFAULT
0x88575460  0x18cc1460  \SystemRoot\System32\Config\SECURITY
0x885cb3d8  0x183063d8  \SystemRoot\System32\Config\SAM
0x8f4ef008  0x20d43008  \Device\HarddiskVolume1\Boot\BCD
0x8f589510  0x20d9e510  \SystemRoot\System32\Config\SOFTWARE
0x9140b9c8  0x180ae9c8  \??\C:\Windows\ServiceProfiles\NetworkService\NTUSER.DAT
0x914619c8  0x184a79c8  \??\C:\Windows\ServiceProfiles\LocalService\NTUSER.DAT
0x9687a198  0x0d4af198  \??\C:\Users\hello\ntuser.dat
0x96923648  0x0d44d648  \??\C:\Users\hello\AppData\Local\Microsoft\Windows\UsrClass.dat
```

Timeliner

This plugin usually creates a timeline from the various artifacts found in the memory dump. To locate the artifacts according to the timeline, you can use the following command:

```
volatility -f ram.mem --profile=Win7SP1x64 timeliner
```

```
  ┌──(v⬤kali)-[~/Documents]
  └─$ vol -f Challenge.raw --profile=Win7SP1x86 timeliner
Volatility Foundation Volatility Framework 2.6.1
2018-10-23 08:30:51 UTC+0000|[LIVE RESPONSE]| (System time)|
2018-10-23 08:29:31 UTC+0000|[PROCESS]| VBoxService.ex| PID: 652/PPID: 484/POffset: 0x3d441708
2018-10-04 08:37:27 UTC+0000|[Handle (Key)]| MACHINE\CONTROLSET001\CONTROL\NLS\SORTING\VERSIONS| VBoxService.ex PID: 652/PPID: 484/POf
fset: 0x3d441708
2018-10-19 10:51:38 UTC+0000|[Handle (Key)]| MACHINE\CONTROLSET001\CONTROL\SESSION MANAGER| VBoxService.ex PID: 652/PPID: 484/POffset:
 0x3d441708
2018-10-23 08:29:29 UTC+0000|[Handle (Key)]| MACHINE| VBoxService.ex PID: 652/PPID: 484/POffset: 0x3d441708
2009-07-14 04:37:06 UTC+0000|[Handle (Key)]| USER\CONTROL PANEL\INTERNATIONAL| VBoxService.ex PID: 652/PPID: 484/POffset: 0x3d441708
2009-07-14 04:37:09 UTC+0000|[Handle (Key)]| MACHINE\CONTROLSET001\CONTROL\NLS\LOCALE| VBoxService.ex PID: 652/PPID: 484/POffset: 0x3d
441708
2009-07-14 04:37:09 UTC+0000|[Handle (Key)]| MACHINE\CONTROLSET001\CONTROL\NLS\LOCALE\ALTERNATE SORTS| VBoxService.ex PID: 652/PPID: 4
84/POffset: 0x3d441708
2009-07-14 04:37:09 UTC+0000|[Handle (Key)]| MACHINE\CONTROLSET001\CONTROL\NLS\LANGUAGE GROUPS| VBoxService.ex PID: 652/PPID: 484/POff
set: 0x3d441708
2018-09-13 00:39:48 UTC+0000|[Handle (Key)]| MACHINE\CONTROLSET001\SERVICES\WINSOCK2\PARAMETERS\PROTOCOL_CATALOG9| VBoxService.ex PID:
 652/PPID: 484/POffset: 0x3d441708
2010-11-20 21:41:12 UTC+0000|[Handle (Key)]| MACHINE\CONTROLSET001\SERVICES\WINSOCK2\PARAMETERS\NAMESPACE_CATALOG5| VBoxService.ex PID
: 652/PPID: 484/POffset: 0x3d441708
2018-04-27 09:37:11 UTC+0000|[PE HEADER (dll)]| VBoxService.exe| Process: VBoxService.ex/PID: 652/PPID: 484/Process POffset: 0x3d44170
8/DLL Base: 0x009f0000
2018-04-27 09:37:11 UTC+0000|[PE DEBUG]| VBoxService.exe| Process: VBoxService.ex/PID: 652/PPID: 484/Process POffset: 0x3d441708/DLL B
ase: 0x009f0000
1970-01-01 00:00:00 UTC+0000|[DLL LOADTIME (dll)]| VBoxService.exe| Process: VBoxService.ex/PID: 652/PPID: 484/Process POffset: 0x3d44
```

Hashdump

This plugin can be used to extract, and decrypt cached domain credentials stored in the registry which can be availed from the memory dump. The hashes that are availed from the memory dump can be cracked using John the Ripper, Hashcat, etc. To gather the hashdump, you can use the command:

```
volatility -f ram.mem --profile=Win7SP1x64 hashdump
```

```
  ┌──(v⬤kali)-[~/Documents]
  └─$ vol -f Challenge.raw --profile=Win7SP1x86 hashdump
Volatility Foundation Volatility Framework 2.6.1
Administrator:500:aad3b435b51404eeaad3b435b51404ee:31d6cfe0d16ae931b73c59d7e0c089c0:::
Guest:501:aad3b435b51404eeaad3b435b51404ee:31d6cfe0d16ae931b73c59d7e0c089c0:::
hello:1000:aad3b435b51404eeaad3b435b51404ee:101da33f44e92c27835e64322d72e8b7:::
```

Lsadump

This plugin is used to dump LSA secrets from the registry in the memory dump. This plugin gives out information like the default password, the RDP public key, etc. To perform a lsadump, you can type the following command:

```
volatility -f ram.mem --profile=Win7SP1x64 lsadump
```

```
┌──(v👁kali)-[~/Documents]
└─$ vol -f Challenge.raw --profile=Win7SP1x86 lsadump
Volatility Foundation Volatility Framework 2.6.1
DefaultPassword
0x00000000   00 00 00 00 00 00 00 00 00 00 00 00 00 00 00 00   ................
0x00000010   ae fa b4 46 c8 f1 2c 9b b9 44 aa 45 3c 4f 3f d1   ...F..,..D.E<O?.

NL$KM
0x00000000   40 00 00 00 00 00 00 00 00 00 00 00 00 00 00 00   @...............
0x00000010   a9 d4 73 b5 38 9f 03 cb 7a 7d a8 d7 b7 ff e6 0c   ..s.8...z}......
0x00000020   ec e6 16 34 a4 04 74 f2 b7 84 ce 3f 33 83 ef 28   ...4..t....?3..(
0x00000030   aa 07 7b fb 28 f7 fe 0a 5f 17 96 d7 60 9d a3 17   ..{.(.._...`...
0x00000040   c0 97 96 9e 98 5d ed ff dc d8 4c 59 dc 65 36 f5   .....]....LY.e6.
0x00000050   df ee 9d 49 19 50 cf b8 f3 1c bc f7 83 6a 86 c9   ...I.P.......j..

DPAPI_SYSTEM
0x00000000   2c 00 00 00 00 00 00 00 00 00 00 00 00 00 00 00   ,...............
0x00000010   01 00 00 00 8e 2e 91 3a ab f2 1d 05 06 2e 9d 60   .......:.......`
0x00000020   7c 47 aa c1 08 fc 59 01 bd ed 59 7a 5a 00 ef ce   |G....Y...YzZ...
0x00000030   ff 35 32 22 89 26 bb 59 9a 58 32 a8 00 00 00 00   .52".&.Y.X2.....
```

Modscan

This plugin is used to locate kernel memory and its related objects. It can pick up all the previously unloaded drivers and also those drivers that have been hidden or have been unlinked by rootkits in the system.

```
volatility -f ram.mem --profile=Win7SP1x64 modscan
```

```
┌──(v👁kali)-[~/Documents]
└─$ vol -f Challenge.raw --profile=Win7SP1x86 modscan
Volatility Foundation Volatility Framework 2.6.1
Offset(P)            Name              Base         Size     File
------------------   --------------    ----------   ------   ----------
0x000000003d2e39b0   spsys.sys         0x978a4000   0x6a000  \SystemRoot\system32\drivers\spsys.sys
0x000000003d429b30   luafv.sys         0x91000000   0x1b000  \SystemRoot\system32\drivers\luafv.sys
0x000000003d4381f8   peauth.sys        0x96160000   0x98000  \SystemRoot\system32\drivers\peauth.sys
0x000000003d4ea4a0   lltdio.sys        0x9101b000   0x10000  \SystemRoot\system32\DRIVERS\lltdio.sys
0x000000003d4f0478   rspndr.sys        0x8fc00000   0x13000  \SystemRoot\system32\DRIVERS\rspndr.sys
0x000000003d52bcd0   mrxsmb10.sys      0x96108000   0x3c000  \SystemRoot\system32\DRIVERS\mrxsmb10.sys
0x000000003d52e318   HTTP.sys          0x96036000   0x85000  \SystemRoot\system32\drivers\HTTP.sys
0x000000003d5560f0   mrxsmb.sys        0x960e5000   0x23000  \SystemRoot\system32\DRIVERS\mrxsmb.sys
0x000000003d5609a0   bowser.sys        0x960bb000   0x18000  \SystemRoot\system32\DRIVERS\bowser.sys
0x000000003d560ec8   mpsdrv.sys        0x960d3000   0x12000  \SystemRoot\system32\DRIVERS\mpsdrv.sys
0x000000003d564008   mrxsmb20.sys      0x96144000   0x1c000  \SystemRoot\system32\DRIVERS\mrxsmb20.sys
0x000000003d5a5f88   srvnet.sys        0x96000000   0x22000  \SystemRoot\System32\DRIVERS\srvnet.sys
0x000000003d5acc68   tcpipreg.sys      0x96022000   0xd000   \SystemRoot\System32\drivers\tcpipreg.sys
0x000000003d5c32a8   srv.sys           0x97851000   0x53000  \SystemRoot\System32\DRIVERS\srv.sys
0x000000003d5c5850   srv2.sys          0x97800000   0x51000  \SystemRoot\System32\DRIVERS\srv2.sys
0x000000003d6d03b0   usbhub.sys        0x9107a000   0x44000  \SystemRoot\system32\drivers\usbhub.sys
0x000000003d6d92b0   win32k.sys        0x82190000   0x25e000 \SystemRoot\System32\win32k.sys
0x000000003d6d9c48   cdd.dll           0x82030000   0x1e000  \SystemRoot\System32\cdd.dll
0x000000003d6e2008   NDProxy.SYS       0x910be000   0x11000  \SystemRoot\System32\Drivers\NDProxy.SYS
0x000000003d70b628   HdAudio.sys       0x910cf000   0x50000  \SystemRoot\system32\drivers\HdAudio.sys
0x000000003d70c190   drmk.sys          0x9114e000   0x19000  \SystemRoot\system32\drivers\drmk.sys
0x000000003d70d3d0   portcls.sys       0x9111f000   0x2f000  \SystemRoot\system32\drivers\portcls.sys
0x000000003d7269e8   cdfs.sys          0x91167000   0x16000  \SystemRoot\System32\DRIVERS\cdfs.sys
0x000000003d7586b0   mouhid.sys        0x911d7000   0xb000   \SystemRoot\system32\DRIVERS\mouhid.sys
0x000000003d75dd18   Dxapi.sys         0x911e2000   0xa000   \SystemRoot\system32\drivers\Dxapi.sys
0x000000003d7814d8   TSDDD.dll         0x82000000   0x9000   \SystemRoot\System32\TSDDD.dll
0x000000003d783c78   DumpIt.sys        0x9790e000   0xc000   \??\C:\Windows\system32\Drivers\DumpIt.sys
0x000000003dc05390   rasppppoe.sys     0x8fb93000   0x18000  \SystemRoot\system32\DRIVERS\rasppppoe.sys
```

Filescan

This plugin is used to find FILE_OBJECTs present in the physical memory by using pool tag scanning. It can find open files even if there is a hidden rootkit present in the files. To make use of this plugin, you can type the following command:

```
volatility -f ram.mem --profile=Win7SP1x64 filescan
```

```
  ┌──(v☻kali)-[~/Documents]
  └─$ vol -f Challenge.raw --profile=Win7SP1x86 filescan
Volatility Foundation Volatility Framework 2.6.1
Offset(P)            #Ptr   #Hnd  Access Name
------------------   -----  ----- ------ ----
0x000000003d2396b0       1      1 RW-r-d \Device\HarddiskVolume2\Windows\System32\LogFiles\SQM\SQMLogger.etl.003
0x000000003d2398d8       8      1 R--r-d \Device\HarddiskVolume2\Windows\System32\en-US\propsys.dll.mui
0x000000003d239a90      17      0 RW-rwd \Device\HarddiskVolume2\$Directory
0x000000003d23e0f8       2      1 ------ \Device\Afd\Endpoint
0x000000003d23e1b0       8      0 R--r-d \Device\HarddiskVolume2\Windows\System32\wbem\wmiutils.dll
0x000000003d23e2c0       7      0 R--r-d \Device\HarddiskVolume2\Windows\System32\wpdbusenum.dll
0x000000003d23f4a0       2      1 R--rwd \Device\HarddiskVolume2\Users\hello\AppData\Roaming\Microsoft\Windows\Printer Shortcuts
0x000000003d242138      10      1 RW-r-- \Device\HarddiskVolume2\Windows\System32\winevt\Logs\Microsoft-Windows-Winlogon%4Operational.e
vtx
0x000000003d242be8       6      0 R--r-d \Device\HarddiskVolume2\Windows\System32\PortableDeviceApi.dll
0x000000003d244330       4      0 R--r-d \Device\HarddiskVolume2\Windows\System32\wbem\repdrvfs.dll
0x000000003d244548       7      0 R--r-d \Device\HarddiskVolume2\Windows\System32\wdi.dll
```

Svcscan

This plugin is used to see the services are registered on your memory image, use the svcscan command. The output shows the process ID of each service the service name, service name, display name, service type, service state, and also shows the binary path for the registered service – which will be a .exe for user-mode services and a driver name for services that run from kernel mode. To find the details on the services

```
volatility -f ram.mem --profile=Win7SP1x64 svcscan
```

```
  ┌──(v☻kali)-[~/Documents]
  └─$ vol -f Challenge.raw --profile=Win7SP1x86 svcscan_
```

```
Offset: 0x5de698
Order: 394
Start: SERVICE_AUTO_START
Process ID: 2032
Service Name: WSearch
Display Name: Windows Search
Service Type: SERVICE_WIN32_OWN_PROCESS
Service State: SERVICE_RUNNING
Binary Path: C:\Windows\system32\SearchIndexer.exe /Embedding

Offset: 0x5de340
Order: 393
Start: SERVICE_AUTO_START
Process ID: -
Service Name: wscsvc
Display Name: Security Center
Service Type: SERVICE_WIN32_SHARE_PROCESS
Service State: SERVICE_STOPPED
Binary Path: -
```

Cmdscan

This plugin searches the memory dump of XP/2003/Vista/2008 and Windows 7 for commands that the attacker might have entered through a command prompt (cmd.exe). It is one of the most powerful commands that one can use to gain visibility into an attacker's actions on a victim system. To conduct a cmdscan, you can make use of the following command:

```
volatility -f ram.mem --profile=Win7SP1x64 cmdscan
```

```
  ┌──(v☻kali)-[~/Documents]
  └─$ vol -f Challenge.raw --profile=Win7SP1x86 cmdscan
Volatility Foundation Volatility Framework 2.6.1
**************************************************
CommandProcess: conhost.exe Pid: 2104
CommandHistory: 0x300498 Application: cmd.exe Flags: Allocated, Reset
CommandCount: 1 LastAdded: 0 LastDisplayed: 0
FirstCommand: 0 CommandCountMax: 50
ProcessHandle: 0x5c
Cmd #0 @ 0x2f43c0: C:\Python27\python.exe C:\Users\hello\Desktop\demon.py.txt
```

IEhistory

This plugin recovers the fragments of Internet Explorer history (assuming they are still using IE) by finding index.dat cache file. To find iehistory files, you can type the following command:

```
volatility -f ram.mem --profile=Win7SP1x64 iehistory
```

In the raw file we had there was no history, likely IE was not being used.

Dumpregistry

This plugin allows one to dump a registry hive into a disk location. To dump the registry hive, you use the following command.

```
volatility -f ram.mem --profile=Win7SP1x64 dumpregistry --dump-dir /root/ramdump/
```

Moddump

This plugin is used to extract a kernel driver to a file, you can do this by using the following command:

```
volatility -f ram.mem --profile=Win7SP1x64 moddump --dump-dir /root/ramdump/
```

Procdump

This plugin is used to dump the executable processes in a single location, if there is malware present it will intentionally forge size fields in the PE header for the memory dumping tool to fail. To collect the dump on processes, you can type:

```
volatility -f ram.mem --profile=Win7SP1x64 procdump --dump-dir /root/ramdump/
```

Memdump

The memdump plugin is used to dump the memory-resident pages of a process into a separate file. You can also look up a particular process using -p and provide it with a directory path -D to generate the output. To take a dump on memory-resident pages, you can use the following command:

```
volatility -f ram.mem --profile=Win7SP1x64 memdump --dump-dir /root/ramdump/
```

Notepad

Notepad files are usually highly looked up files in the ram dump. To find the contents present in the notepad file, you can use the following command:

```
volatility -f ram.mem --profile=WinXPSP2x86 notepad
```

Finding Malicious Artifacts Using Volatility

By: Mossaraf Zaman Khan

Volatility is an Advanced Open-Source Memory Forensics framework produced by The Volatility Foundation. Now let's talk about what is Memory. Memory or Random-access Memory (RAM) is a type of computer memory and a part of essential computer hardware, used to store the data in current use, so it can be quickly accessed by the processor. RAM is a volatile type of memory that means after turning off the computer the data lost. So, it can't store the permanent data. Here the memory forensics comes into picture. Memory forensics is a technique to analyze volatile memory for forensic artifacts.

A memory dump contains the valuable information about the runtime state of the system like Running Processes & Application details, Active Network Connections related information, Kernel Drivers related information, Loaded Modules etc.

Performing memory forensics includes two major steps:

Step 1: Memory Acquisition:

Memory Acquisition is a process of dumping the contents of Volatile Memory (RAM) from a suspect machine.

Tools of the Trade: FTK Imager, Dumpit, Magnet RAM Capture, Belkasoft RAM Capturer etc.

Step 2: Memory Analysis:

Memory Analysis is a procedure of analyzing the memory dump for forensic artifacts or finding malicious artifacts.

Tools of the Trade: Volatility, Redline, Belkasoft Evidence Centre

In this topic, I am going to focus on Volatility Framework. This Open-Source Memory Forensic Tool is available for major operating system like Windows, Mac, Linux etc.

Installation

Volatility can be downloaded from the Official Website and from the official GitHub Page.
Official Site: *www.volatilityfoundation.org/releases*
Github Page: *https://github.com/volatilityfoundation/volatility*

Volatility comes pre-installed with major security operating system like CSI Linux, Kali Linux, Sans Sift, Parrot Sec OS etc.

Installation Process on Linux:

1. Clone the setup file from the Github - git clone https://github.com/volatilityfoundation /volatility
2. Change the permission of the setup file (setup.py) - *chmod 755 setup.py*
3. Installing the volatility - *./setup.py install*
4. Change the permission of Volatility launcher (vol.py) - *chmod 755 vol.py*
5. Launch the Volatility - *./vol.py*

Installation Guide: *https://github.com/volatilityfoundation/volatility/wiki/Installation*

Volatility Usage

For the demonstration purposes I use Parrot Security OS. That comes with pre-installed version of Volatility Framework.

Volatility Available Options

Command: **volatility -h**
This command helps to display the available options and supported plugins

```
┌─[root@parrot]─[/home/markonsec]
└──╼ #volatility -h
Volatility Foundation Volatility Framework 2.6
Usage: Volatility - A memory forensics analysis platform.

Options:
  -h, --help            list all available options and their default values.
                        Default values may be set in the configuration file
                        (/etc/volatilityrc)
  --conf-file=/root/.volatilityrc
                        User based configuration file
  -d, --debug           Debug volatility
  --plugins=PLUGINS     Additional plugin directories to use (colon separated)
  --info                Print information about all registered objects
  --cache-directory=/root/.cache/volatility
                        Directory where cache files are stored
  --cache               Use caching
  --tz=TZ               Sets the (Olson) timezone for displaying timestamps
                        using pytz (if installed) or tzset
  -f FILENAME, --filename=FILENAME
                        Filename to use when opening an image
```

Fig 1: Volatility Help Option

```
Supported Plugin Commands:

        amcache         Print AmCache information
        apihooks        Detect API hooks in process and kernel memory
        atoms           Print session and window station atom tables
        atomscan        Pool scanner for atom tables
        auditpol        Prints out the Audit Policies from HKLM\SECURITY\Policy\PolAdtEv
        bigpools        Dump the big page pools using BigPagePoolScanner
        bioskbd         Reads the keyboard buffer from Real Mode memory
        cachedump       Dumps cached domain hashes from memory
        callbacks       Print system-wide notification routines
        clipboard       Extract the contents of the windows clipboard
        cmdline         Display process command-line arguments
        cmdscan         Extract command history by scanning for _COMMAND_HISTORY
        connections     Print list of open connections [Windows XP and 2003 Only]
        connscan        Pool scanner for tcp connections
        consoles        Extract command history by scanning for _CONSOLE_INFORMATION
```

Fig 2: Plugin Details

Profile and Plugin Availability

Command: **volatility --info | more**

This command helps to display the supported profile and provide details of the available plugin

Profile Determination of a Memory Dump

The first step of any memory analysis using Volatility is to determine the profile of the memory dump. This is the extremely important step for any memory analysis. Profile determination helps to detect the correct profile type of the memory. Profile includes the metadata of the memory image like operating system types, service pack details, system architecture, timestamp etc.
Plugin Required: **imageinfo, kdbgscan**

Usage: volatility -f <file name> <plugin>
Command: **volatility -f sample.vmem imageinfo** [-f: filename]

```
┌─[root@parrot]─[/home/markonsec]
└──╼ #volatility -f sample.vmem imageinfo
Volatility Foundation Volatility Framework 2.6
INFO    : volatility.debug    : Determining profile based on KDBG search...
          Suggested Profile(s) : WinXPSP2x86, WinXPSP3x86 (Instantiated with WinXPSP2x86)
                     AS Layer1 : IA32PagedMemoryPae (Kernel AS)
                     AS Layer2 : FileAddressSpace (/home/markonsec/sample.vmem)
                      PAE type : PAE
                           DTB : 0x319000L
                          KDBG : 0x80544ce0L
          Number of Processors : 1
     Image Type (Service Pack) : 2
                KPCR for CPU 0 : 0xffdff000L
             KUSER_SHARED_DATA : 0xffdf0000L
           Image date and time : 2011-10-10 17:06:54 UTC+0000
     Image local date and time : 2011-10-10 13:06:54 -0400
```

Fig 3: Memory Image Profile Determination

Here, the suggested profile is - **WinXP2x86.**

Instead of **imageinfo** plugin we can also use **kdbgscan** plugin to determine the profile of the memory dump.

Finding running processes from a Memory Dump

Volatility plugin **pslist** is used to display the processes of the system. It displays the Process name, Process ID, Parent process ID, Offset, Timestamp etc. But this plugin cannot detect the hidden and the unlinked processes

Command: **volatility -f sample.vmem --profile=WinXPSP2x86 pslist**

Volatility plugin **pstree** do the same job as **pslist** plugin but it displays the process listing in tree form. It is helpful to detect the parent and child processes as a simple manner. It is also cannot detect the hidden and the unlinked processes like **pslist**.

Command: **volatility -f sample.vmem --profile=WinXPSP2x86 pstree**

PSLIST

```
┌─[root@parrot]─[/home/markonsec]
└──╼ #volatility -f sample.vmem --profile=WinXPSP2x86 pslist
Volatility Foundation Volatility Framework 2.6
Offset(V)  Name                    PID   PPID   Thds     Hnds   Sess  Wow64 Start                          Exit
---------- -------------------- ------ ------ ------ -------- ------ ------ ------------------------------ ------------
0x819cc830 System                    4      0     55      162 ------      0
0x81945020 smss.exe                536      4      3       21 ------      0 2011-10-10 17:03:56 UTC+0000
0x816c6020 csrss.exe               608    536     11      355      0      0 2011-10-10 17:03:58 UTC+0000
0x813a9020 winlogon.exe            632    536     24      533      0      0 2011-10-10 17:03:58 UTC+0000
0x816da020 services.exe            676    632     16      261      0      0 2011-10-10 17:03:58 UTC+0000
0x813c4020 lsass.exe               688    632     23      336      0      0 2011-10-10 17:03:58 UTC+0000
0x81772ca8 vmacthlp.exe            832    676      1       24      0      0 2011-10-10 17:03:59 UTC+0000
0x8167e9d0 svchost.exe             848    676     20      194      0      0 2011-10-10 17:03:59 UTC+0000
0x817757f0 svchost.exe             916    676      9      217      0      0 2011-10-10 17:03:59 UTC+0000
0x816c6da0 svchost.exe             964    676     63     1058      0      0 2011-10-10 17:03:59 UTC+0000
0x815daca8 svchost.exe            1020    676      5       58      0      0 2011-10-10 17:03:59 UTC+0000
0x813aeda0 svchost.exe            1148    676     12      187      0      0 2011-10-10 17:04:00 UTC+0000
0x817937e0 spoolsv.exe            1260    676     13      140      0      0 2011-10-10 17:04:00 UTC+0000
0x81754990 VMwareService.e        1444    676      3      145      0      0 2011-10-10 17:04:00 UTC+0000
0x8136c5a0 alg.exe                1616    676      7       99      0      0 2011-10-10 17:04:01 UTC+0000
0x815c4da0 wscntfy.exe            1920    964      1       27      0      0 2011-10-10 17:04:39 UTC+0000
0x813bcda0 explorer.exe           1956   1884     18      322      0      0 2011-10-10 17:04:39 UTC+0000
0x816d63d0 VMwareTray.exe          184   1956      1       28      0      0 2011-10-10 17:04:41 UTC+0000
0x8180b478 VMwareUser.exe          192   1956      6       83      0      0 2011-10-10 17:04:41 UTC+0000
0x818233c8 reader_sl.exe           228   1956      2       26      0      0 2011-10-10 17:04:41 UTC+0000
0x815e7be0 wuauclt.exe             400    964      8      173      0      0 2011-10-10 17:04:46 UTC+0000
0x817a34b0 cmd.exe                 544   1956      1       30      0      0 2011-10-10 17:06:42 UTC+0000
```

Fig 4: Process detection using PSLIST

PSTREE

```
-[root@parrot]-[/home/markonsec]
 #volatility -f sample.vmem --profile=WinXPSP2x86 pstree
Volatility Foundation Volatility Framework 2.6
Name                                                  Pid   PPid   Thds   Hnds Time
-------------------------------------------------- ------ ------ ------ ------ ----
 0x819cc830:System                                      4      0     55    162 1970-01-01 00:00:00 UTC+0000
. 0x81945020:smss.exe                                 536      4      3     21 2011-10-10 17:03:56 UTC+0000
.. 0x816c6020:csrss.exe                               608    536     11    355 2011-10-10 17:03:58 UTC+0000
.. 0x813a9020:winlogon.exe                            632    536     24    533 2011-10-10 17:03:58 UTC+0000
... 0x816da020:services.exe                           676    632     16    261 2011-10-10 17:03:58 UTC+0000
.... 0x817757f0:svchost.exe                           916    676      9    217 2011-10-10 17:03:59 UTC+0000
.... 0x81772ca8:vmacthlp.exe                          832    676      1     24 2011-10-10 17:03:59 UTC+0000
.... 0x816c6da0:svchost.exe                           964    676     63   1058 2011-10-10 17:03:59 UTC+0000
..... 0x815c4da0:wscntfy.exe                         1920    964      1     27 2011-10-10 17:04:39 UTC+0000
..... 0x815e7be0:wuauclt.exe                          400    964      8    173 2011-10-10 17:04:46 UTC+0000
.... 0x8167e9d0:svchost.exe                           848    676     20    194 2011-10-10 17:03:59 UTC+0000
.... 0x81754990:VMwareService.e                      1444    676      3    145 2011-10-10 17:04:00 UTC+0000
.... 0x8136c5a0:alg.exe                              1616    676      7     99 2011-10-10 17:04:01 UTC+0000
.... 0x813aeda0:svchost.exe                          1148    676     12    187 2011-10-10 17:04:00 UTC+0000
.... 0x817937e0:spoolsv.exe                          1260    676     13    140 2011-10-10 17:04:00 UTC+0000
.... 0x815daca8:svchost.exe                          1020    676      5     58 2011-10-10 17:03:59 UTC+0000
... 0x813c4020:lsass.exe                              688    632     23    336 2011-10-10 17:03:58 UTC+0000
 0x813bcda0:explorer.exe                             1956   1884     18    322 2011-10-10 17:04:39 UTC+0000
. 0x8180b478:VMwareUser.exe                           192   1956      6     83 2011-10-10 17:04:41 UTC+0000
. 0x817a34b0:cmd.exe                                  544   1956      1     30 2011-10-10 17:06:42 UTC+0000
. 0x816d63d0:VMwareTray.exe                           184   1956      1     28 2011-10-10 17:04:41 UTC+0000
. 0x818233c8:reader_sl.exe                            228   1956      2     26 2011-10-10 17:04:41 UTC+0000
```

Fig 5: Process detection using PSTREE

Volatility plugin **psscan** is used to enumerate the processes with the help of pool tag scanning. It can detect the hidden and the unlinked processes. This plugin is always helpful during malware investigation.

Command: **volatility -f sample.vmem --profile=WinXPSP2x86 psscan**

We can also output the processes list as a graphical view to present or understand the processes simpler manner.

Command: **volatility -f sample.vmem --profile=WinXPSP2x86 psscan -output=dot -out-file=sample.dot**

PSCAN

```
-[root@parrot]-[/home/markonsec]
 #volatility -f sample.vmem --profile=WinXPSP2x86 psscan
Volatility Foundation Volatility Framework 2.6
Offset(P)          Name                PID   PPID PDB        Time created                   Time exited
------------------ ---------------- ------ ------ ---------- ------------------------------ ------------
0x000000000156c5a0 alg.exe            1616    676 0x05e001e0 2011-10-10 17:04:01 UTC+0000
0x00000000015a9020 winlogon.exe        632    536 0x05e00060 2011-10-10 17:03:58 UTC+0000
0x00000000015aeda0 svchost.exe        1148    676 0x05e00180 2011-10-10 17:04:00 UTC+0000
0x00000000015bcda0 explorer.exe       1956   1884 0x05e00220 2011-10-10 17:04:39 UTC+0000
0x00000000015c4020 lsass.exe           688    632 0x05e000a0 2011-10-10 17:03:58 UTC+0000
0x00000000017c4da0 wscntfy.exe        1920    964 0x05e00240 2011-10-10 17:04:39 UTC+0000
0x00000000017daca8 svchost.exe        1020    676 0x05e00140 2011-10-10 17:03:59 UTC+0000
0x00000000017e7be0 wuauclt.exe         400    964 0x05e002c0 2011-10-10 17:04:46 UTC+0000
0x000000000187e9d0 svchost.exe         848    676 0x05e000e0 2011-10-10 17:03:59 UTC+0000
0x00000000018c6020 csrss.exe           608    536 0x05e00040 2011-10-10 17:03:58 UTC+0000
0x00000000018c6da0 svchost.exe         964    676 0x05e00120 2011-10-10 17:03:59 UTC+0000
0x00000000018d63d0 VMwareTray.exe      184   1956 0x05e00160 2011-10-10 17:04:41 UTC+0000
0x00000000018da020 services.exe        676    632 0x05e00080 2011-10-10 17:03:58 UTC+0000
0x0000000001954990 VMwareService.e    1444    676 0x05e001c0 2011-10-10 17:04:00 UTC+0000
0x0000000001972ca8 vmacthlp.exe        832    676 0x05e000c0 2011-10-10 17:03:59 UTC+0000
0x00000000019757f0 svchost.exe         916    676 0x05e00100 2011-10-10 17:03:59 UTC+0000
0x00000000019937e0 spoolsv.exe        1260    676 0x05e001a0 2011-10-10 17:04:00 UTC+0000
0x00000000019a34b0 cmd.exe             544   1956 0x05e00200 2011-10-10 17:06:42 UTC+0000
0x0000000001a0b478 VMwareUser.exe      192   1956 0x05e00260 2011-10-10 17:04:41 UTC+0000
0x0000000001a233c8 reader_sl.exe       228   1956 0x05e00280 2011-10-10 17:04:41 UTC+0000
0x0000000001b45020 smss.exe            536      4 0x05e00020 2011-10-10 17:03:56 UTC+0000
0x0000000001bcc830 System                4      0 0x00319000
```

Fig 6: Enumerating Process using PSSCAN

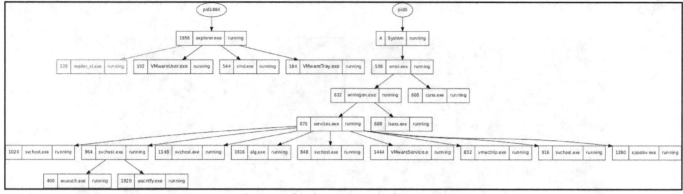
Fig 7: Graphical presentation of Processes

Result: **reader_sl.exe** is a malicious process. It runs under **explorer.exe** process.

Finding executed commands from a Memory Dump

CMDSCAN

Volatility plugin **cmdscan** is used to find the suspected executed commands by the attacker or the malicious user. It helps to gain visibility into an attacker's action on a victim system. Whether they opened command prompt (cmd.exe) or not. It is use **COMMAND_HISTORY** Structure to display the results.

Command: **volatility -f sample.vmem --profile=WinXPSP2x86 cmdscan**

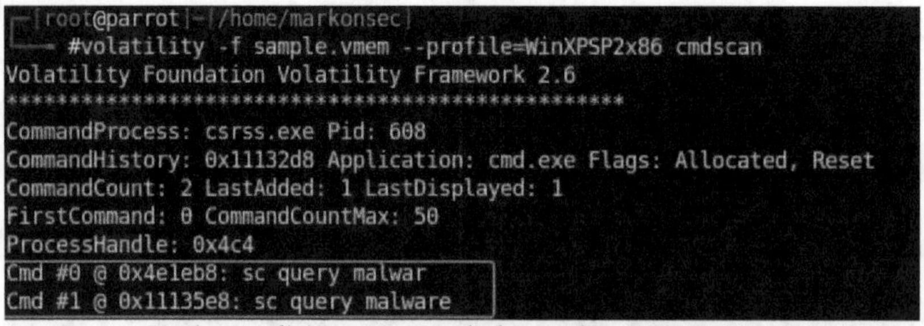

```
┌──[root@parrot]─[/home/markonsec]
└──➤ #volatility -f sample.vmem --profile=WinXPSP2x86 cmdscan
Volatility Foundation Volatility Framework 2.6
**************************************************
CommandProcess: csrss.exe Pid: 608
CommandHistory: 0x11132d8 Application: cmd.exe Flags: Allocated, Reset
CommandCount: 2 LastAdded: 1 LastDisplayed: 1
FirstCommand: 0 CommandCountMax: 50
ProcessHandle: 0x4c4
Cmd #0 @ 0x4e1eb8: sc query malwar
Cmd #1 @ 0x11135e8: sc query malware
```
Fig 8: Malicious commands detected by CMDSCAN

CONSOLES

Volatility plugin **consoles** is similar to the **cmdcan**. It is use **CONSOLE_INFORMATION** to display the results. It is useful for finding commands that is used by attacker or executed by some malware or backdoor.

Command: **volatility -f sample.vmem --profile=WinXPSP2x86 consoles**

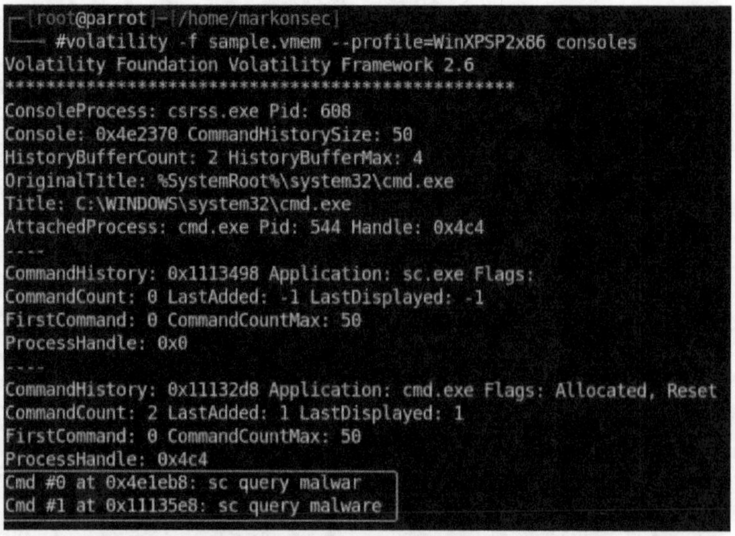

```
┌──[root@parrot]─[/home/markonsec]
└──➤ #volatility -f sample.vmem --profile=WinXPSP2x86 consoles
Volatility Foundation Volatility Framework 2.6
**************************************************
ConsoleProcess: csrss.exe Pid: 608
Console: 0x4e2370 CommandHistorySize: 50
HistoryBufferCount: 2 HistoryBufferMax: 4
OriginalTitle: %SystemRoot%\system32\cmd.exe
Title: C:\WINDOWS\system32\cmd.exe
AttachedProcess: cmd.exe Pid: 544 Handle: 0x4c4
----
CommandHistory: 0x1113498 Application: sc.exe Flags:
CommandCount: 0 LastAdded: -1 LastDisplayed: -1
FirstCommand: 0 CommandCountMax: 50
ProcessHandle: 0x0
----
CommandHistory: 0x11132d8 Application: cmd.exe Flags: Allocated, Reset
CommandCount: 2 LastAdded: 1 LastDisplayed: 1
FirstCommand: 0 CommandCountMax: 50
ProcessHandle: 0x4c4
Cmd #0 at 0x4e1eb8: sc query malwar
Cmd #1 at 0x11135e8: sc query malware
```
Fig 9: Malicious Commands detected by CONSOLES

Fig 10: Executed Commands dumps by CONSOLES

Results: sc query malwar & **sc query malware** are the malicious commands are executed by the malware.

Except from that **dlllist** plugin is used to display the loaded DLLs from a process and the **dlldump** plugin is used to dump the DLL file from the processes.

Dumping the Process Executable and Memory Section from a Memory Image:

ProcDump

Volatility plugin **procdump** is used to dump a process to the executable file format. This executable file can be further analysis for the addition information like PE header details, strings information etc.

Command: **volatility -f sample.vmem --profile=WinXPSP2x86 procdump -p 228 --dump-dir=./**
[**-p**: Process ID, **./**: Dump the file into the current directory]

Fig 11: Process dumping using PROCDUMP

Memdump

Volatility plugin **memdump** is used to dump the memory sections from a given Process ID.

Command: **volatility -f sample.vmem --profile=WinXPSP2x86 memdump -p 228 --dump-dir=./**
[**-p**: Process ID, **./**: Dump the file into the current directory]

Fig 12: Memory section extraction by MEMDUMP

Finding Networking related activity from a Memory Dump

Connscan

Volatility plugin **connscan** is used to finding artifacts from previously disconnected connections.

Command: **volatility -f sample.vmem --profile=WinXPSP2x86 connscan**

Fig 13: Network Related Artifacts using CONNSCAN

```
┌─[root@parrot]─[/home/markonsec]
└─▶ #volatility -f sample.vmem --profile=WinXPSP2x86 connscan
Volatility Foundation Volatility Framework 2.6
Offset(P)   Local Address                Remote Address              Pid
---------- -------------------------- -------------------------- --------
0x01a25a50 0.0.0.0:1026                 172.16.98.1:6666           1956
```

Netscan

Here malicious PID **1956** is communicated with the Remote IP **172.16.98.1** and port **6666**. Volatility plugin **netscan** is used to find TCP & UDP listener, endpoints. But it will not work with the WinXPSP2x86 profile.

Volatility plugin sockets is used to detect the listening sockets for any TCP, UDP or RAW protocols.

Command: **volatility -f sample.vmem --profile=WinXPSP2x86 sockets**

```
┌─[root@parrot]─[/home/markonsec]
└─▶ #volatility -f sample.vmem --profile=WinXPSP2x86 sockets
Volatility Foundation Volatility Framework 2.6
Offset(V)    PID   Port  Proto Protocol      Address      Create Time
---------- ------ ------ ----- -----------   -----------  ------------------------
0x8177e3c0  1956  1026     6  TCP           0.0.0.0      2011-10-10 17:04:39 UTC+0000
0x81596a78   688   500    17  UDP           0.0.0.0      2011-10-10 17:04:00 UTC+0000
0x8166a008   964  1029    17  UDP           127.0.0.1    2011-10-10 17:04:42 UTC+0000
0x818ddc08     4   445     6  TCP           0.0.0.0      2011-10-10 17:03:55 UTC+0000
0x818328d8   916   135     6  TCP           0.0.0.0      2011-10-10 17:03:59 UTC+0000
0x81687e98  1616  1025     6  TCP           127.0.0.1    2011-10-10 17:04:01 UTC+0000
0x817517e8   964   123    17  UDP           127.0.0.1    2011-10-10 17:04:00 UTC+0000
0x81753b20   688     0   255  Reserved      0.0.0.0      2011-10-10 17:04:00 UTC+0000
0x8174fe98  1148  1900    17  UDP           127.0.0.1    2011-10-10 17:04:41 UTC+0000
0x81753008   688  4500    17  UDP           0.0.0.0      2011-10-10 17:04:00 UTC+0000
0x816118d8     4   445    17  UDP           0.0.0.0      2011-10-10 17:03:55 UTC+0000
```

Fig 14: List of Listening Sockets

Finding Networking related activity from a Memory Dump

Timeliner

Volatility plugin **timeliner** is used to parses timestamped objects from memory images. It shows process name, PID, Timestamps, related DLLs, Registry hives information, sockets etc.

Command: **volatility -f sample.vmem --profile=WinXPSP2x86 timeliner --outfile-file itsoutput.body --output=body**

```
┌─[root@parrot]─[/home/markonsec]
└─▶ #volatility -f sample.vmem --profile=WinXPSP2x86 timeliner --output-file itsoutput.body --output=body
Volatility Foundation Volatility Framework 2.6
Outputting to: itsoutput.body
WARNING : volatility.debug    : No ShimCache data found
┌─[root@parrot]─[/home/markonsec]
└─▶ #ls -l
total 331372
-rw-r--r-- 1 root      root      70377472 Feb  5 20:21 228.dmp
drwxr-xr-x 1 markonsec markonsec       90 Jan 28 18:42 Desktop
drwxr-xr-x 1 markonsec markonsec        0 Oct 10 14:13 Documents
drwxr-xr-x 1 markonsec markonsec       98 Feb  5 19:48 Downloads
drwxr-xr-x 1 markonsec markonsec       12 Nov 10 10:57 go
-rw-r--r-- 1 markonsec markonsec        0 Dec  7 02:34 history
-rw-r--r-- 1 root      root        500334 Feb  5 20:35 itsoutput.body
drwxr-xr-x 1 markonsec markonsec        0 Oct 10 14:13 Music
```

Fig 15: Extract the timestamp info using TIMELINER

```
┌─[markonsec@parrot]─[~]
└──╼ $cat itsoutput.body | grep "PID: 228"
0|[PROCESS] reader_sl.exe PID: 228/PPID: 1956/POffset: 0x01a233c8|0|---------------|0|0|0|1318266281|0|1318266281|1318266281
0|[PROCESS LastTrimTime] reader_sl.exe PID: 228/PPID: 1956/POffset: 0x01a233c8|0|---------------|0|0|0|1318266281|1318266281|1318266281|1318266281
0|[Handle (Key)] MACHINE reader_sl.exe PID: 228/PPID: 1956/POffset: 0x01a233c8|0|---------------|0|0|0|1318266238|1318266238|1318266238|1318266238
0|[Handle (Key)] USER reader_sl.exe PID: 228/PPID: 1956/POffset: 0x01a233c8|0|---------------|0|0|0|1318266402|1318266402|1318266402|1318266402
0|[PE HEADER (dll)] Reader_sl.exe Process: reader_sl.exe/PID: 228/PPID: 1956/Process POffset: 0x01a233c8/DLL Base: 0x00400000|0|---------------|0|0|0|12132634
73|1213263473|1213263473|1213263473
0|[PE DEBUG] Reader_sl.exe Process: reader_sl.exe/PID: 228/PPID: 1956/Process POffset: 0x01a233c8/DLL Base: 0x00400000|0|---------------|0|0|0|-|-|-|-
0|[PE HEADER (dll)] ntdll.dll Process: reader_sl.exe/PID: 228/PPID: 1956/Process POffset: 0x01a233c8/DLL Base: 0x7c900000|0|---------------|0|0|0|1091606196|1
091606196|1091606196|1091606196
0|[PE DEBUG] ntdll.dll Process: reader_sl.exe/PID: 228/PPID: 1956/Process POffset: 0x01a233c8/DLL Base: 0x7c900000|0|---------------|0|0|0|-|-|-|-
0|[PE HEADER (dll)] MSVCR80.dll Process: reader_sl.exe/PID: 228/PPID: 1956/Process POffset: 0x01a233c8/DLL Base: 0x78130000|0|---------------|0|0|0|1165042232
|1165042232|1165042232|1165042232
0|[PE DEBUG] MSVCR80.dll Process: reader_sl.exe/PID: 228/PPID: 1956/Process POffset: 0x01a233c8/DLL Base: 0x78130000|0|---------------|0|0|0|1165042232|116504
2232|1165042232|1165042232
0|[PE HEADER (dll)] USER32.dll Process: reader_sl.exe/PID: 228/PPID: 1956/Process POffset: 0x01a233c8/DLL Base: 0x77d40000|0|---------------|0|0|0|1091606200|
1091606200|1091606200|1091606200
0|[PE DEBUG] USER32.dll Process: reader_sl.exe/PID: 228/PPID: 1956/Process POffset: 0x01a233c8/DLL Base: 0x77d40000|0|---------------|0|0|0|-|-|-|-
0|[PE HEADER (dll)] MSVCP80.dll Process: reader_sl.exe/PID: 228/PPID: 1956/Process POffset: 0x01a233c8/DLL Base: 0x7c420000|0|---------------|0|0|0|1165042376
|1165042376|1165042376|1165042376
```

Fig 16: Timestamp based Memory artifacts

Fig 16 shows the related artifact of malicious PID 228 based on timeline manner.

Malicious Process Analysis using MALPROCFIND

Malprocfind

Volatility plugin **malprocfind** is used to extracting the malicious processes based on predefined rules.

Command: **volatility -f sample.vmem --profile=WinXPSP2x86 malprofind**

```
┌─[root@parrot]─[/home/markonsec]
└──╼ #volatility -f sample.vmem --profile=WinXPSP2x86 malprocfind
Volatility Foundation Volatility Framework 2.6
Offset     ProcessName     PID  PPID Name Path Priority Cmdline User  Sess Time CMD  PHollow SPath
---------- --------------- ---- ---- ---- ---- -------- ------- ----- ---- ---- ---- ------- -----
0x819cc830 system             4 True True True True     True    True  None True True True    True
0x817757f0 svchost.exe      916 True True True True     True    True  True True True True    True
0x81945020 smss.exe         536 True True True True     True    True  None True True True    True
0x817a34b0 cmd.exe          544 True True True True     True    False True True True True    True
0x816da020 services.exe     676 True True True True     True    True  True True True True    True
0x813c4020 lsass.exe        688 True True True True     True    True  True True True True    True
0x816c6da0 svchost.exe      964 True True True True     True    True  True True True True    True
0x8167e9d0 svchost.exe      848 True True True True     True    True  True True True True    True
0x816c6020 csrss.exe        608 True True True True     True    True  True True True True    True
0x813aeda0 svchost.exe     1148 True True True True     True    True  True True True True    True
0x817937e0 spoolsv.exe     1260 True True True True     True    True  True True True True    True
0x813a9020 winlogon.exe     632 True True True True     True    True  True True True True    True
0x813bcda0 explorer.exe    1956 True True True True     True    True  True True True True    True
0x815daca8 svchost.exe     1020 True True True True     True    True  True True True True    True

Unusual process counts:
-----------------------

Processes without running parent process:
-----------------------------------------
PID 1956 Offset: 0x813bcda0 Name: explorer.exe
PID 4 Offset: 0x819cc830 Name: System
```

Fig 17: Looking for malicious processes using MALPROCFIND

Process Hollowing detection using HOLLOWFIND

Hollowfind

Process hollowing is a technique used to inject the malicious code into legitimate processes to evade detection or misguide the forensic analysis. This technique is generally used by malware or attackers. Volatility plugin **hollowfind** is used to automatically detects the process hollowing techniques.

Command: **volatility -f sample.vmem --profile=WinXPSP2x86 hollowfind**

You can download the Hollowfind plugin from here - ***https://github.com/monnappa22/HollowFind***

How to Install a Volatility Plugin:

Step 1: Download the plugin from the Website [Ex. Hollowfind] –
https://github.com/monnappa22/HollowFind/blob/master/hollowfind.py
[You can Download normally or using **git clone** command from terminal]

Step 2: Copy the plugin file to the Volatility Folder

$ sudo cp hollowfind.py /usr/lib/python2.7/dist-packages/volatility/plugins/malware

Resources:

Volatility Command Reference: *https://github.com/volatilityfoundation/volatility/wiki/Command-Reference*

Frameworks

"Researchers and developers in the community have also created frameworks that build on top of Volatility. These aren't necessarily Volatility plugins (that you would import with --plugins) and usually they contain additional modules, configurations, and components. For that reason, we don't feature those frameworks in this repository, but we'd still like to reference them:" https://github.com/volatilityfoundation/community

- Autopsy Plugins by Mark McKinnon
- PyREBox by Xabier Ugarte-Pedrero at Cisco Talos
- Cuckoo Sandbox uses Volatility for its Memory module
- VolDiff Malware Memory Footprint Analysis by @aim4r
- Evolve Web interface for the Volatility Memory Forensics Framework by James Habben
- GVol Lightweight GUI (Java) by EG-CERT
- LibVMI Simplified Virtual Machine Introspection
- DAMM Differencial Analysis of Malware in Memory
- YaraVol GUI for Volatility Framework and Yara
- VolUtility Web Interface for Volatility by Kevin Breen
- ROPMEMU A framework to analyze, dissect and decompile complex code-reuse attacks by Mariano Graziano
- VolatilityBot An automated memory analyzer for malware samples and memory dumps by Martin Korman
- ProfileScan Profile detection for Volatility by Stanislas Lejay (P1kachu)

"In 2019, the Volatility Foundation released a complete rewrite of the framework, Volatility 3. The project was intended to address many of the technical and performance challenges associated with the original code base that became apparent over the previous 10 years. Another benefit of the rewrite is that Volatility 3 could be released under a custom license that was more aligned with the goals of the Volatility community, the Volatility Software License (VSL). See the LICENSE file for more details." - https://github.com/volatilityfoundation/volatility3

Fast Incident Response I

Cedarpelta Build

By: Carlyle Collins

Regardless of the size of your organization, plans and policies should be instituted to direct decision making under the pressures of a cyber incident. One aspect of planning for a cyber incident involves determining possible tools which may be helpful in gathering evidence to understand the cause and effects of the breach. This article and the following explore some of the tools which can help with data collection.

Incident response is the process by which an organization deals with a data breach or cyber-attack. This includes the technical aspects, such as gathering evidence in a Forensically robust manner, as well as the management of the consequences of the incident, which may include Public Relations strategies.

Cedarpelta Build

Cedarpelta collects volatile data and creates a memory dump. This tool may be used in an automated manner during a live incident. It supports Windows, OSX/ Mac OS, and *nix based operating systems.

You can download the latest build here. Be careful not to just Google search 'cedarpelta' because you may find yourself with some strange results in a completely different field. Who knows? Maybe you may find that information interesting!

Download and Installation

This tool is simple to download, install and use. You can download by going to https://brimorlabs.com/tools. There may be a GUI version available for Windows OS, but I'll be utilizing the command line options on a Linux based OS.

After downloading, change to the folder that you saved the zipped file to, and unzip it. I chose to unzip the contents in the same folder, but you may choose to save the resulting files in a different location.

```
c@c:~/Downloads$ unzip LiveResponseCollection-Cedarpelta.zip
Archive:  LiveResponseCollection-Cedarpelta.zip
```

After extraction you should see three folders. Each of these folders correspond to the scripts for different OS.

```
c@c:~/Downloads$ ls
COPYING.txt                          Mac_Live_Response   Windows_Live_Response
Live_Response_Collection_ReadMe.txt  nix_Live_Response
```

Walkthrough

Since I'm on a Linux OS I changed into the nix_Live_Response directory using the command:

```
cd nix_Live_Response
```

Within this directory were two (2) directories: Checklists and Modules and a shell script: nix_Live_Response.sh. These can be seen by using the following command:

```
ls
```

The Checklists directory contains directions of what information needs to be collected during a live incident response. For example: contents of the 'log' folders should be copied; date on the system should be noted; users logged on to the system should be determined; running processes etc. This information may be gathered manually or may be automated by running the nix_Live_Response.sh script.

In order to run the script, it first needs to be changed into an executable. This is done using the following command:

```
chmod +x nix_Live_Response.sh
```

Then the file is executed using the command:

```
sudo ./nix_Live_Response.sh
```

```
c@c:~/Downloads$ cd nix_Live_Response/
c@c:~/Downloads/nix_Live_Response$ ls
Checklists  Modules  nix_Live_Response.sh
c@c:~/Downloads/nix_Live_Response$ chmod +x nix_Live_Response.sh
c@c:~/Downloads/nix_Live_Response$ ./nix_Live_Response.sh
```

After the data has been collected, the hashes are computed. So, this can inform you when the data collection process has been completed.

```
./nix_Live_Response.sh: li
netstat -rn
./nix_Live_Response.sh: li
arp -an
./nix_Live_Response.sh: li
ifconfig -a
cat /etc/hosts.allow
cat /etc/hosts.deny
Computing hashes of files
```

Upon completion of the data collection process an output folder (which has the same name as the computer analyzed along with the date of collection) is stored in the same location as the executable file.

NB- In a real-life scenario, the storage of the Cedarpelta tool may be on a USB drive which is connected to the system under investigation.

Resources

https://www.hackingarticles.in/fast-incident-response-and-data-collection/
https://www.brimorlabs.com/tools/
https://www.ncsc.gov.uk/collection/incident-management/cyber-incident-response-processes
https://digitalguardian.com/blog/what-incident-response

Fast Incident Response II
Cyber Defense Institute Incident Response Collector
By: Carlyle Collins

The Cyber Defense Institute Incident Response (CDIR) Collector is the second tool in our Fast Incident Response (IR) series.

The CIDR Collector was created by the Cyber Defense Institute, Japan. It is another effective, yet lightweight tool to be used for live IR. It works on the Windows OS and the following are the lists of some data which it can collects information:

- RAM
- NTFS ($MFT, $SECURE:$SDS, $UsnJrnl:$J)
- Prefetch
- Eventlog
- Registry (Amcache.hve, NTUser.dat, UsrClass.dat)
- Web (History (Chrome), cookies.sqlite, places.sqlite (Firefox), WebCacheV01.dat (IE, Edge))

Download and Installation

The zipped format of the tool can be downloaded from github.com/CyberDefenseInstitute/CDIR/releases. The installation process only involves unzipping the contents to the preferred storage location. In practice this would be on an external USB device.

Walkthrough

After the installation process, you should see the following in the location where you chose to extract the contents of the zipped file.

cdir	18/11/2020 15:02	Configuration setti...	1 KB
cdir-collector	18/11/2020 15:02	Application	520 KB
libcrypto-41.dll	18/11/2020 15:02	Application extens...	1,360 KB
libssl-43.dll	18/11/2020 15:02	Application extens...	296 KB
NTFSParserDLL.dll	18/11/2020 15:02	Application extens...	136 KB
winpmem	18/11/2020 15:02	Application	2,411 KB
winpmem-2.1.post4	18/11/2020 15:02	Application	2,203 KB

To start data collection, you need to click on the cdir-collector file and start the command prompt in Admin mode. The following shows how this appears.

```
C:\Users\New User\Downloads\cdir-collector_1.3.5\cdir-collector\cdir-collector.exe    —    □

CDIR Collector v1.3.5 - Data Acquisition Tool for First Response
Cyber Defense Institute, Inc.

Loading C:\Users\New User\Downloads\cdir-collector_1.3.5\cdir-collector\cdir.ini...
MemoryDump is undefined
MemoryDump (1:ON 2:OFF 0:EXIT)
>
```

At this point the collector is waiting for instructions. Three instructions may be given:
- To initiate the memory dump process (Press 1)
- To end the memory dump process (Press 2)
- To exit the tool (Press 3)

I pressed 1 to start the memory dump process.

After the process is complete you should see the following in the command prompt window.

```
2020-11-18 15:15:04 : writing central Dire
Finished collecting memory dump
Start collecting data for analysis
metadata is saved C:\$MFT
$SECURE:$SDS is saved C:\$SECURE:$SDS
journal is saved C:\$Extend\$UsnJrnl:$J
event log is saved
prefetch is saved
registry is saved
wmi data is saved
srum is saved
internet artifact data is saved
Finished collecting data for analysis
Press Enter key to continue...
```

CIDR creates a folder named in format 'COMPUTERNAME_YYYYMMDDhhmmss' in the location where the executable is. Within this folder you can see the following (in the picture below) and begin your analysis of the collected information.

Name	Date modified	Type	Size
Evtx	18/11/2020 15:14	File folder	
NTFS	18/11/2020 15:13	File folder	
Prefetch	18/11/2020 15:14	File folder	
Registry	18/11/2020 15:15	File folder	
SRUM	18/11/2020 15:15	File folder	
Web	18/11/2020 15:15	File folder	
WMI	18/11/2020 15:15	File folder	
collector-log	18/11/2020 15:15	Text Document	114 KB
RAM_DESKTOP-	18/11/2020 15:13	AFF4 File	7,734,808 ...

Resources

https://github.com/CyberDefenseInstitute/CDIR/blob/master/README_en.md
https://github.com/CyberDefenseInstitute/CDIR/releases
https://www.hackingarticles.in/fast-incident-response-and-data-collection/

Fast Incident Response III:

DG Wingman

By: Carlyle Collins

This tool, developed by Digital Guardian (DG), was created to assist in forensically harvesting important artefacts such as $MFT, Event Logs, Registry etc. from Windows OSes. To compliment the aforementioned features, there are options which enable you to run custom commands as SYSTEM or execute a full scan of an endpoint system. DG Wingman may be used remotely or locally to gather the needed information.

By default, the following information may be collected with a variety of commands:

System Information
- Prefetch
- Scheduled Tasks

Active Scan Data
- Open Handles
- Recently Opened/ Closed Files

Static Scan Data
- Binary Attribute/ Version Information
- Binary Import/ Export Sections
- Digital Certificate Information

Network Information

Event Log Entries
- System Event Log
- Application Event Log
- Security Event Log

Registry Hives
- System Hive
- Software Hive
- Security Hive
- SAM Hive
- NTUSER Hives (Current User data)

Web History

Master File Table

Download and Installation

You can get the download the tool from here: info.digitalguardian.com/wingman. However, in order to download the program, you'll need to provide an email address. After downloading the Wingman archive, extract the files to a location of your choosing. After extraction you should see the following.

Name	Date modified	Type	Size
browserhistoryfiles.dat	01/08/2019 15:03	DAT File	3 KB
wingman	31/07/2019 14:17	Application	1,526 KB

Walkthrough

Wingman may be used to gather information remotely or locally. In this example we'll do a local collection.

Firstly, open the Command prompt and change into the directory where the Wingman application resides using the **cd** command. Then use the **dir** command to list the contents of the folder to ensure you're in the correct location.

```
C:\Users\New User>cd C:\Users\New User\Downloads\wingman

C:\Users\New User\Downloads\wingman>dir
 Volume in drive C has no label.
 Volume Serial Number is ▮▮▮▮▮▮▮▮

 Directory of C:\Users\New User\Downloads\wingman

09/12/2020  13:12    <DIR>          .
09/12/2020  13:12    <DIR>          ..
01/08/2019  14:03             2,206 browserhistoryfiles.dat
31/07/2019  13:17         1,561,944 wingman.exe
               2 File(s)      1,564,150 bytes
               2 Dir(s)  329,795,051,520 bytes free
```

Launch the Wingman application by typing the command **wingman.exe**. Add the **/h** flag to show the various options available to use.

```
C:\Users\New User\Downloads\wingman>wingman.exe /h
Unknown option ( /h ).. Aborting.

wingman [Version 1.0]
(c) Digital Guardian, Inc. All rights reserved.


Usage:
  wingman [-p pid] [-ph] [-e] [-f pathname] [-s] [-la] [-le] [-ly] [-lt] [-lw]
          [-mft] [-pre] [-sup] [-h] [-j] [-r] [-ry] [-ro] [-re] [-ra] [-ru] [-k key]
          [-b] [-d] [-bf filename] [-pf filename] [-pn name]
          [-ac command] [-acf filename]
          [-cap filename] [-capf filename]
          [-x savefile] [-nj num]
          [-ob] [-oh] [-ov] [-oc] [-ox] [-os]
```

I have perused the list of options and decided I want to gather all system information **(s)** and all registry information **(r)**. So, I'll run the command **wingman.exe -s -r** in order to gather this data. At the end of the process, you should see a similar message as below and then you are returned to the command prompt.

```
--Saving MetaData...
done in 15 ms

--Finalizing...
Compressing $MFT
```

Upon completion of the collection of data, a folder called EDR is made in the directory where the Wingman executable is stored. You can now analyze your files using various other tools!

Name	Date modified	Type	Size
RegistryOut	09/12/2020 13:42	File folder	
$MFT	29/11/2076 08:54	File	605,696 KB
.NET Framework NGEN v4.0.30319	05/12/2020 21:29	30319 File	4 KB
.NET Framework NGEN v4.0.30319 64	05/12/2020 21:27	File	4 KB
.NET Framework NGEN v4.0.30319 64 Crit...	27/11/2020 15:58	File	3 KB
.NET Framework NGEN v4.0.30319 Critical	27/11/2020 15:58	File	3 KB
_IU14D2N.TMP-B90B29AD.pf	05/12/2020 17:09	PF File	7 KB
_wmic_BASEBOARD.lst	09/12/2020 13:41	LST File	1 KB
_wmic_BIOS.lst	09/12/2020 13:41	LST File	2 KB
_wmic_BOOTCONFIG.lst	09/12/2020 13:41	LST File	1 KB

Resources

https://www.hackingarticles.in/fast-incident-response-and-data-collection/
https://digitalguardian.com/blog/introducing-dg-wingman-free-forensics-tool
https://info.digitalguardian.com/wingman

NetDiscover :Network Scanning Tool

By: Frederico Ferreira

Network discovery is an important part of Information Gathering: it is the process of identifying live hosts on the network. Its purpose is to understand their logical location inside the network. Mapping your systems is extremely useful to model network infrastructure and identify possible rogue devices. Using Netwflow of F-Flow are better, but you you do not have the budget for such architecture, this works too.

Netdicover is an active/passive ARP reconnaissance tool, initially developed to gain information about wireless networks without DHCP servers in wardriving scenarios. It can also be used on switched networks. Built on top of libnet and libpcap, it can passively detect online hosts or search for them by sending ARP requests. Furthermore, it can be used to inspect network's ARP traffic or find network addresses using auto-scan mode, which will scan for common local networks.[1] Netdiscover was written by Jaime Penalba Estebanez.[1]

Netdiscover features:

- Simple Arp Scanner
- Works in both Active & Passive modes
- Produces a live display of identified hosts
- Able to scan multiple subnets
- Timing Options

Netdiscover command-line options:[1]

-I *device* The network interface to sniff and inject packets. If no interface is specified, first available will be used.

-r *range* Scan a given *range* instead of auto scan. Valid *range* values area for example: 192.168.0.0/24, 192.168.0.0/16 or 192.168.0.0/8.
Currently, acceptable ranges are /8, /16, and /24 only.

-l *file* Scan ranges contained on the given *file*. It must contain only one *range* per line.

-p Enable passive mode. In passive mode, netdiscover does not send anything but does only sniff.

-m *file* Scan a list of known MACs and hostnames.

-F *filter* Customize pcap *filter* expression (default: "arp").

-s *time* Sleep given *time* in milliseconds between each ARP request injection. (default 1)

-c *count* Number of times to send each ARP request. Useful for networks with packet loss, so it will scan given times for each host (default 1)

-n *node* Last IP octet of the source IP used for scanning. You can change it if the default host (x.x.x.67) is already used. (allowed *range* is 2 to 253, default 67)

-d Ignore configuration files at home dir (for autoscan and fast mode only). This will use default ranges and IPs for autoscan and fast mode. See below for information about configuration files.

-f Enable fast mode scan. This will only scan for .1, .100, and .254 on each network. This mode is useful while searching for ranges being used. After you found such *range* you can make a specific *range* scan to find online boxes.

-P Produces an output suitable to be redirected into a *file* or to be parsed by another program, instead of using interactive mode. Enabling this option, netdiscover will stop after scanning given ranges.

-L Similar to **-P** but continue program execution to capture ARP packets passively after the active scan. phase to capture ARP packets passively.

-N Do not print header. Only valid when **-P** or **-L** is enabled.

-S (DEPRECATED) Enable sleep *time* suppression between each request. If set, netdiscover will sleep after having scanned 255 hosts instead of sleeping after each one. This mode was used in netdiscover 0.3 beta4 and before. Avoid this option in networks with packet loss, or in wireless networks with low signal level. (also called hardcore mode)

Libnet and Libpcap

Netdiscover is built on top of 2 powerful libraries libnet and libpcap. Libnet is an API to help with the construction and injection of network packets. It provides a portable framework for low-level network packet writing and handling. Libnet includes packet creation at the IP layer and at the link layer as well as a host of supplementary and complementary functionality. Libnet is very handy with which to write network tools and network test code.[2] Some projects, available made using libnet are:

- arping
- ettercap/bettercap
- ipguard
- isic
- nemesis
- packit
- tcptraceroute
- yersinia

Libpcap is an open-source library that provides a high-level interface to network packet capture systems. It was created in 1994 by McCanne, Leres, and Jacobson – researchers at the Lawrence Berkeley National Laboratory from the University of California at Berkeley as part of a research project to investigate and improve TCP and internet gateway performance. Libpcap authors' main objective was to create a platform-independent API to eliminate the need for system-dependent packet capture modules in each application, as virtually every OS vendor implements its own capture mechanisms.[3]

The libpcap API is designed to be used from C and C++. However, the are many wrappers that allow its use from languages like Perl, Python, Java, C# or Ruby. Libpcap runs on most UNIX-like operating systems (Linux, Solaris, BSD, HP-UX, etc). There is also a Windows version named Winpcap. Libpcap is maintained by the Tcpdump Group[3], and NPCAP is maintained by the NMAP team.

Netdiscover Quick Guide

Netdiscover can be found on the Project website: github.com/netdiscover-scanner/netdiscover

We can scan a specific range with -r option, in the example we will perform an active ARP reconnaissance on my lab environment subnet:

```
root@csi-iwc:~# netdiscover -r 192.168.10.0/24
 Currently scanning: Finished!    |   Screen View: Unique Hosts
 4 Captured ARP Req/Rep packets, from 4 hosts.   Total size: 240
 _____
   IP            At MAC Address     Count    Len   MAC Vendor / Hostname
 ---------------------------------------------------------------------------
 192.168.10.1     00:00:00:07:50c      1       10   Cisco
 192.168.10.50    00:0c:32:59:72:xv    1       60   VMware, Inc.
 192.168.10.120   00:0c:32:3a:cb:gf    1       60   VMware, Inc.
 192.168.10.180   00:0c:32:a2:56:2e    1       90   VMware, Inc.
```

We can scan multiple ranges at the same time. The ranges are defined on a file like the example below.

RangeTestFile.txt - Bloco de notas

Ficheiro Editar Formatar Ver Ajuda
192.168.10.0/24
10.10.0.1/24

```
root@csi-iwc:~# netdiscover -l RangeTestFile

 Currently scanning: Finished!   |   Screen View: Unique Hosts

 4 Captured ARP Req/Rep packets, from 10 hosts.   Total size: 790
 _____

   IP            At MAC Address     Count    Len   MAC Vendor / Hostname
 --------------------------------------------------------------------

 192.168.10.1       00:00:00:07:50c       1      10   Cisco
 192.168.10.50      00:0c:32:59:72:xv     1      120  VMware, Inc.
 192.168.10.120     00:0c:32:3a:cb:gf     1      120  VMware, Inc.
 192.168.10.180     00:0c:32:a2:56:2e     1      120  VMware, Inc.
 192.168.10.190     00:0c:36:3a:cb:ed     1      70   VMware, Inc.
 192.168.10.200     00:0c:21:b3:56:2f     1      70   VMware, Inc.
 10.10.0.1          50:b7:22:f5:75:55     1      70   VMware, Inc.
 10.10.0.3          00:27:ee:4b:98:xv     1      70   VMware, Inc.
 10.10.0.4          00:0c:27:c5:cb:gf     1      70   VMware, Inc.
 10.10.0.1          80:00:27:69:56:2e     1      70   VMware, Inc.
```

We can also use passive scanning; this will take longer than the active scanner because it will only be listening for ARP requests and responses on the network.

```
root@csi-iwc:~# netdiscover -p

 Currently scanning: (passive)     |   Screen View: Unique Hosts

 10 Captured ARP Req/Rep packets, from 4 hosts.   Total size: 320
 _____

   IP            At MAC Address     Count    Len   MAC Vendor / Hostname
 --------------------------------------------------------------------

 192.168.10.1       00:00:00:07:50c       1      10   Cisco
 192.168.10.50      00:0c:32:59:72:xv     1      120  VMware, Inc.
 192.168.10.120     00:0c:32:3a:cb:gf     1      120  VMware, Inc.
 192.168.10.180     00:0c:32:a2:56:2e     1      70   VMware, Inc.
```

This is the ideal tool if you want to scan only your local network for active hosts. With this tool, we can get the host IP and Mac Address.

There are more complete tools on the wild like nmap, but certainly, Netdiscover earn its spot on the Information Gathering Tools Category

Resource

- [1] manpages.debian.org/unstable/netdiscover/netdiscover.8.en.html
- [2] github.com/libnet/libnet
- [3] http://recursos.aldabaknocking.com/libpcapHakin9LuisMartinGarcia.pdf

Swimming with the Wireshark

By Richard Medlin

Wireshark is a cross-platform open-source network protocol analyzer and traffic sniffer that operates in a GUI to make interpreting network traffic a breeze. Likewise, it is one of the most trusted industry standards for providing static and dynamic analysis of any and all network traffic. Wireshark offers a three-pane packet browsing GUI, and can read, or write to many different capture file formats. Overall, it provides a lot of features, and outputs that you can really dive into in order to get a good view of what's happening or has been happening on your network.

If you've heard about Wireshark, you're probably wondering why it's such a great tool, and why it's referenced in just about every certification prep that involves cyber security, pentesting, or networking. Wireshark is the go-to network traffic analyzer, and can be used by security professionals, and system administrators to analyze network traffic — best of all, it's free. Wireshark isn't just used to capture traffic and see potential security issues, it's also a great tool that lets you see dropped packets and latency issues, which can help you troubleshoot. Imagine having the ability to see things under a microscope, it's a lot easier to notice things that would normally go undetected — this is the exact capability that Wireshark affords an administrator or analyst in regard to network traffic. A lot of the time attackers are trying to steal data and you can see that with Wireshark.

Wireshark does a lot of things, and we will take an in-depth look into how to use some of the powerful features of Wireshark, and also cover what we are looking at while we are going through it. In order to do that, we need to understand what Wireshark is doing. Wireshark captures binary traffic and converts it into an output that we can easily decipher. Moreover, it's kind of hard to tell what we are looking at if it is all zeros and ones.

Some of the features of Wireshark are as follows:

- Support for thousands of network protocols
- Analysis of packets
- Filter out traffic based on areas of interest
- Inspect specific traffic
- Network protocol analyzer provides search tools
- Color highlighting
- Creating baselines
- Narrow down abnormal traffic after malicious traffic has been identified by an IDS
- Ability to capture wired, and wireless traffic
- Following TCP streams
- Coloring Rules
- Writing protocol dissectors in LUA programming language

This write-up will cover the following:

- Understanding Wireshark
  - Wireshark Collection Methods
  - The OSI Model and How it Applies to Wireshark
    - OSI Layers
      - Layer 1 — Physical Layer
      - Layer 2 — Data-Link Layer
      - Layer 3 — Network Layer
      - Layer 4 — Transport Layer
      - Layer 5 — Session Layer
      - Layer 6 — Presentation Layer
      - Layer 7 — Application Layer
    - Encapsulation
- Installing Wireshark
  - MacOS Big Sur Installation
  - Windows 10 Wireshark Installation
- Performing Basic Captures
  - Setting up Filters
- Analyzing Network Traffic
  - ICMP (PING Request and Reply)
  - ARP Request
  - Transmission Control Protocol Captures
  - HTTP Traffic

Understanding Wireshark

In order to review network traffic, you have to capture it, or analyze it — this is where Wireshark comes into play. Wireshark allows us to analyze protocols using Packet Capture (PCAP), which is sometimes known as libpcap [in Unix like systems], WinPcap [that is used by old versions of Windows and is no longer supported], Npcap [used with Windows 7], or Win10Pcap [that hasn't been support since 2016] that all use an Application Programing Interface (API) that is captured from live network packet data that is used in OSI Layers 2-7. Wireshark actually creates. pcap files from collected and recorded packet data and allows you to analyze it. PCAP files are written in C, and the other languages that use this data actually apply a wrapper to it. Moreover, this wrapper is not used for libpcap or WinPcap files, and C++ programs will directly link to C APIs or they will apply an object-oriented wrapper to these files. Many packet sniffers, and protocol analyzers will use these types of files for analysis.

Libcap itself was originally developed for use by tcpdump — a powerful command-line packet analyzer — and is a very popular way to analyze network traffic too. There are several different programs that use libpcap, and PCAP files.

Network Taps are used to monitor the local network and are usually a dedicated hardware device that can be placed between two points on the network to sniff or analyze network traffic. Taps typically passthrough network traffic even if they result in a failed state. A lot of people refer to traffic that is monitored using a network tap as pass-through-traffic. There are other ways to tap network traffic by using software, SNMP, port-mirroring, switch sniffer, and hardware taps.

What are some of the advantages of using a physical Network TAP? Most network taps are passive and provide a fail-safe when something breaks, they require no configuration, they're secure, and they provide an exact duplicate of the original network traffic. At the end of the day, the only downside is that you have to pay for new hardware, and when encryption is used, they are essentially useless. Likewise, you can simply encrypt your communications when you want to ensure your data can't be read when someone may be using a network tap.

Let's put on our red team hat now and go over a couple of techniques we can use to gain access to network traffic. One simple way is MAC flooding, and this is a tactic that we use to actively sniff packets by flooding a switch with MAC Addresses making it fill it's CAM table so that the switch no longer accepts new MAC addresses. Furthermore, resulting in the switch sending out packets to all ports on the switch instead of the intended port — what good is a switch that acts like a hub. Let's put on our blue team hat now and look at how we stop this from happening. Moreover, one easy way is to enable a feature called port security that limits the number of MACs that a given port can learn when connected to end stations. You can use discovered MAC addresses that are bounced off a AAA server, and filtered, or you can implement the IEEE 802.1x suites that provides port-based Network Access Control (PNAC). Furthermore, PNAC is an authentication method that is used for devices that are requesting to connect to the network. Likewise, PNAC involves three key pieces, the Supplicant, Authenticator, and Authentication Server. The supplicant is the device making the request to the Authenticator — the switch, or WAP — and the authentication server is a trusted server, and it tells the authenticator if the connection is allowed or not. Furthermore, authentication servers usually run RADIUS or EAP protocols and can reside directly on the Authenticator itself.

The last method we will cover is ARP Poisoning, or ARP Spoofing. ARP poisoning is a task that we can use to sniff packets by redirecting traffic from its hosts to the machine we monitor from. This doesn't create as much noise as MAC flooding will, and it's less stressful to the network equipment. Additionally, this attack is conducted by sending malicious ARP packets to the default gateway to change the pairing of IP and MAC Addresses within the ARP table. We basically trick the device into thinking our new IP and MAC combo is trusted by spoofing [our IP address and MAC address] or poisoning the ARP tables information [on the device we want to sniff traffic from]. However, both methods gain the trust of the target device and allow us to sniff traffic from that part of the network. Remember too, you can collect the data live, or you can simply view saved . pcap files later as well. Likewise, there are a few factors you must consider when capturing traffic, you need to have the compute power that is required for the network size, and you need to have enough disk space to save the pcap files.

Note: Make sure you place your network TAP in an essential location to get access to the traffic that you need and want access to. Likewise, the same goes for ARP poisoning, and MAC flooding. If you gain access to traffic and it's not in a place you can see your intended target, you've wasted your time, and made a lot of noise while doing it.

The OSI Model and How It Applies to Wireshark

Wireshark analyzes network traffic, and it's important that we apply the concept of the associated layers of the OSI Model to the network traffic so we can understand what is happening. Likewise, it's important to note that Wireshark works in promiscuous mode, and it sniffs everything that goes across the network. The OSI model provides a framework that lets us understand what we are seeing traverse the physical layer. The OSI Model consists of 7 layers and they are the Application, Presentation, Session, Transport, Network, Data Link, and Physical layers.

It is important to understand the OSI model because every layer serves the layer above it, and sometimes they overlap depending on what is happening on the device itself. We use the OSI model to talk about how devices communicate because it gives us a quick way to reference what is happening, and provides the ability to describe it, and analyze it. We will cover the layers of the OSI model, and then break down how encapsulation works, and how packets are built using the OSI model.

OSI Layers:

- Layer 1 — Physical Layer
  - Layer 1 Protocol Data Unit (PDU)s — bits, or the act of transmission and reception over a physical medium or airwaves.
  - The lowest layer of the OSI model that consists of electrical or optical signals that are raw and unstructured data bits that traverse a network on the physical medium that is sent from a sending device, to a receiving device.
  - Layer 1 specifications determine what the voltage level, timing of voltage changes, the distance of transmission, data rates, and physical connections are. Layer 1 is also responsible for determining the transmission mode of either full duplex, half duplex, or simplex.
  - Network topology is the description of the physical layer in regard to the physical layout of a given network.

- Layer 2 — Data-Link Layer
  - Layer 2 PDUs — Frame — a protocol data unit that is a segment of data that generally consists of a header containing a preamble — start of the frame that is flagged — a destination and source address, the payload, and a form of error checking. Frames are generally assembled and created by the data-link layer of the OSI reference model. Furthermore, this process is usually referred to as "framing." A frame is created by the process of encapsulating packets that are formed at the Layer 3.
    - Responsible for providing node-to-node data transfer, while making a connection between two nodes. This part of the OSI model is also equally responsible for detecting errors in Layer 1 transmissions and providing error correction.
    - The IEEE 802 standard uses two sublayers for Layer 2:
  - Medium Access Control (MAC) layer — determines how devices gain access to network media and authorization of those communications.
  - Logical Link Control (LLC) layer — provides encapsulation for network layer protocols and provides error checking and synchronizes frames.
  - Defines the protocols that devices will use to access the network for transmitting or receiving messages using protocols like the Serial Line Internet Protocol (SLIP), Address Resolution Protocol (ARP), and Point-to-Point Protocol (PPP)s to transfer data.

- Layer 3 — Network Layer
  - Layer 3 PDUs — Packet — streams of data bits that are sent as electrical or optical signals on physical media that is used to transmit the data. This same concept applies to over the air and WIFI transmissions. The electrical signals are comprised of zeros and ones, and they make up the packet of information.
  - Packets are always comprised of a header, and a payload no matter what protocol is sending them.
  - Header — has a specific structure, and this ensures that it can be interpreted by the recipient and also ensures that the communication is handled properly.
  - Payload — Is the actual data or information that you are sending.
    - Revolves around the Internet Protocol and is the standard for routing packets between networks and interconnected networks. Layer 3 encapsulates just like the data-link layer.
    - Responsible for defining how packets and data are routed between devices while providing routing error correction and control.
  - Uses protocols like the Internet Protocol (IP), Internet Control Messaging Protocol (ICMP), Open Shortest Path First (OSPF), and Routing Information Protocol (RIP) to name a few.

- Layer 4 — Transport Layer
  - Layer 4 PDUs — Segments are used for Transmission Control Protocol (TCP) or Datagrams used for UDP:
  - Segments — are blocks of data that have been prepped for transmission using the Transmission Control Protocol (TCP). Likewise, segments carry logical address information — IP Address — port numbers, and the logical connection identifiers of the devices that sent the communication. TCP creates a session using a 3-way handshake which consists of a Syn, Syn-Ack, Ack. This can be seen in Wireshark by downloading the 3-way handshake file from this link: https://wiki.wireshark.org/TCP_3_way_handshaking?action=AttachFile&do=view&target=3-way+handshake.pcap
  - TCP 3-way handshake: is used to establish a reliable connection between two devices. This requires both sides to synchronize (SYN) and acknowledge (ACK) each other using a full duplex connection. There is a four-flag exchange that is performed in 3 steps, thus creating a 3-way handshake using a SYN, SYN-ACK, and finally an ACK.
    - The first SYN packet contains an initial sequence number as shown below:

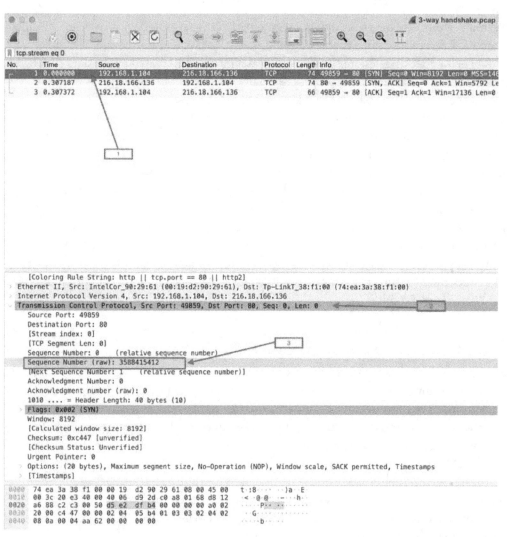

Note: Left Click the first line with where step 1 is, then Left Click the Transmission Control Protocol line in the 2nd pane labeled 2, and then Left Click the Sequence Number.

- The recipient will choose an initial sequence number and respond with a SYN / ACK packet. Furthermore, each side will acknowledge the other's sequence number incrementally and that is referred to as the acknowledge number as shown below:

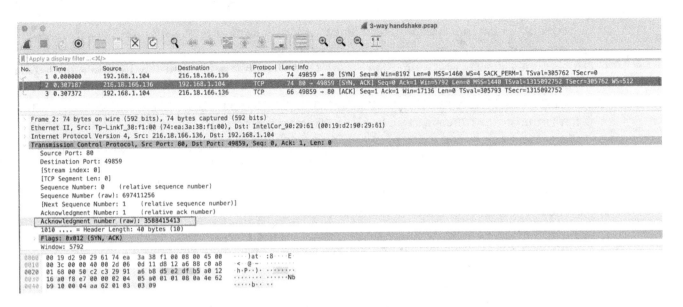

View the picture below to see how a 3-way handshake would look. Take note that 192.168.1.104 is sending a TCP SYN packet to 216.18.16.136, and then 216.18.16.136 responds with a SYN, ACK, and then 192.168.1.104 sends an ACK that finalizes the 3-way handshake. This process will leave that communication open until a FIN packet is transmitted by either side of the communication stream. Furthermore, an RST (reset) packet can be used to abruptly stop the communication stream.

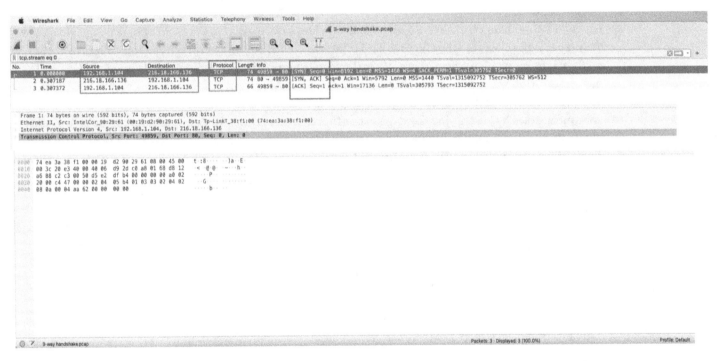

- Datagrams — is a generic term used for IP network protocols and is the actual data unit. At Layer 2, this is the User Datagram Protocol UDP, that is sometimes called a UDP datagram.
  - It's important to know that an IP Datagram is built from data that is already in the form of TCP or UDP data that has a TCP or UDP header and is then encapsulated into the body of an IP datagram. IP Datagrams differ from UDP Datagrams in this way.
  - Some of the common protocols used at the transport layer are AEP, AH over IP or IPSec, ESP, and NetBIOS to name a few.

- Layer 5 — Session Layer
  - Layer 5 PDU — Data or Payload — is combined with Layer 6 and Layer 7. This is the Data or Payload that you are sending.
  - This is the layer where your connection between two systems is established and the data is formatted for transfer between two nodes.
  - The session layer is responsible for setting up full-duplex, half-duplex, or simplex operation and it also helps terminate the TCP connection from the Transport layer.
  - Layer 5, 6 and 7 are all combined together in the TCP/IP model.
  - Some of the common protocols used at the Session Layer are SDP, RPC, SMB, SOCKS, H.245 and PAP.

- Layer 6 — Presentation Layer
  - Layer 6 PDU – Data or Payload — combined with layers 5 and 7.
  - The presentation layer is responsible for presenting data to the Application layer and works much like a translator from the computer to the human and provides a readable format that we can understand. This layer provides a context for the Application layer
  - This layer provides a large variety of coding and conversation functions that tie into Layer 7. Likewise, this ensures that information sent from the application layer is readable once it reaches the application layer of the other system it's communicating with — that's where it gets its name, it presents the data in a way both sides can understand it.
  - This area of the OSI model doesn't typically have any protocols but uses formats like HTTP, TIFF, MIDI, MPEG, and JPEG.

- Layer 7 — Application Layer
  - Layer 7 PDU — shares with layers 5 and 6 and provides information in the form of data or a payload.
  - This layer is the closest to the end user, and it interacts with our inputs directly — it is the software or applications we use. This area of the OSI is the software applications that provide some form of communication via user input, or through processes and APIs from other programs and the OS itself. Think of it like the part of the application that determines resource availability, or that synchronizes communication by identifying the two parties that intend to transmit data back and forth. How does it determine resource availability? It has to ensure that sufficient resources on the network exist to establish communications with another node. There are two forms of applications, TCP/IP model and OSI model applications.
  - Some of the internetworking applications are email, bulletin boards, DNS, FTP, WWW, and Electronic Data Exchange.

Another way to look at how two nodes communicate is the TCP/IP Model:

1. Layer 4 is the application layer, and it combines layers 7 through 5 of the OSI model.
2. Layer 3 is the TCP or Transport Layer (Layer 4 of the OSI).
3. Layer 2 is the Internet layer (Layer 3 of the OSI).

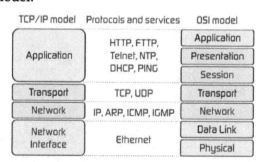

Layer 1 is the Network Access or Data Link Layer (combines Layer 1 and 2 of the OSI model).

The TCP/IP model is similar to the OSI model, but they just merged the top 3 layers together. The communicating nodes will always perform the same functions — no matter what model you use to describe it — it's just a different way of communicating those functions. In order to better understand how the OSI bits traverse the network we need to take a look at how encapsulation works. We will look at encapsulation first through the lens of the OSI model, but the same concept applies to the TCP/IP model which we will cover too.

Encapsulation

Encapsulation is sometimes referred to as packaging because each layer is packaged by the next one. Think of it like sticking a letter into an envelope, and then put that envelope into another envelope and so on. We can look at both layers to see how data encapsulation works, but they are essentially the same. So, the Data plus the header of an upper layer is packaged into the data of the layer below it, and when a machine receives incoming packets, it strips these headers off and determines what to do with it based off the payload beneath it. See the following diagram for an idea of how this process works.

The following diagram shows encapsulation in the OSI model:

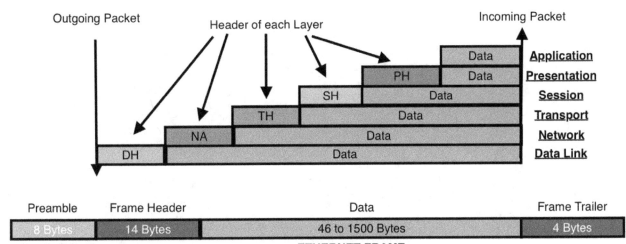

Note: The preamble is 62 bits of alternating 1s and 0s that are followed by two 1s.

During encapsulation under the TCPI/IP model it works just like the OSI model, but there are less layers. Essentially, it's just a different way of looking at the same thing. The packet will be the same across the network, these are just reference models. The following diagram shows encapsulation using the TCP/IP Model:

During encapsulation, every protocol will add a header to the packet, and the previous layer is treated as a payload. When receiving data, it will do the opposite and strip the header at each layer revealing the payload. The application itself doesn't have to worry about how each layer below it works, it just sends the packet to the transport layer, and the rest will be taken care of.

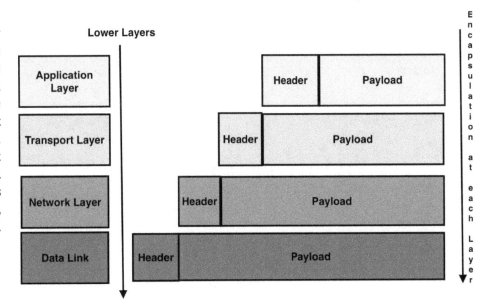

Installing Wireshark
MacOS Big Sur Installation

Before we get started, we need to install Wireshark. This section of the walkthrough will cover the installation process on MacOS Big Sur version 11.0.1.

1. Go to your web browser and input the following address:

    1. *https://www.wireshark.org*

2. Left Click Download:

3. Left Click the Big Sur users should use 3.4.0 link:

4. **Double Left Click** the **.dmg** file and open the installer:
5. Left Click and hold and drag the Wireshark icon to the Applications folder:

    Note: If you don't get an output saying anything happened, that's ok. You must perform the next step and install ChmodBPF on MacOS in order to capture packets.

6. **Double Left Click** the **Install CHmodBPF.pkg** and a new install window will pop up. **Left Click Continue** in the installer:

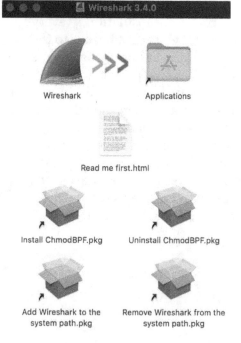

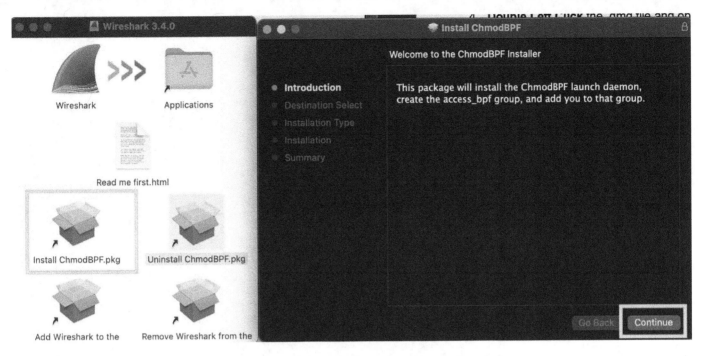

Note: My installer skipped the destination select tab, if it pops up just select where you want it saved. Also, you can click change location to pick a new location.

7. Left Click Install and enter your password or biometric fingerprint to finish the installation
8. Left Click Close.

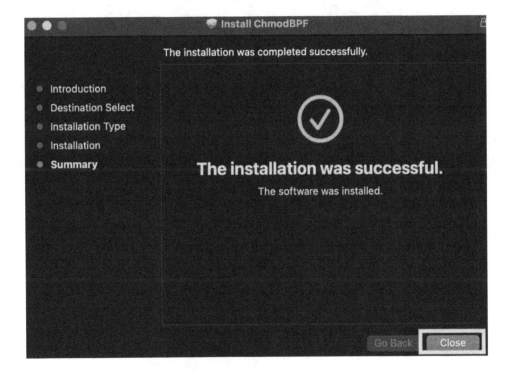

Windows 10 Wireshark Installation

1. Go to your web browser and input the following address:

   https://www.wireshark.org

2. Left Click Download:

3. Left Click the Windows Installer (64 - bit) link:

4. Left Click Run:

Do you want to run or save **Wireshark-win64-3.4.1.exe** (58.6 MB) from **2.na.dl.wireshark.org**?

This type of file could harm your computer.

    [Run] [Save] [▼] [Cancel]

5. Left Click Yes:

6. Left Click Next:

7. Left Click Noted:

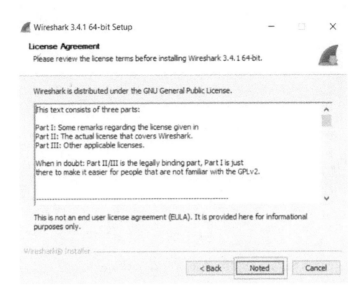

8. Leave the default components selected unless you want to take some away and **Left Click Next**:

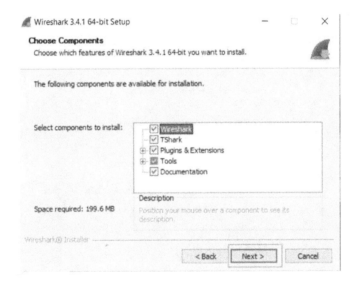

9. Ensure you have the same settings below and **Left Click Next**:

10. Ensure you have the destination folder set to where you want to install the program and **Left Click Next**:

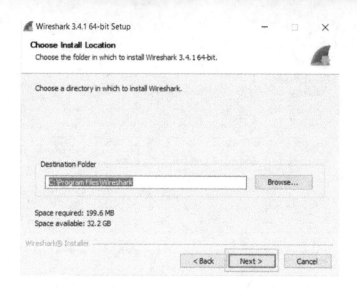

11. Left Click the radio box to check Install PCAP, and then Left Click Next:

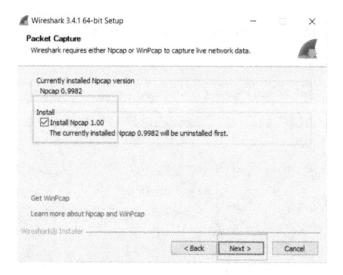

12. I chose not to use the USB PCAP and **Left Clicked Install**:

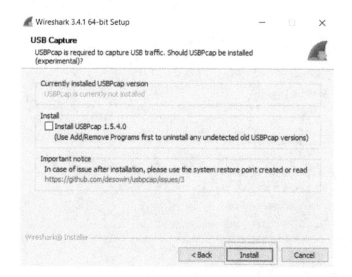

13. Left Click I Agree:

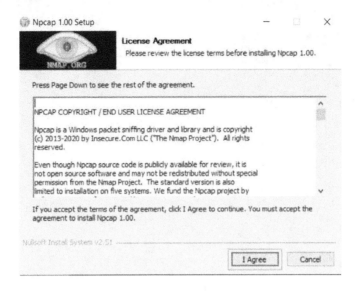

14. **Left Click Install** after choosing which options you want:

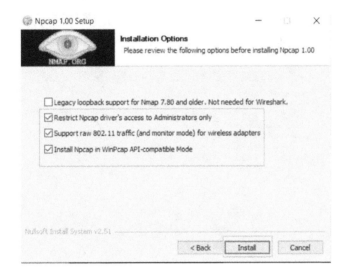

15. Left Click Next:

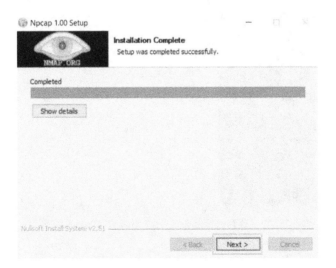

16. Left Click Finish:

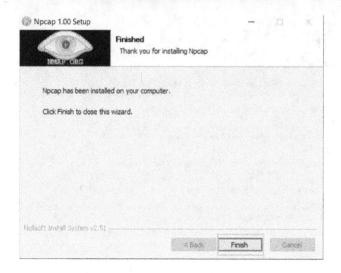

17. Left Click Next:

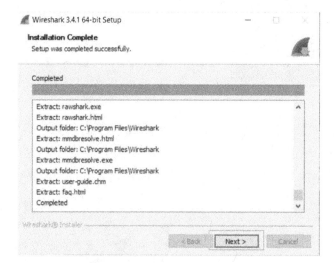

18. **Left Click Finish** to complete the installation:

Performing Basic Captures

1. **Double Left Click** on the capture interface you wish to use — in my case Wi-Fi: en1:

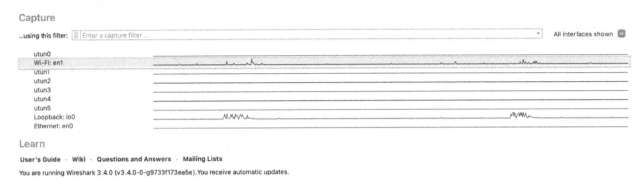

Note: You will now see the capture screen. On this version of Wireshark on MacOS Big Sur the capture will start automatically with the default configuration. If not, just click the blue shark fin to start the capture, the red square to stop it, and the green shark fin to restart the current capture as shown below.

If you mouse over any of the tool bar icons, they will tell you what they are for, and you can navigate the menus to become familiar with Wireshark.

Setting up Filters

At this point we are going to setup a capture filter — to filter out unwanted traffic captures. Do not confuse a capture filter with a Display Filter. The Capture Filter will filter what Wireshark actually captures. Likewise, the Display Filter will display the content you want to filter out in order to look at something specific. If you use a Capture Filter you will only get content related to what you are filtering for. Wireshark also uses the same syntax as other capture tools when applying filters; the sytanx for these capture filters will be the same as TCP dump, WinDump, Analyzer, and Libpcap tools.

1. At the welcome screen Left Click on the green ribbon and Left Click Manage Capture Filters.

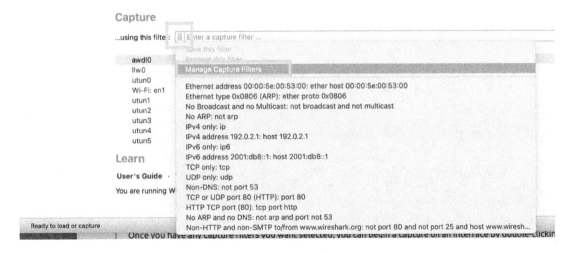

2. At the Wireshark Capture Filters window, **Double Left Click HTTP TCP port (80)** and **Left Click** the **OK** button as shown below:

Note: *Please don't make any changes to the filters — I'm just showing you that you can edit them.*

Note: *This is just a listing of filters, and you can add new ones, or remove them. The next step will show you how to actually use the capture filters that are available.*

3. At the Welcome screen **Left Click** the **Green Ribbon**, and this time select **TCP or UDP Port 80 (HTTP): port 80**, and then **Double Left Click** the **interface** you want to capture on — I used Wi-FI: en1:

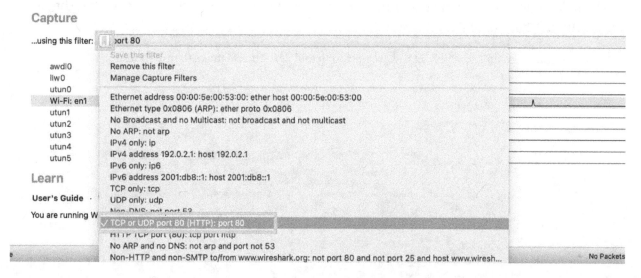

Note: *Once you capture Wireshark data, notice that all traffic is to, or from port 80 as shown below. Please note I covered the IP addresses from the capture and highlight the information area that shows the ports for this current capture.*

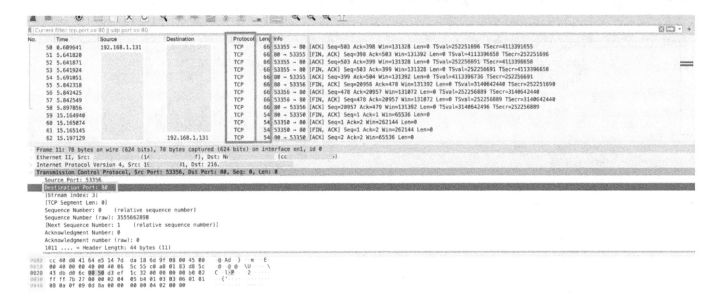

Next, we will go over the capture screen above to get a little more familiar with Wireshark. The red highlight box shows the protocol type, the purple highlight box shows the length of the frame and the green highlight box shows the port that is being used under the info column. Notice below, that the highlighted packet number 62 has a length of 54 and the frame area in the 2nd pane shows that frame 62 has 54 bytes on wire.

```
 62 15.197129          192.168.1.131     TCP     54 80 → 53350 [ACK] Seq=2 Ack=2 Win=65536 Len=0
∨ Frame 62: 54 bytes on wire (432 bits), 54 bytes captured (432 bits) on interface en1, id 0
    Interface id: 0 (en1)
    Encapsulation type: Ethernet (1)
    Arrival Time: Nov 30, 2020 19:54:35.298433000 EST
    [Time shift for this packet: 0.000000000 seconds]
    Epoch Time: 1606784075.298433000 seconds
    [Time delta from previous captured frame: 0.031984000 seconds]
    [Time delta from previous displayed frame: 0.031984000 seconds]
    [Time since reference or first frame: 15.197129000 seconds]
    Frame Number: 62
    Frame Length: 54 bytes (432 bits)
    Capture Length: 54 bytes (432 bits)
    [Frame is marked: False]
    [Frame is ignored: False]

0000  14 7d da 18 6d 9f cc 48  d0 41 64 e5 08 00 45 00   ·}··m··H ·Ad···E·
0010  00 28 00 00 40 00 35 06  76 fb 68 1b a4 8e c0 a8   ·(··@·5· v·h·····
0020  01 83 00 50 d0 66 dd c3  d6 9f 97 f7 e9 71 50 10   ···P·f·· ·····qP·
0030  00 40 da 3b 00 00                                  ·@·;··
```

The frame or packet is what is being represented in the picture above. This is the information that is presented from Layer 1. The next screen shot is of the Ethernet II section of Wireshark that shows the information from Layer 2.

```
> Frame 61: 54 bytes on wire (432 bits), 54 bytes captured (432 bits) on interface en1, id 0
∨ Ethernet II, Src: Apple 18      14:          f), Dst: Ne        64:e5 (cc:4       i)
    > Destination: Net        4:e5 (cc:4(          )
    > Source: Ap              (14:7            )
      Type: IPv4 (0x0800)
> Internet Protocol Version 4, Src: 192.168.1.131, Dst: 104.2
> Transmission Control Protocol, Src Port: 53350, Dst Port: 80, Seq: 1, Ack: 2, Len: 0
```

Likewise, you can see that this section shows the destination and source mac addresses — Layer 2 information — I greyed out the Mac addresses for anonymity. The next screen shot below shows the Layer 3 information. This is the Internet Protocol Version 4, drop down. This section is used to display the source and destination IPv4 addresses.

```
∨ Internet Protocol Version 4, Src: 192.168.1.131, Dst:
    0100 .... = Version: 4
    .... 0101 = Header Length: 20 bytes (5)
  > Differentiated Services Field: 0x00 (DSCP: CS0, ECN: Not-ECT)
    Total Length: 40
    Identification: 0x0000 (0)
  > Flags: 0x40, Don't fragment
    Fragment Offset: 0
    Time to Live: 64
    Protocol: TCP (6)
    Header Checksum: 0x6bfb [validation disabled]
    [Header checksum status: Unverified]
    Source Address: 192.168.1.131
    Destination Address: ...........
```

117

This area gives the flags, lengths, and protocol being used; you can see if there is a checksum in being performed as well. Checksums are used to detect errors in a transmission and verify if the data integrity is intact. The next screen shot shows the Layer 4 protocol being used TCP or UDP, and it also shows the port information for the source and destination from the transport layer.

```
> Internet Protocol Version 4, Src: 192.168.1.131, Dst:
∨ Transmission Control Protocol, Src Port: 53350, Dst Port: 80, Seq: 1, Ack: 2, Len: 0
     Source Port: 53350
     Destination Port: 80
     [Stream index: 0]
     [TCP Segment Len: 0]
     Sequence Number: 1     (relative sequence number)
     Sequence Number (raw): 2549606768
     [Next Sequence Number: 2     (relative sequence number)]
     Acknowledgment Number: 2     (relative ack number)
     Acknowledgment number (raw): 3720599199
     0101 .... = Header Length: 20 bytes (5)
   > Flags: 0x011 (FIN, ACK)
     Window: 4096
     [Calculated window size: 262144]
     [Window size scaling factor: 64]
     Checksum: 0xca7b [unverified]
     [Checksum Status: Unverified]
```

The next screen shot shows the application protocol or (OSI layer 5). This gives you the HTTP information. This is information is from the application layer.

```
∨ Hypertext Transfer Protocol
   > HTTP/1.1 404 Not Found\r\n
     Date: Tue, 01 Dec 2020 00:54:20 GMT\r\n
     Server: Apache\r\n
   > Content-Length: 196\r\n
     Keep-Alive: timeout=5, max=100\r\n
     Connection: Keep-Alive\r\n
     Content-Type: text/html; charset=iso-8859-1\r\n
     \r\n
     [HTTP response 1/1]
     [Time since request: 0.060462000 seconds]
     [Request in frame: 38]
     [Request URI: http://www.tcpipguide.com/space.gif]
     File Data: 196 bytes
```

Please note that if you're looking at a TCP packet, you are looking at a Layer 4 protocol, and you won't get information from the layers above that. The above picture is looking at an HTTP transmission, you won't see this kind of information in a TCP 3-way handshake sequence for instance, you will just see what is specific to that packet. Let's look at the next screen shot; this screen shot shows you the application data.

```
∨ Line-based text data: text/html (7 lines)
     <!DOCTYPE HTML PUBLIC "-//IETF//DTD HTML 2.0//EN">\n
     <html><head>\n
     <title>404 Not Found</title>\n
     </head><body>\n
     <h1>Not Found</h1>\n
     <p>The requested URL was not found on this server.</p>\n
     </body></html>\n
```

Note: the information we have just covered is for reference and to give you a better understanding of the basics of viewing OSI information using Wireshark. We will dig deeper into the HTTP traffic a little further on in this article.

Analyzing Network Traffic

ICMP

Now we are going to analyze some Internet Control Message Protocol (ICMP) traffic with Wireshark. First, I need you to go to the following link and download the dns+icmp.pcapng file:
https://wiki.wireshark.org/SampleCaptures?action=AttachFile&do=get&target=dns%2Bicmp.pcapng.gz

Note: The following link also has many different forms of network traffic that you can analyze. All of the traffic used for this write up will come from this page:

https://wiki.wireshark.org/SampleCaptures#Captures_used_in_Wireshark_testing

Go to File and **Left Click Open** and select the **dns+icmp.pcapng** file in Wireshark and **Left Click Open** to get started to get started.

Note: In MacOS you can just drag the PCAP file you want to open into your Wireshark GUI, and it will automatically open it.

If you've ever used the PING command in any OS, you are using ICMP. ICMP is used for error reporting and helps determine whether a communication is reaching its destination or not. Likewise, ICMP is used to perform traceroute functions. Traceroute shows the path taken between two communicating hosts on networks, and or the internet. The path is the physical path that is connected between networks and the logical routing techniques. When communications happen between routers it is called a hop; each time a communication goes from one point to a router, to another router, to another router is a hop — a hop is performed from point to point and reoccurs until it meets its destination. The following is an example of the output you receive from performing a ping:

```
PING 192.168.1.130 (192.168.1.130): 56 data bytes
64 bytes from 192.168.1.130: icmp_seq=0 ttl=64 time=38.119 ms
64 bytes from 192.168.1.130: icmp_seq=1 ttl=64 time=70.800 ms
64 bytes from 192.168.1.130: icmp_seq=2 ttl=64 time=82.626 ms
64 bytes from 192.168.1.130: icmp_seq=3 ttl=64 time=99.688 ms
64 bytes from 192.168.1.130: icmp_seq=4 ttl=64 time=20.795 ms
64 bytes from 192.168.1.130: icmp_seq=5 ttl=64 time=44.531 ms
^X^C
--- 192.168.1.130 ping statistics ---
6 packets transmitted, 6 packets received, 0.0% packet loss
round-trip min/avg/max/stddev = 20.795/59.427/99.688/27.254 ms
```

The following is a traceroute output [In MacOS or Linux] — or tracert in windows:

```
traceroute to 191.168.1.1 (191.168.1.1), 64 hops max, 52 byte packets
 1  192.168.1.1 (192.168.1.1)  6.915 ms  1.840 ms  2.197 ms
 2  * * *
 3  09              .com (9        2)  19.719 ms  12.212 ms  12.652 ms
 4  dtr(                    .com (9       )) 16.858 ms  23.008 ms  13.194 ms
 5  096             com (          3)  26.728 ms  22.048 ms  24.003 ms
 6  bbr01s|                :.com (           )  31.392 ms  26.551 ms  31.888 ms
 7  cha-b1-lin|                 | 42.504 ms  35.949 ms  38.712 ms
 8  as                  (62.1        4)  46.321 ms  41.424 ms  44.343 ms
 9  a               et (6       .21)  35.472 ms  35.155 ms  34.101 ms
10  tel                         a.net (2        )  34.797 ms  35.615 ms  42.610 ms
^X^C
```

This is a simple way of showing network delay or seeing if a packet is routing on an unintended path. ICMP is an echo-request, and an echo-reply. ICMP doesn't require a TCP or UDP connection, and because of that it can be used maliciously with tactics like ICMP flood attacks, Ping of Death attacks, and Smurf Attacks. Additionally, ICMP does not use a specific port for its communication either. Now that you have a little background on ICMP we can use Wireshark to analyze the ICMP process used with the PING command.

PING Request and Reply

1. **Double Left Click** the **fourth capture** to open it — it should be a PING request:

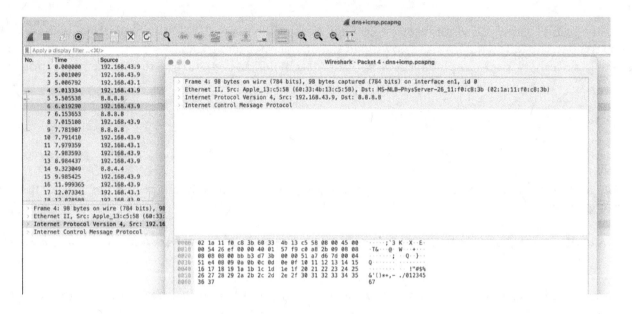

2. Left Click the Drop down for Internet Control Message Protocol:

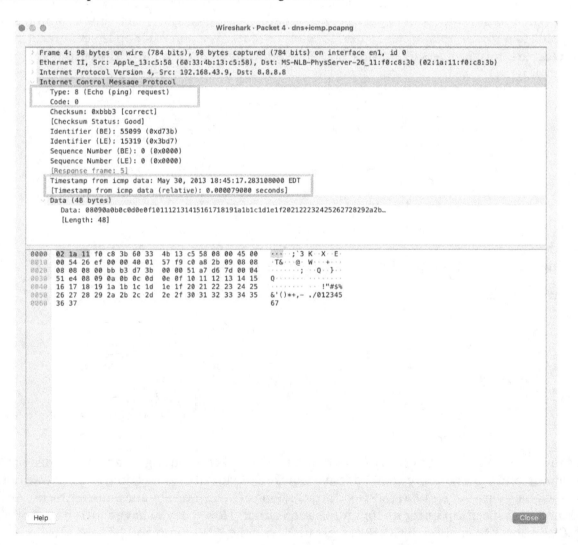

This ICMP packet is a PING request, and you can see that by looking at the type. Likewise, there are different types that's you can google. We are looking at a Type 8 Ping Request, and next we will look at a Type 0 Echo Reply. I highlighted the Echo Request, and the Timestamp. A timestamp is important for trouble shooting potential issues, or malicious activity.

3. **Double Left Click** the **fifth capture** to open it — it should be a PING reply:

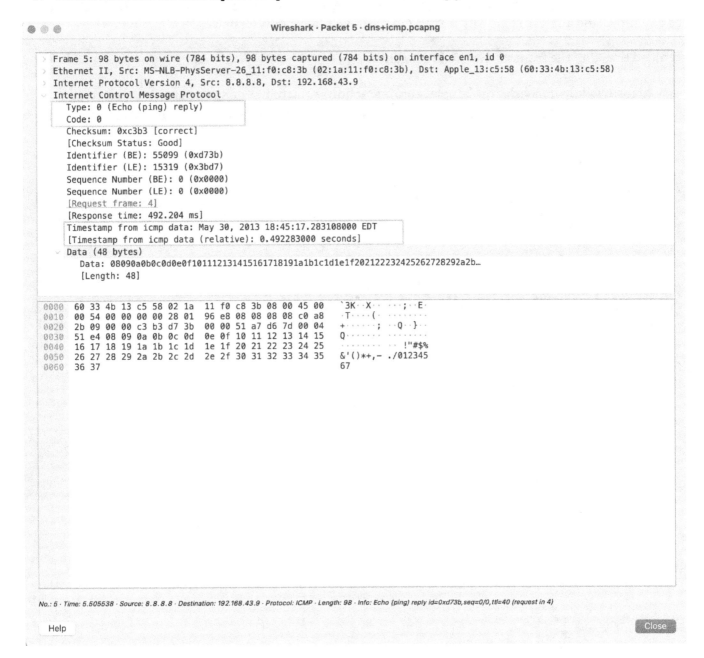

Notice the Type 0 Echo Reply, and the Time Stamp — the Data field is usually a random string of data.

ARP Request

The next capture we are going to look at is an ARP broadcast storm that contains more than 20 ARP requests per second. Before we dig into the sample libcap file, lets cover what an Address Resolution Protocol (ARP) is. This is a Layer 2 protocol that is used to place IP Addresses with a respective MAC address. This is an important protocol and is one of the fundamental pieces of the Internet Protocol (IP) suite. ARP uses a request-response protocol, and these messages are encapsulated by the Link Layer protocol. IPv4 uses ARP, while IPv6 uses a method called Network Discovery Protocol, or Secure Neighbor Discovery instead of the ARP method that is used in IPv4. Furthermore, this was changed in the new IPv6 suite because of secure issues with ARP spoofing. Let's download and analyze some ARP traffic and see how it looks in Wireshark.

Download the PCAP file from the two-following links:

- https://wiki.wireshark.org/SampleCaptures?action=AttachFile&do=get&target=nb6-startup.pcap
- https://wiki.wireshark.org/SampleCaptures?action=AttachFile&do=get&target=arp-storm.pcap

1. Open the nb6-startup.pcap.

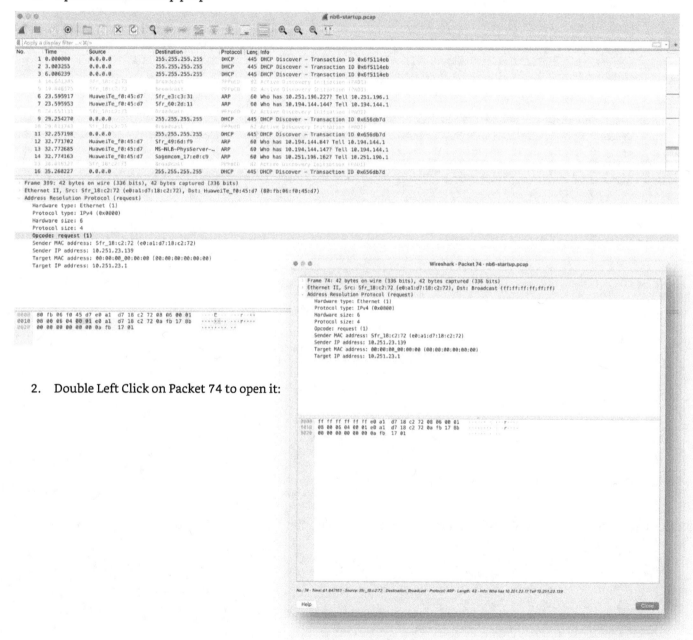

2. Double Left Click on Packet 74 to open it:

3. Left Click the Address Resolution Protocol (Request) drop down:

```
●●●                        Wireshark · Packet 74 · nb6-startup.pcap

  Frame 74: 42 bytes on wire (336 bits), 42 bytes captured (336 bits)
  Ethernet II, Src: Sfr_18:c2:72 (e0:a1:d7:18:c2:72), Dst: Broadcast (ff:ff:ff:ff:ff:ff)
  Address Resolution Protocol (request)
        Hardware type: Ethernet (1)
        Protocol type: IPv4 (0x0800)
        Hardware size: 6
        Protocol size: 4
        Opcode: request (1)
        Sender MAC address: Sfr_18:c2:72 (e0:a1:d7:18:c2:72)
        Sender IP address: 10.251.23.139
        Target MAC address: 00:00:00_00:00:00 (00:00:00:00:00:00)
        Target IP address: 10.251.23.1



0000  ff ff ff ff ff ff e0 a1  d7 18 c2 72 08 06 00 01    ·········· ···r····
0010  08 00 06 04 00 01 e0 a1  d7 18 c2 72 0a fb 17 8b    ·········· ···r····
0020  00 00 00 00 00 00 0a fb  17 01                      ········ ··


Help                                                                    Close
```

The opcode that is highlighted above will tell you whether the ARP packet is a request packet or a reply packet. I highlighted the Target MAC because this shows where the request is going to, and this one is a broadcast because there is no specified address.

1. Double Left Click on Packet 76 to open it:

```
●●●                        Wireshark · Packet 76 · nb6-startup.pcap

  Frame 76: 60 bytes on wire (480 bits), 60 bytes captured (480 bits)
  Ethernet II, Src: HuaweiTe_f0:45:d7 (80:fb:06:f0:45:d7), Dst: Sfr_18:c2:72 (e0:a1:d7:18:c2:72)
  Address Resolution Protocol (reply)
        Hardware type: Ethernet (1)
        Protocol type: IPv4 (0x0800)
        Hardware size: 6
        Protocol size: 4
        Opcode: reply (2)
        Sender MAC address: HuaweiTe_f0:45:d7 (80:fb:06:f0:45:d7)
        Sender IP address: 10.251.23.1
        Target MAC address: Sfr_18:c2:72 (e0:a1:d7:18:c2:72)
        Target IP address: 10.251.23.139



0000  e0 a1 d7 18 c2 72 80 fb  06 f0 45 d7 08 06 00 01    ·····r··· ··E·····
0010  08 00 06 04 00 02 80 fb  06 f0 45 d7 0a fb 17 01    ········ ··E·····
0020  e0 a1 d7 18 c2 72 0a fb  17 8b 00 22 00 5c 00 00    ·····r··· ···"·\··
0030  00 00 00 00 00 00 aa aa  00 00 00 3c                ········ ···<
```

This is an OPCODE reply and has the MAC from the responding host. The ARP process is fairly easy to understand and you need to focus on the request, and the response. Open the arp-storm.pcap file that is linked above to see what an ARP broadcast storm looks like — here is the sample screen capture:

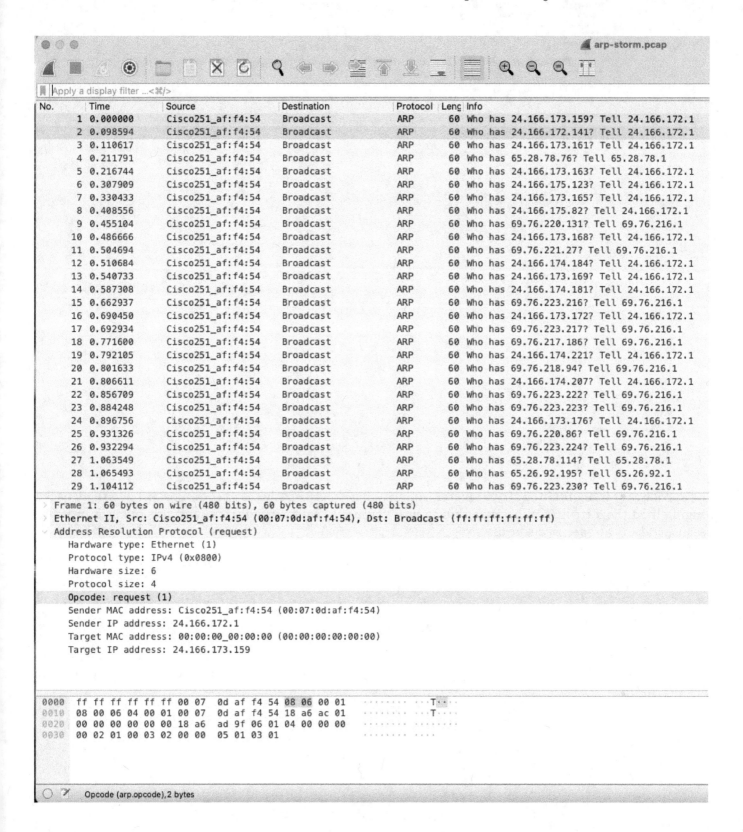

Transmission Control Protocol Captures

We covered how the TCP 3-way handshake occurs, now let's look at it in action. Open the nb6-startup-pcap file, and notice that I have highlighted the 3-way handshake being displayed in Wireshark. TCP traffic in Wireshark is color coded based of the amount of perceived danger. With that being said, Wireshark will color RST, ACK packets red. This a picture from the nb6-startup.pcap that shows the red packet:

Note: Wireshark highlights the TCP drop down yellow, and the RST, ACK so you know why the packet is red.

We talked about the TCP handshake when going over the OSI model earlier. The next picture is from a TCP handshake that is typically seen:

Notice the SYN, SYN-ACK, ACK and then PSH that has occurred in the picture above. This is what we typically do in an NMAP scan. If you see this and there is an RST packet in the middle of this process, you might want to look into why. This could be malicious activity, like scanning, or mapping out the services on the machine you're analyzing.

In the next example, we will see how a SYN Packet looks. I have highlighted the interesting information that we can gain, and that's the sequence number, and the acknowledgement number.

1. Left Click Wireshark at the menu and Left Click Preferences:

    Note: If you are on a Windows Machine it's under the edit tab.

2. Left Click Protocols to expand the selection:

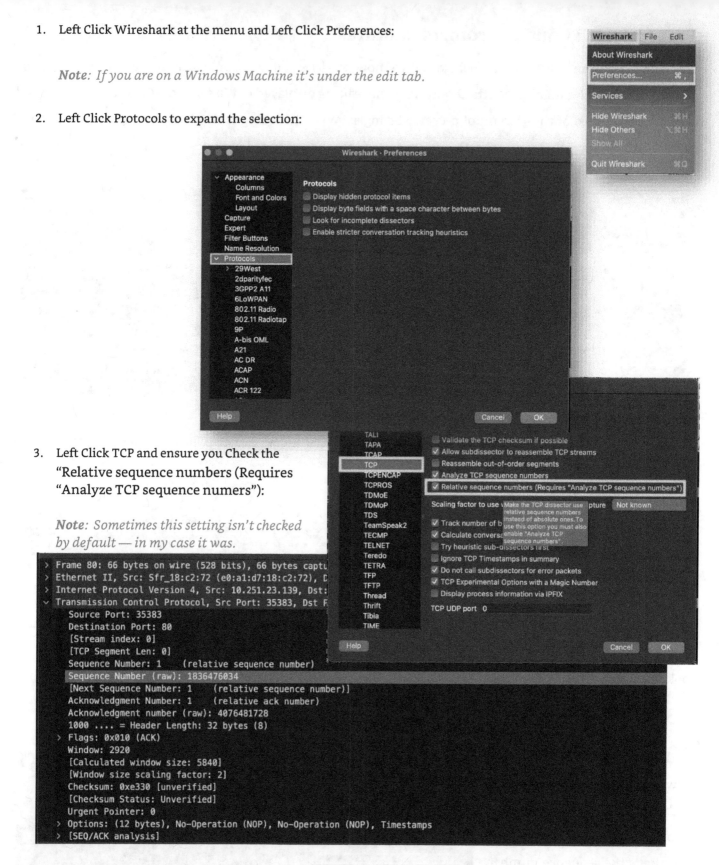

3. Left Click TCP and ensure you Check the "Relative sequence numbers (Requires "Analyze TCP sequence numers"):

    Note: Sometimes this setting isn't checked by default — in my case it was.

Please note in the photo above, that the Sequence Number for the Ack transmission is 1 number higher than the last from the same host. The acknowledgement number is now 1 because it is acknowledging if it wasn't the number would be 0. The SYN-ACK sequence number will be different because it is from the responding host, and the sequence numbers will be in-line on that device as well. Make sure you're paying attention to the communication flow, and where it's coming from and where it is going. This all tells a story when transmissions are going across your network.

HTTP Traffic

Go to the Wireshark sample captures and download the http.cap file or get it from this link:

https://wiki.wireshark.org/SampleCaptures?action=AttachFile&do=get&target=http.cap

Open the http.cap file so you can follow along. Most of you know what HTTP traffic is, but if you don't it is use on the World Wide Web (www), and it tells your web browser how to format the messages that it is reading and sending. Your browser sends HTTP commands to the server and the server replies with the appropriate command. This is important to know when analyzing traffic so we will go over some of the HTTP methods. The common methods are GET, POST, PUT, DELETE, OPTION, TRACE, and CONNECT.

The GET command requests data from a webserver and this is the common method for document retrieval. The POST command is used when a browser is sending information to the server. HTTP uses port 80 and works with the TCP that we discussed earlier. After the TCP 3-way handshake is completed the HTTP GET request is sent to the server. The graphic below shows the TCP sequence highlighted in pink, and then the HTTP GET request in orange. The data itself is listed below in the Hyper Text Transfer Protocol area of the middle pane. The GET request is shown for /download.html, and the Request Method shows GET. The Request URI shows /download.html, the full request URI shows that it is trying to GET the http://www.ethereal.com/download.html page. The Request Version is HTTP/1.1, and the accept data tells the server what file types the browser can accept. In our case, it's trying to GET an HTML document. The Accept-Encoding is gzip,deflate and it is the accepted encoding by the client side. The other thing to note is the connection flag is set to keep alive, and this controls the network connection and enables it to stay open after the transaction is complete.

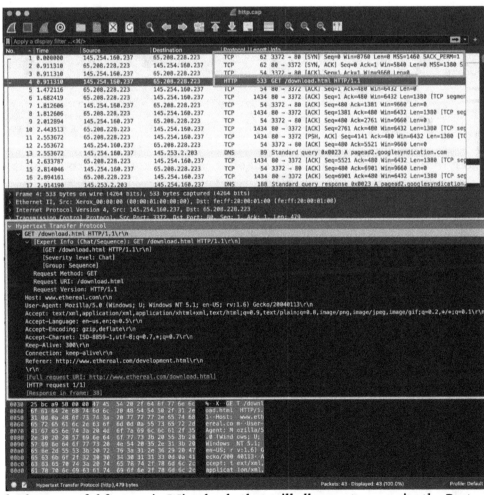

Now we need to look at a useful feature in Wireshark, that will allow us to organize the Protocol Hierarchy.

1. Left Click Statistics and then Left Click Protocol Hierarchy.

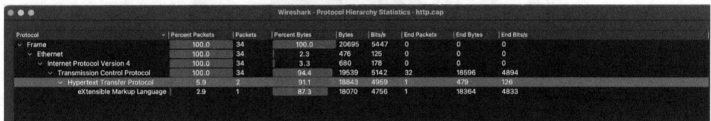

This data can be used to find anomalies, and you will oftentimes see multiple protocols used in conjunction with one another.

Conclusion

Wireshark is a great tool that lets you see how data is being sent across the network. It can be used for trouble shooting, and general awareness of what is happening in your network environment. Wireshark can also be used for malicious purposes, and while this concludes the current article where we discussed how the OSI model applies to Wireshark, and how to install the application, next time we will cover some malicious uses. We analyzed ICMP, ARP, TCP, and HTTP captures, and saw the basic functionality of Wireshark. Try to look at some of the sample captures and start looking at the different types of network traffic and how it is viewed in Wireshark.

Protecting Linux Systems with iptables
Discussion and Application
By: Kevin John O. Hermosa

iptables is an administration tool designed to manage and maintain the built-in IPV4 and IPV6 packet filter rules in the Linux kernel. The tool is currently being maintained by **Netfilter**.

iptables allow a systems/Linux administrator to implement a host-based Firewall which is a basic necessity in cybersecurity.

Before we get ahead of ourselves, I would like the readers to become familiar of what exactly firewalls are because a proper understanding of firewalls is essential for the creation of ideal sets of firewall rules using iptables.

Firewalls

Firewalls are devices that were traditionally designed to filter packets whose destination is the device behind it or the network behind it. Cybersecurity back in the day focused on defending the workplace from external threats, all the while assuming an all-encompassing trust on everything inside – which is no longer applicable to today's Cybersecurity.

Fast-forward to today where Firewalls have vastly evolved and are now commonly incorporated into **Unified Threat Management (UTM)** devices which are designed to have a rich collection of features designed defend against today's cyber threats.

That said, UTMs won't be today's topic and the main focus will be firewalls. Firewalls are commonly categorized into either of these 3:

- Stateless firewalls – These are early conceptions of Firewalls which are only **designed to drop packets according to either its source, destination, or both**. This kind of firewall is no longer common these days because it is no longer enough for a "sound" approach in Cybersecurity and the capabilities of Stateless firewalls are fully covered by Stateful firewalls already.
- Stateful firewalls – These are firewalls designed with the **capability of tracking a connection** in order to be able to tell apart packets part of an established TCP connection and packets that belong to something else. This capability became necessary in order to aid the need for proper network traffic monitoring. A prime example of this kind of firewall is the packet filter managed by the **iptables** tool that we will be discussing further down the road.
- Next-generation firewalls (NGFW) – These firewalls are not only stateful firewalls, but they are also **packed with many other features** like deep packet inspection, intrusion prevention/detection system (IPS/IDS), comprehensive zone management, application-aware traffic monitoring, beautiful statistical graphs, graphically rich interactive user interface, and many more.

Some examples of NGFWs that I know of are:

- OPNSense – Berkeley Software Distribution(bsd) based + Free and Open source + paid subscription for support/IPS rules.
- PfSense – bsd-based + Free and Open source + paid subscription for support/IPS rules.
- Fortigate – paid and subscription-based NGFW by Fortinet.
- GNU/Linux-based ipFire – Free and Open source.

There are many other NGFWs out there and some notable names that produce these are Palo Alto and Juniper.

Features and cost vary from each NGFW to another and by no means can anyone say easily that a certain NGFW is better than the rest as it greatly varies from a case-to-case basis. I hope the readers are enthusiastic about doing their own extensive research about this!

iptables

With that out of the way, let's get started in configuring iptables in order to serve as a worthy layer of cybersecurity for ourselves!

But wait! You need to first understand the general idea of how it works.

The framework of iptables revolves around the use of 5 tables along with built-in chains but for the sake of getting your basics solid, I will only be focusing on 3 tables namely:

- <u>filter</u> – "This is the default table (if no -t option is passed)." as written in the manpage of iptables(8). Basically, this is the first thing that any user should configure before any other table.
- <u>mangle</u> – "This table is used for specialized packet alteration." as written in the manpage of iptables(8). Packets can be allowed/dropped/forwarded as early as it enters the processing scope of the mangle table before it even reaches the filter table. Dropping packets in the mangle table isn't commonly discussed on publicly available articles tackling iptables but I perceive dropping packets in the mangle table to be a very useful defense-in-depth approach. Altering of packets before it leaves the machine is also done on the mangle table.
- <u>nat</u> - "This table is consulted when a packet that creates a new connection is encountered." as written in the manpage of iptables (8). This table is consulted after the mangle table when a packet that creates a new connection is encountered.

Each table has a set of built-in chains that divide the processing of packets according to the category implied by the built-in chain's name. filter has 3 built-in chains, nat has 4, and mangle has 5:

- <u>PREROUTING</u> – Present in both mangle and nat. According to the iptables manpage, **mangle's** prerouting is **for altering incoming packets before routing**. While **nat's** prerouting is **for altering packets as soon as they come in**.
- <u>INPUT</u> – Present in filter, mangle, and nat. According to the iptables manpage, filter's input is for packets destined to local sockets, mangle's input is for packets coming into the box itself, and nat's input is for altering packets destined for local sockets.
- <u>FORWARD</u> – Present in filter and mangle. According to the iptables manpage, **filter's** forward is **for packets being routed through the box**. While **mangle's** forward is **for altering packets being routed through the box.**
- <u>OUTPUT</u> – Present in filter, mangle, and nat. According to the iptables manpage, filter's output is for locally generated packets, mangle's output is for altering locally generated packets before routing, and nat's output is for altering locally generated packets before routing.
- <u>POSTROUTING</u> – Present in both mangle and nat. According to the iptables manpage, mangle's postrouting is for altering packets as they are about to go out. While nat's postrouting is for altering packets as they are about to **go... out**.

That last one sounds confusing but disregarding the very same sentences used, **mangle's** postrouting is **for altering packets as they are about to go out of the machine and unto the wire/wifi towards where it needs to go. nat's** postrouting on the other hand, is **for altering packets as they are about to go out of the nat table** – which is before proceeding to be processed by the mangle table.

Refer to the chart in the next page in order ensure your complete understanding.

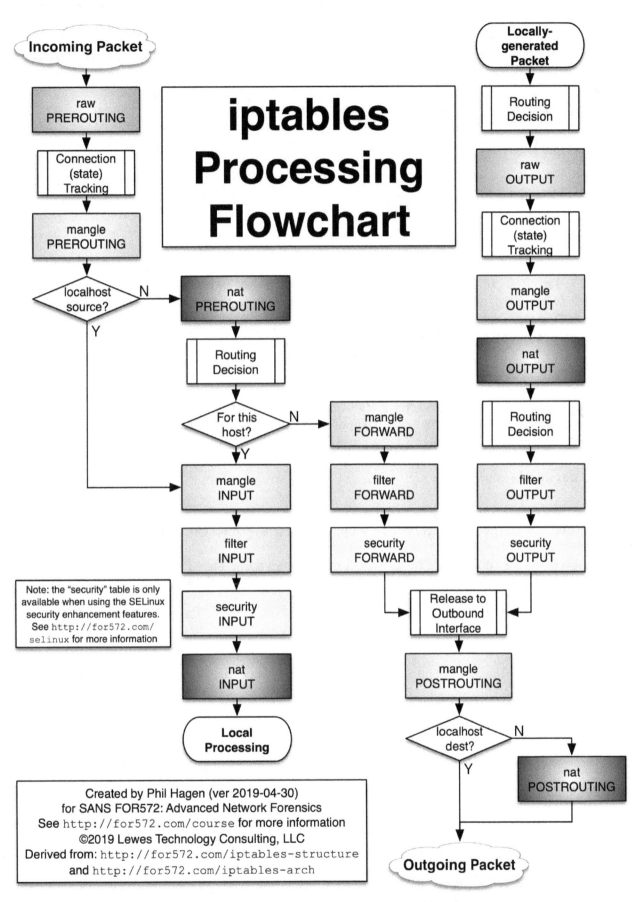

iptables Processing Flowchart

Note: the "security" table is only available when using the SELinux security enhancement features. See http://for572.com/selinux for more information

Created by Phil Hagen (ver 2019-04-30)
for SANS FOR572: Advanced Network Forensics
See http://for572.com/course for more information
©2019 Lewes Technology Consulting, LLC
Derived from: http://for572.com/iptables-structure
and http://for572.com/iptables-arch

https://stuffphilwrites.com/wp-content/uploads/2014/09/FW-IDS-iptables-Flowchart-v2019-04-30-1.png

As you may have observed already, the names of the chains are practically the same across tables but the implication of each varies depending on the table.

Basic usage of the iptables involves the creation of rules for the appropriate chains in order to serve the intended use-case. One big thing to note is the fact that rules are processed by in the order of top-to-bottom.

For example: You have a rule that accepts any packet as rule#1 and a rule that drops any packet as rule#2. The end result is that all packets are accepted, and no packet ever gets processed by rule#2 because they have already been accepted by rule#1.

I hope you haven't cowered through everything just yet because I have yet to teach you through iptables by providing examples, dissecting it, and help you understand it every step of the way!

For beginners to GNU/Linux terminal, please do not include the dollar sign in your commands. The $ is merely there to indicate the start of a terminal command.

BIG BIG NOTE: I'm 95% confident that the GNU/Linux distro that you are using right now has the "sudo" command on it and you will need to use it by **typing sudo before the iptables command** because any interaction using iptables **requires you to have** "root" privileges AKA "higher than administrator" privileges else you will be getting error messages like "permission denied". So basically:

> $ sudo iptables .... etc.

I didn't include sudo to the iptables commands because in order to reach the highest level of security in a GNU/Linux system, you would need to be able to operate a GNU/Linux system without having to rely on "sudo" but instead, rely on "su" or other cybersecurity-ethical methods of reaching a root terminal session. There's no need to rush with this, so please take your time in skilling-up in Linux administration until you can confidently live without the cursed sudo!

As a side note, su=superuser, command that allows you to login as root. sudo=superuserdo, command to execute a command with root privileges even if all you need to provide is the current user's password.

Finally, it's high noon for application. Do your best to analyze a complete run of examples that I'm giving you from here, complete with explanations! Go ahead, deploy it and put it to the test!

Iptables syntax and usage examples

1. Command to display all iptables rules in their respective syntax format. Also includes policies set to each chain:

```
$ iptables -S
      OR
$ iptables --list-rules
```

2. Command to list all iptables rules in table format:

```
$ iptables -L
      OR
$ iptables -list
```

3. Command to list all iptables rules in table format + numeric display of IP addresses and respective port numbers will be displayed instead of protocols:

```
$ iptables -L -n
      OR
$ iptables -L --numeric
```

4. You can explicitly specify a chain when listing rules:

```
$ iptables -S INPUT
$ iptables -L FORWARD
$ iptables --list OUTPUT
```

5. Command to add a basic iptables rule that allows outbound packets with a destination port of 443. Note that the filter table is implied by default when you do not explicitly specify a table.

```
$ iptables -A OUTPUT -p tcp -m tcp --dport 443 -j ACCEPT
      OR
$ iptables --append OUTPUT --protocol tcp --match tcp --destination-port 443 -jump
  ACCEPT
```

-A appends the rule to the chain specified. Using -A on a chain with 4 rules will effectively make it the 5th rule – adding the rule at the end of the list of rules.
-p defines the protocol of the packets that should match with this iptables rule.
-m defines a special parameter with various uses. This can be freely omitted as defaults are automatically set whenever you define a specific protocol using -p.
--destination-port defines the destination port of the packets that should match
       with this iptables rule.
-j defines the action to be taken against packets that match this iptables rule.

There is a myriad of accepted values for -j but we will focus on ACCEPT, REJECT, DROP, LOG, and DNAT. The difference between REJECT and DROP is that REJECT makes the computer **notify** the **machine where the packet came from** that its sent packet was **rejected**. While DROP will outright drop the packet without even notifying the source machine about it.

LOG will make a kernel log entry about the packet that matched the iptables rule which can be viewed using the "dmesg" command.

Finally, DNAT is used strictly on the **PREROUTING** and **OUTPUT chains** of the **nat table** in order to modify the destination address of the packet, which will result in tcp connections being established to the newly defined destination through DNAT modification (udp packets do not establish a connection, so all udp packets that match the parameters will still be processed by the DNAT iptables rule).

Do note that a packet must match **ALL parameters** defined in an iptables rule for it to be processed using the action defined at -j.

Now let us proceed on making iptables rules that check the source and destination ports as well as rules that can act against a range of ports instead of just one port.

6. Command to add an iptables rule that allows SSH (tcp port 22) connections coming from the 1.1.1.1 ip address:

```
$ iptables -A INPUT -s 1.1.1.1 -p tcp --dport 22 -j ACCEPT
      OR
$ iptables --append --source 1.1.1.1 --protocol tcp --destination-port 22 -jump
  ACCEPT
```

-s defines which ip address the packet should come from in order to match with a rule.

7. Command to add an iptables rule that allows HTTPS (tcp port 443) connections coming from the 1.1.1.1 ip address:

```
$ iptables -A INPUT -s 1.1.1.1 -p tcp --dport 443 -j ACCEPT
```

8. For allowing HTTPS connections coming from ANY ip address, simply omit the -s from example#7:

```
$ iptables -A INPUT -p tcp --dport 443 -j ACCEPT
```

Allowing a connection through your firewall on port 443 is not enough for functional HTTPS or SSH communication to be established as the nature of established tcp connections in networking is a give-and-take… in other words, the packets going back to the requester (popular example is a web browser like Mozilla Firefox) must be allowed in the firewall as well.

I can't stress enough just how lazy people are about this by just outright defining a default policy of ACCEPT on the OUTPUT chain of the filter table!

9. Command to add an iptables rule that allows ONLY THE packets locally generated as a response to the request/s made by 1.1.1.1:

```
$ iptables -A OUTPUT -d 1.1.1.1 -p tcp -m conntrack --ctstate ESTABLISHED -j ACCEPT
```

-d or --destination defines the ip address destination of the packet to match to this iptables rule
-m conntrack means that you are using an **iptables extension** for the match parameter   and   the **extension's name is "conntrack"**. As its name suggests, it's a connection   tracking   extension   that allows iptables to match according to the defined parameters in   its built-in module/s. **ctstate** is the conntrack module used in the command, which is   used in order to specify a connection state to match with the iptables rule.

There are many states that can be defined using **ctstate,** but we will be focusing on NEW, ESTABLISHED, and RELATED.

- o   NEW – Matches packets that starts a new connection or packets that are "otherwise associated with a connection which has not seen packets in both directions." as written in the manpage of iptables-extensions(8).
- o   ESTABLISHED – Matches packets that "is associated with a connection which has seen packets in both directions." as written in the manpage of iptables-extensions(8).
- o   RELATED – Matches packets that "is starting a new connection, but is associated with an existing connection, such as an FTP data transfer or an ICMP error." as written in the manpage of iptables-extensions(8). This is useful for cases where multiple connections are used to fetch a specific resource and Persepolis/aria2c is one just one of the many applications that utilize this method.

10. Command to add an iptables rule that allows 1.1.1.1 to established HTTPS (tcp port 443) connections AS WELL AS allow packets that are part of the established connection and also associated/related to the established connection through the firewall:

```
$ iptables -A INPUT -s 1.1.1.1 -p tcp -m tcp --dport 443 -m conntrack --ctstate
  NEW,ESTABLISHED,RELATED -j ACCEPT
```

11. Command to add an iptables rule that strictly allows ONLY the packets locally generated to respond to connections established by 1.1.1.1:

```
$ iptables -A OUTPUT -d 1.1.1.1 -p tcp -m tcp -m conntrack --ctstate ESTABLISHED -j
  ACCEPT
```

Do note that the iptables rule created by the syntax above allows not only the packets being sent to respond to 1.1.1.1's HTTPS connection but also allows packets that are being sent to respond to ALL connections established by 1.1.1.1 to the server.

A ctstate of ESTABLISHED is absolutely needed in order to match the packets made in response to a new tcp connection request as well as future packets sent as part of the established tcp connection. So, for the case of endpoints connecting to the internet, an iptables rule with ctstate of ESTABLISHED should be placed on either mangle PREROUTING, INPUT, filter INPUT, or across all of them for multiple layers of processing – something that you will only do if the level of security needed is on the level of paranoia because more rules also means more CPU power is needed to process packets against the iptables rules. So please consider that in mind when you are working with low processing power devices like early generation Raspberry Pis.

Packets coming from a destination host/server that are expected to come after your computer sends the initial NEW TCP packet will be considered to match with the ESTABLISHED ctstate.

12. Command to add an iptables rule that allows packets part of an ESTABLISHED connection in the PREROUTING chain of the mangle table:

```
$ iptables -t mangle -A PREROUTING -p tcp -m tcp -m conntrack --ctstate ESTABLISHED
  -j ACCEPT
```

13. Command to add an iptables rule that allows packets part of an ESTABLISHED connection in the INPUT chain of the mangle table:

```
$ iptables -t mangle -A INPUT -p tcp -m tcp -m conntrack --ctstate ESTABLISHED -j
  ACCEPT
```

14. Command to add an iptables rule that allows packets part of an ESTABLISHED connection in the INPUT chain of the filter table:

```
$ iptables -A INPUT -p tcp -m tcp -m conntrack --ctstate ESTABLISHED -j ACCEPT
```

Notice that the iptables command above did not use the -t parameter. This is because the iptables command defaults to the filter table when you don't specify a table using -t.

Let's backtrack for a bit about ports because I still have yet to teach you about rules for specifying source ports and covering a port range.

15. Command to add an iptables rule that allows clients to connect to the server via port 443:

```
$ iptables -A INPUT -p tcp --dport 443 -j ACCEPT
      or better yet
$ iptables -A INPUT -i [internet interface] -p tcp --dport 443 -j ACCEPT
```

INPUT's good now so all we have to do is best practice for the OUTPUT.

16. Command to add an iptables rule that allows a web server software i.e., httpd to respond to clients accessing web content on port 443 HTTPS:

```
$ iptables -A OUTPUT -p tcp -m tcp -m conntrack --ctstate ESTABLISHED,RELATED -j
  ACCEPT
```

I added RELATED on this one because you will always want your clients to be loading your web content as fast as possible and multiple connections are needed for that purpose.

Now let's move on to one of the most important parts of this guide and that is utilizing the ability to apply a single rule against a port range which is invaluable on certain situations.

We will be utilizing the **multiport** iptables extension to serve the purpose of covering a port range.

17. Command to add an iptables rule that allows outbound connections toward ports 1024 up to 65535:

```
$ iptables -A OUTPUT -p tcp -m multiport --dports 1024:65535 -j ACCEPT
```

This can be extended with single port specifics as well as additional port ranges for up to a set of 15 port specifics/port ranges.

18. Command to add an iptables rule that allows outbound connections towards port 53 as well as ports 1024 to 65535:

```
$ iptables -A OUTPUT -p tcp -m multiport --dports 53,1024:65535 -j ACCEPT
```

19. Command to add an iptables rule that allows outbound connections toward ports 53 to 80 as well as ports 1024 to 65535:

```
$ iptables -A OUTPUT -p tcp -m multiport --dports 53:80,1024:65535 -j ACCEPT
```

It's finally time to be dropping those baddie packets.

20. Command to drop TCP packets whose defined destination port is POP3 (port 110):

```
$ iptables -A INPUT -p tcp -m tcp --dport 110 -j DROP
```

21. Command to literally drop ALL packets processed by the INPUT chain of filter table:

```
$ iptables -A INPUT -j DROP
```

22. Command to drop UDP packets whose defined destination port is DNS (port 53):

```
$ iptables -A INPUT -p udp -m udp --dport 53 -j DROP
```

23. Command to drop all packets going out of the computer whose destination is a computer/host that is part of the 192.168.1.0/24 subnet:

```
$ iptables -A OUTPUT -d 192.168.1.0/24 -j DROP
```

Note: that for iptables rules that need to have a defined destination or source port, you need two iptables rules in order to match both TCP and UDP packets.

Now let's teach you about setting default policies on iptables chains. By default, all iptables chains are set with the ACCEPT policy. This means that packets that do not match a rule are ACCEPTED by default. You don't want to have it on ACCEPT by default because that literally means letting yourself get shot in the foot!

WARNING: Be careful with changing the default policies when you're dealing with a machine that you are connected to using SSH, VNC, or some sort of remote shell/control protocol. You may accidentally lock yourself out of the machine if you did not prepare sure-fire working iptables rules that properly handles the packets involved in your connection.

24. Command to set a default policy of DROP to the FORWARD chain of the filter table:

```
$ iptables -P FORWARD DROP
      OR
$ iptables --policy FORWARD DROP
```

You should always set FORWARD to DROP on endpoints because it's unnecessary for these computers to be forwarding packets not unless they have virtual machines running inside of them. On the other hand, it's common for a router to have the FORWARD policy on ACCEPT until appropriate iptables rules have already been deployed and adequately tested on it.

25. Command to set a default policy of REJECT to the FORWARD chain of the mangle table:

$ iptables -t mangle -P FORWARD DROP

In order to lend you a hand in experimenting with the setting of a drop policy on a VPS, here's the rules that you should set for your SSH connection:

```
$ iptables -I INPUT 1 -p tcp -m tcp --dport 22 -m conntrack --ctstate
  NEW,ESTABLISHED,RELATED -j ACCEPT
$ iptables -I OUTPUT 1 -p tcp -m tcp -m conntrack --ctstate ESTABLISHED -j ACCEPT
```

Noticed something different? This time around I used an -I instead of an -A. This is for inserting rules in the iptables rule list instead of appending it to the bottom of the list. This is useful when you are modifying an already configured iptables setup or when you have made some mistakes in the rules you made. You may use --insert instead of using -I.

The general rule of thumb when figuring out the number to use for --insert is that the old rule placed in this number is moved downwards before the new rule is inserted in order to take the old rule's place.

For example, you have 4 rules as listed using iptables -S:

-A INPUT -p tcp -m tcp --dport 110 -j DROP
-A INPUT -j DROP
-A INPUT -p udp -m udp --dport 53 -j DROP
-A INPUT -d 192.168.1.0/24 -j DROP

And you added this rule using --insert INPUT 3:

$ iptables -I INPUT 3 -p tcp -m tcp --dport 1194 -m conntrack --ctstate ESTABLISHED -j ACCEPT

You would see the following list using iptables -S:

-A INPUT -p tcp -m tcp --dport 110 -j DROP
-A INPUT -j DROP
-A INPUT -p tcp -m tcp --dport 1194 -m conntrack --ctstate ESTABLISHED -j ACCEPT
-A INPUT -p udp -m udp --dport 53 -j DROP
-A INPUT -d 192.168.1.0/24 -j DROP

I hope that helped you understand how the -I parameter works in iptables.

About the iptables rules for your SSH connection, you can specify your internet connection's assigned public ip address in the iptables rule, but it is generally not advised as the ip address assigned to you does dynamically change over-time and there is usually an added cost for a static public ip address allocation for your internet plan/package. Your ip address dynamically changing would mean that an SSH connection from your computer will no longer match the SSH iptables rule with --destination parameter that you made, effectively locking you out.

Don't be too afraid of locking yourself out though, a Linux administrator with a good security sense is those who have already locked themselves out a couple of times and learned the good lesson behind it!

That said, performing double checks is a healthy habit and one good way of verifying the effectiveness of your iptables rules is by checking the number of packets processed by your new rules.

26. Command to list all iptables rules in table format and display the number of packets and total size of the data processed:

```
$ iptables -L -v
        OR
$ iptables --list -v
```

The command will display you the usual with added information about packet count processed by the default policy of a chain as well as the packet count processed by each iptables rule.

Now let's proceed to processing packets coming from specific network adapters.

First off, you should remember the "ifconfig" command:

```
$ ifconfig
```

which lets you see the network adapters that you use. If you have a machine that has an Ethernet network adapter and a Wireless network adapter then you should see something like "eth0", "wlan0", "eno1", and etc. "eth0" is used to refer to Ethernet network adapters while "wlan0" is used to refer Wireless network adapters.

Other GNU/Linux distributions use stuff like "wlp3 bla bla" or "enp3 bla bla", pardon me for not being able to remember the whole thing but I hope you get the gist of it. Asides from that, you should be able to see a "lo" which is the loopback adapter that is used to send packets to the machine itself. The "lo" adapter is always used when packets have a destination address of 127.0.0.1 AKA localhost.

Now let's get started in processing packets specific to a network adapter!

27. Command to add an iptables rule that allows outbound HTTPS packets to threatpost.com through the eth0 network adapter:

```
$ iptables -A OUTPUT -o eth0 -d threatpost.com -p tcp -m tcp --dport 443 -j ACCEPT
```

If you have a DROP policy in OUTPUT and you're trying to connect to threatpost.com using a **wifi connection**, I'm pretty sure you won't be loading that website anytime soon because an ethernet interface was specified using the -o parameter.

Do note that it's generally not a good idea to put a domain name in place of an ip address because this can be dangerous in the event that your DNS server gets compromised. You could be given spoofed DNS responses which is really dangerous!

You should instead, perform DNS lookup using a vps or through sources you can really trust and use the ip address provided by the response for your iptables rule.

The case is different when you're making a rule for the INPUT chain.

28. Command to add an iptables rule that allows ESTABLISHED tcp packets coming from the wlan0 network adapter to go through the firewall:

```
$ iptables -A INPUT -i wlan0 -p tcp -m tcp -m conntrack --ctstate ESTABLISHED -j
   ACCEPT
```

Remember, -o for OUTPUT and -i for INPUT. That said, you'll be notified anyways when you make the mistake of using the wrong parameter for this.

I hope you are still with me because there are still 2 things left for me to discuss and that is the usage of -j LOG and -j DNAT

It's always important to have logs whenever you are troubleshooting networks or simply want to be alerted when there are attempts to connect to ports that hackers are always attacking like ports 22, 23, and 3389.

29. Command to LOG incoming TCP 3389 packets:

```
$ iptables -A INPUT -p tcp -m tcp -dport 3389 -j LOG
```

It is good practice to specify the "level" of what gets written to the kernel logs so as to help you sort things out:

```
$ iptables -A INPUT -p tcp -m tcp --dport 3389 -j LOG --log-level alert
$ iptables -A INPUT -p tcp -m tcp --dport 22 -j LOG --log-level warning
```

Log levels are from 0-7 or in this ascending order:

- emerg (0)
- alert (1)
- crit (2)
- error (3)
- warning (4)
- notice (5)
- info (6)
- debug (7)

The lower the level, the easier it is to see it using the "dmesg" command. Higher log levels are only displayed when you have specified it with the -l or --level parameter.

Finally, it's time to settle the score with -j DNAT.

This is used to make TCP connections establish to a different computer/host by directly changing the destination of the TCP packet. UDP packets on the other hand, are merely passed along as no connections are ever made using UDP.
Here's a scenario for this:
You have a DNS-over-TLS proxy running on your computer and it's listening at port 5353. You want this to also serve DNS queries coming from other computers within the same network by redirecting packets meant for this computer's port 53 towards port 5353.
Your computer is connected to this network through the eth0 interface.

30. Command to do what needs to get done as described in the scenario above:

```
$ iptables -t nat -A PREROUTING -i eth0 -p udp -m udp --dport 53 -j DNAT --to-
   destination 127.0.0.1:5353
```

The above command will effectively change the destination port of all UDP packets with a dport of 53 going through nat table's PREROUTING chain into having a dport of 5353.

Using -j DNAT in the nat table is most applicable to firewalls that guard a network segmented by a router.

Now of course you wouldn't want your csec party to be ruined by a reboot because as it is right now, your iptables rules will go poof after a reboot. So yes, there are additional steps to perform in order to ensure that your iptables rules will be restored upon reboot.

First things first, let's go ahead and save your iptables rules to a file.

31. Command to save the iptables rules to a file:

```
$ iptables-save -f [filename]
      example:
$ iptables-save -f myIptablesRulesFile
```

Don't forget to invoke this using <u>sudo</u> or you'll end up with 0 bytes AKA an empty file. Also, invoking this with sudo will give you a file owned by root, so you won't be deleting or moving that file anytime soon using your non-root user.

Now you need to know how to restore your iptables rules using the file that you saved earlier.
32. Command to restore the iptables rules using a saved file:

```
$ iptables-restore [filename]
      example:
$iptables-restore myIptablesRulesFile
```

And this is where things get a little bit complicated. You see, GNU/Linux systems are really flexible to the point that even the initialization system AKA the first program that runs to load all other programs on startup can be freely customized and changed according to one's preferences.

Examples of these init systems are:

o   OpenRC – a modern init system made by the developers of the Gentoo Linux distro. Used by Gentoo Linux, Artix Linux, Redcore Linux, and etc.
o   SystemD – used by well-known GNU/Linux distributions like RHEL, CentOS, and OpenSUSE.
o   Sysvinit – used by legacy or tradition-respecting GNU/Linux systems like MX Linux.

So now, I will guide you through the steps in ensuring that iptables-restore is executed during startup in order to save you from the trouble of either doing it yourself or being had by hackers simply because you forgot to restore your firewall up to shape.

33. Steps to restore the iptables rules on startup for a GNU/Linux system using openrc as init:
The first step is to find out where openrc-run and iptables-restore executable files are located because you will need to use the full path of these in the script. This can be done by invoking:

```
$ which openrc-run
$ which iptables-restore
```

I am using Artix Linux for the creation of this guide and the full paths of these two in my system were:

```
/usr/bin/openrc-run
/usr/bin/iptables-restore
```

This may be different in your system so please pay attention to the full paths given to you by the which command and duly note them.

The second step is to write the script at /etc/init.d/ and setting permissions for it to be executable. There are many ways to create the script there, but I will be using nano for this example.

```
$ nano /etc/init.d/iptables-startup
```

This will turn your terminal into a terminal-based text editor where you can start typing out the contents of your script.

Now please review the script below and you will notice that the full path of openrc-run is used at the beginning of this script then the full path of the iptables-restore was used inside the start() function. Should the full paths given to you were different, please change these accordingly before writing it into the terminal-based text editor.

```
#!/usr/bin/openrc-run

depend() {
        after localmount
        before loopback
}

start()
{
        ebegin "Restoring iptables rules"
        /usr/bin/iptables-restore /home/[your username]/myIptablesRulesFile
        return 0
}
```

You may be stuck right now because you don't know what to place on the **[your username]** section but you can easily find it out by opening another terminal and invoking this command:

```
$ whoami
```

Oh and, **please don't invoke that using sudo** or else you will get "root" which isn't where the script was saved earlier.

After placing your system's username, please press CTRL+O then press enter after typing all that in order to save the script. To exit out of the text editor, press CTRL+X.

Now you have to set executable permissions for the script using this command:

```
$ chmod 755 /etc/init.d/iptables-restore
```

Finally, the script has to be added to the boot runlevel so that it will execute during startup. This can be done by invoking the following command:

```
$ rc-update add iptables-restore boot
```

34. Steps to restore the iptables rules on startup for a GNU/Linux system using systemd as init:
The steps to take for Systemd is going to be completely different. I will be using Linode.com's tutorial about this as reference and the link to it is written at the references section.

First things first, the script has to be created and placed at /usr/bin/ which is followed by a chmod command to give it executable permissions.

```
$ nano /usr/bin/iptables-startup.sh
```

This will turn your terminal into a terminal-based text editor where you can start typing out the contents of your script.

Command not found. I'm afraid to say that you will have to use another text editor like vi or running a graphical text editor as root using sudo and here are a few examples that will most likely work on Linux distros:

```
$ sudo kate /usr/bin/iptables-startup.sh
$ sudo gedit /usr/bin/iptables-startup.sh
$ sudo kwrite /usr/bin/iptables-startup.sh
```

Please type the following lines of shell commands on the text editor:

#!/bin/bash
iptables-restore /home/[your username]/myIptablesRulesFile

You may be stuck right now because you don't know what to place on the **[your username]** section but you can easily find it out by opening another terminal and invoking this command:

$ whoami

Oh and, **please don't invoke that using sudo** or else you will get "root" which isn't where the script was saved earlier.

After placing your system's username, please press CTRL+O then press enter after typing all that in order to save the script. To exit out of the text editor, press CTRL+X.

Saving with the graphical text editors should be as simple as the typical notepad's CTRL+S.

Now you have to set executable permissions for the script using this command:

```
$ chmod 755 /usr/bin/iptables-startup
```

The next step is creating a Unit file in order to define a systemd service:

```
$ nano /lib/systemd/system/iptables-startup.service
```

Type in the content below:

```
[Unit]
Description=Systemd service to restore iptables rules on startup.

[Service]
Type=simple
ExecStart=/usr/bin/iptables-startup.sh

[Install]
WantedBy=multi-user.target
```

And just like earlier, CTRL+O, press enter, then CTRL+X. Or CTRL+S with the gui text editors.

After that you will have to copy that service file to /etc/systemd/system/ which is another important directory of Systemd. Use the command below:

```
$ cp /lib/systemd/system/iptables-startup.service /etc/systemd/system/
```

At long last, you're all set to test your shiny new Systemd service!

```
$ systemctl start iptables-startup
```

After that, do kindly check the status of your service:

```
$ systemctl status iptables-startup
```

Please compare it to the output shown below as a successful start should resemble it.

```
mint@mint:~$ sudo cp /lib/systemd/system/iptables-startup.service /etc/systemd/system/
mint@mint:~$ systemctl start iptables-startup
mint@mint:~$ systemctl status iptables-startup
● iptables-startup.service - Systemd service to restore iptables rules on startup.
   Loaded: loaded (/etc/systemd/system/iptables-startup.service; disabled; vendor preset: enabled)
   Active: inactive (dead)

Nov 20 17:02:35 mint systemd[1]: Started Systemd service to restore iptables rules on startup..
mint@mint:~$ sudo iptables -S INPUT
-P INPUT DROP
mint@mint:~$ systemctl enable iptables-startup
Created symlink /etc/systemd/system/multi-user.target.wants/iptables-startup.service → /etc/systemd/system/iptables-startup.service.
```

Systemd service unit creation reference; Featured distro: Linux Mint

Should there be no problems then it should be all good to have it run on startup by invoking this command:

```
$ systemctl enable iptables-startup
```

Your iptables rules should now be reloaded every time your installed Linux instance reboots.

35. Steps to restore the iptables rules on startup for a GNU/Linux system using sysvinit as init:
The steps to take for Sysvinit is actually the same as OpenRC but the only difference is that you will no longer have to invoke rc-update because Sysvinit will literally execute anything placed in /etc/init.d as long as you don't forget to set it as executable using chmod.

Main topic closure

I hope that taught you a whole lot about how to properly configure the host-based iptables firewall of GNU/Linux and I sincerely hope you'll be able to put this to good use in securing your GNU/Linux endpoints and servers.

Should you find the need to do a more in-depth study about iptables then I highly suggest you use the man command to view the man pages of iptables that already comes with the iptables program itself in GNU/Linux.

Accessing the man pages is as easy as invoking:

```
$ man iptables
```

For accessing iptables' extensions and modules, invoke:

```
$ man iptables-extensions
```

Extras

Basic protection from reconnaissance

One of the first things that you are told when it comes to red teaming/penetration testing is that the very first step would always be about reconnaissance AKA gathering as much information as you can about a target through various methods available to you.

Good blue teamers know the fact that it is of utmost importance to erect as much deterrence as you can against all possible threats there is against your infrastructure and one of those should always be preventing the enemy from gathering essential information against you or adding difficulties to their efforts in possibly knowing what's beyond the horizons that they are trying to infiltrate.

The less they know, the less prepared they could possibly be in trying to perform a planned/coordinated attack.

That said, one of the most basic ways of reconaissance is through the use of icmp packets and I must mention that nmap, a renowned pentesting reconnaissance tool, uses icmp packets (along with special tcp packets) to gather information about a target system.

For the application of this using iptables, these rules should do the trick:

```
$ iptables -t raw -A OUTPUT -p icmp -j DROP
$ iptables -t mangle -I OUTPUT 1 -p icmp -j DROP
```

I added the same rule to mangle because at the end of the day, the filtering system of the Linux kernel is also a program by nature and you never know when a vulnerability suddenly appears one day that allows malicious packets to skip a rule or two. But please be advised, you should not set the mangle rule on devices that have low processing power as more rules mean potentially greater performance demands.

Finally, I encourage you to research more about reconnaissance, icmp, icmp packet types. Knowing icmp packet types enabled you to determine which icmp packets to allow through the firewall in order to help occasional troubleshooting efforts such as the use of the ping and traceroute command. Don't forget that some programs actually rely on the use of icmp packets for their own functionality so always remember to occasionally include that in your research scope when new programs malfunction/are unable to perform certain actions.

Uncomplicated Firewall (ufw) in GNU/Linux

Uncomplicated Firewall, **ufw** in short, is a program that provides an easy-to-use terminal-based interface for the user to configure the iptables firewall in Linux. It has a graphical counterpart called **gufw** and as its name, graphical ufw, implies, it provides a graphical user interface (GUI) to configure iptables firewall rules through the terminal-based interface provided by ufw.

I will not be discussing the usage of ufw because it discourages the potential growth of critical thinking that occurs through the learning of iptables' in-depth usage. I have chosen to add it for the sake of general knowledge.

Just to let you know, not all GNU/Linux distributions come with ufw and/or gufw by default – which forces you to connect out into the dangerous internet just for the sake of downloading and installing ufw/gufw... providing an adequate time frame for hackers to easily pwn you as most GNU/Linux distributions come with avahi-daemon, samba, and cups printing service by default and for your information, these services are easy open tickets of pwnage for hackers.

Protips:

- o You can make ufw block ipv6 and set default policies by editing the textfile located at → /etc/default/ufw
- o The set of default ipv4 rules that ufw/gufw sets as soon as you enable it is listed at the textfile located at → /etc/ufw/before.rules
- o For default ipv6 rules that would be → /etc/ufw/before6.rules
- o There are many other firewalls rule related stuff located at /etc/ufw/ so I highly encourage you to explore it!

ufw vs gufw

The main difference between ufw and gufw is the fact that gufw provides a graphical user interface (GUI).

How the gufw looks like as shown

It is common knowledge that most beginners in GNU/Linux are used to always having a graphical/visual interface in order to help them navigate and get stuff done. With respect to that, gufw was made in order to help beginners embrace GNU/Linux instead of scaring them away by forcing them to use the terminal.

Deep Packet Inspection (DPI)

As an added bonus to iptables as a topic, I wanted to briefly discuss deep packet inspection because it is typically used alongside firewalls or as a feature that comes with an NGFW.

As its name implies, deep packet inspection literally means an in-depth inspection of packets in order to potentially determine the application that sent the packet as well as finding out the nature and purpose of the packet.

It's a very useful feature that goes hand-in-hand along with other NGFW features that allows a user to allow/block connections made by specific applications.

For example, a company is worried about its users' productivity being affected by social media and they have found out that **blocking ports** alone **wasn't enough** to prevent its users from getting through to social media networks – hinting at the fact that users were using VPNs that connect through to the HTTPS standard port of 443.

Blocking port 443 is no good because that would effectively block ALL HTTPS connections being attempted by web browsers to all websites that support HTTPS and sticking to port 80 HTTP connections is VERY DANGEROUS because data is unencrypted and can easily fall victim to Man-in-the-middle (MITM) attacks.

Deep packet inspection to the rescue! DPI allows the firewall to tell which packets headed to port 443 are from a VPN and effectively intercept it to prevent VPNs from working.

Note: Deep packet inspection is an independent feature and does not necessarily need to come with a firewall. It can be an independent program of its own that provides an interface for other programs to use.

Resources

https://stuffphilwrites.com/2014/09/iptables-processing-flowchart/
As the source of the image that shown the order of table processing by iptables.
https://www.linode.com/docs/guides/start-service-at-boot/
As reference for the iptables-restore Systemd service section
Information written in this article are written in my own words according to my own understanding that was cultivated through years of experience of the various tech discussed in this article except for the part about adding a Systemd service where I used Linode's tutorial about it. The said understanding was cultivated and is aided by information coming from manual pages which come with its respective programs in GNU/Linux and all 3 of which are accessible by using the man command in GNU/Linux.

Special thanks to these amazing authors of programs and manpages:

iptables authors:
- "**Rusty Russell** originally wrote iptables, in early consultation with **Michael Neuling**."
- "**Marc Boucher** made Rusty abandon ipnatctl by lobbying for a generic packet selection framework in iptables, then wrote the mangle table, the owner match, the mark stuff, and ran around doing cool stuff everywhere."
- "**James Morris** wrote the TOS target, and tos match."
- "**Jozsef Kadlecsik** wrote the REJECT target."
- "**Harald Welte** wrote the ULOG and NFQUEUE target, the new libiptc, as well as the TTL, DSCP, ECN matches and targets."

"The Netfilter Core Team is: **Jozsef Kadlecsik**, **Pablo Neira Ayuso**, **Eric Leblond**, **Florian Westphal** and **Arturo Borrero Gonzalez**. Emeritus Core Team members are: **Marc Boucher**, **Martin Josefsson**, **Yasuyuki Kozakai**, **James Morris**, **Harald Welte** and **Rusty Russell**."

Excerpts are from the AUTHOR section of iptables' manpage in GNU/Linux → iptables(8)
The manual page was originally written by **Herve Eychenne <rv@wallfire.org>**.
Manual pages as of this writing applies to iptables/ip6tables version 1.8.2.
This entry also includes the manual pages of iptables-extensions(8)

ufw authors
"ufw is Copyright 2008-2014, **Canonical Ltd.**"
Excerpt from the AUTHOR section of ufw's manpage in GNU/Linux → ufw(8)
The manual page was originally written by **Jamie Strandboge <jamie@canonical.com>**
Manual pages version date as of this writing is February 2016

gufw author
"Gufw is (C) 2008-2018, **Marcos Alvarez Costales <https://launchpad.net/~costales>**." - Excerpt from the AUTHOR section of gufw's manpage in GNU/Linux → gufw(8)
The manual page was originally written by the same author.
Manual pages version date as of this writing is 23 June 2018

openrc authors:
"**Roy Marples <roy@marples.name>**"
"**The OpenRC Team <openrc@gentoo.org>**"
- Excerpt from the AUTHOR section of rc-update's manpage in GNU/Linux → RC-UPDATE(8)
The manual pages were originally written by the same author/s.
rc-update's manual page version date as of this writing is 13 January 2014

systemd authors
Systemd authors are not mentioned in its respective manpages but you should be able to know them by visiting Freedesktop.org.

sysvinit author:
"**Miquel van Smoorenburg <miquels@cistron.nl>**"
- Excerpt from the copyright file found at /usr/share/doc/sysvinit-core/ of MX Linux
There are many varying authors and maintainers of sysvinit packages on each major distro like debian, arch, and gentoo which is too many to include in this book, but they are appropriately credited on each distro's respective sysvinit copyright/AUTHORS file.

SSH Server Hardening

By: Carlyle Colins

Commands to know/use for reference:

- ps -ef | grep 'sshd' --this command looks for the ssh server running on the Linux machine. This command also works for looking for pretty much anything in the active process list. Just replace the sshd with the name of the software or service you are looking for.
- sshd -t --this command test runs the ssh software's configuration file.
- sshd -T --this command shows the current configuration variables for the ssh software
- ping 1.2.3.4 --- this command tests connectivity between the machine you run this from and the destination IP address you use (in place of 1.2.3.4)
- systemctl reload ssh.service -This command reloads to sshd config file (like a reboot of the SSH server)
- sudo lsb_release -a -This checks the version and codename of the OS
- sudo apt-get --purge remove sshd --this removes the sshd software. I wouldn't type this as is...it may break the lab. But using this command with a different service name may just be what you need to do.
- ls - this command lists the software packages installed on the system and the 2nd command "grep" filters for anything you want to look for. This is very useful in showing proof that certain services/software are no longer installed.
- Sudo apt-get update
- Sudo apt-get upgrade – both of these commands are a part of patch management. They will even tell you when there are packages that are no longer needed, but you still need to run the command to remove those packages.
- nmap -sS x.x.x.a,b,c this command is for port scans
- ls – directory listing
- cp - to copy a file from one place to another
- location of key pairs: /home/midterm/.ssh/id*
- ssh x.x.x.x is the format of the command to connect to the server

Task – Harden SSH Server

Network defense requires a deep tool set of both network and system administration. Understanding remote login protocols, their strengths and weaknesses is important. In this lab we are going to look at **ssh or secure shell**. **SSh** is a secure remote protocol which is used to work remotely on other machines or transfer data between computers using SCP (secure copy) command.

Confirm which VM is client and which VM is server. How do you do this? The process list in Linux is similar to the task manager in Windows. It shows what processes are running, what the process ID is (if you want to kill/stop it) and other information about processes running at the time you run the command.

Client IP: ifconfig 192.168.174.134
Server IP: ifconfig 192.168.174.136 (this IP can change during the lab, watch out)

How did you determine the IP of each machine? In ta terminal window on each virtual machine, an ifconfig command was issued to ascertain each IP Address

```
                                                   midterm@Client: ~
File  Edit  View  Search  Terminal  Help
midterm@Client:~$ ifconfig
ens33: flags=4163<UP,BROADCAST,RUNNING,MULTICAST>  mtu 1500
        inet 192.168.174.134  netmask 255.255.255.0  broadcast 192.168.174.255
        inet6 fe80::93d0:461:9dd5:63c0  prefixlen 64  scopeid 0x20<link>
        ether 00:0c:29:5e:81:d1  txqueuelen 1000  (Ethernet)
        RX packets 753  bytes 868661 (868.6 KB)
        RX errors 0  dropped 0  overruns 0  frame 0
        TX packets 355  bytes 39951 (39.9 KB)
        TX errors 0  dropped 0 overruns 0  carrier 0  collisions 0

lo: flags=73<UP,LOOPBACK,RUNNING>  mtu 65536
        inet 127.0.0.1  netmask 255.0.0.0
        inet6 ::1  prefixlen 128  scopeid 0x10<host>
        loop  txqueuelen 1000  (Local Loopback)
        RX packets 204  bytes 17573 (17.5 KB)
        RX errors 0  dropped 0  overruns 0  frame 0
        TX packets 204  bytes 17573 (17.5 KB)
        TX errors 0  dropped 0 overruns 0  carrier 0  collisions 0

midterm@Client:~$
```

```
                                                   midterm@server: ~
File  Edit  View  Search  Terminal  Help
midterm@server:~$ ifconfig
ens33: flags=4163<UP,BROADCAST,RUNNING,MULTICAST>  mtu 1500
        inet 192.168.174.136  netmask 255.255.255.0  broadcast 192.168.174.255
        inet6 fe80::7712:d233:e319:679f  prefixlen 64  scopeid 0x20<link>
        ether 00:0c:29:7d:87:4a  txqueuelen 1000  (Ethernet)
        RX packets 1596  bytes 1861805 (1.8 MB)
        RX errors 0  dropped 0  overruns 0  frame 0
        TX packets 1071  bytes 79743 (79.7 KB)
        TX errors 0  dropped 0 overruns 0  carrier 0  collisions 0

lo: flags=73<UP,LOOPBACK,RUNNING>  mtu 65536
        inet 127.0.0.1  netmask 255.0.0.0
        inet6 ::1  prefixlen 128  scopeid 0x10<host>
        loop  txqueuelen 1000  (Local Loopback)
        RX packets 230  bytes 19239 (19.2 KB)
        RX errors 0  dropped 0  overruns 0  frame 0
        TX packets 230  bytes 19239 (19.2 KB)
        TX errors 0  dropped 0 overruns 0  carrier 0  collisions 0

midterm@server:~$
```

Confirm network communications from client to server. Do you have network connectivity? Yes yes/no
What did you do check connectivity? In a terminal window in each virtual machine, a ping command was issued to the opposing IP Address to test connectivity.

```
                                                   midterm@Client:
File  Edit  View  Search  Terminal  Help
midterm@Client:~$ ping 192.168.174.136
PING 192.168.174.136 (192.168.174.136) 56(84) bytes of data.
64 bytes from 192.168.174.136: icmp_seq=1 ttl=64 time=0.296 ms
64 bytes from 192.168.174.136: icmp_seq=2 ttl=64 time=0.520 ms
64 bytes from 192.168.174.136: icmp_seq=3 ttl=64 time=0.767 ms
64 bytes from 192.168.174.136: icmp_seq=4 ttl=64 time=0.457 ms
64 bytes from 192.168.174.136: icmp_seq=5 ttl=64 time=0.699 ms
^C
--- 192.168.174.136 ping statistics ---
5 packets transmitted, 5 received, 0% packet loss, time 106ms
rtt min/avg/max/mdev = 0.296/0.547/0.767/0.171 ms
midterm@Client:~$
```

```
                              midterm@server: ~                              _  □  ⊗
 File Edit View Search Terminal Help
midterm@server:~$ ping 192.168.174.134
PING 192.168.174.134 (192.168.174.134) 56(84) bytes of data.
64 bytes from 192.168.174.134: icmp_seq=1 ttl=64 time=0.264 ms
64 bytes from 192.168.174.134: icmp_seq=2 ttl=64 time=0.283 ms
64 bytes from 192.168.174.134: icmp_seq=3 ttl=64 time=0.411 ms
64 bytes from 192.168.174.134: icmp_seq=4 ttl=64 time=0.748 ms
64 bytes from 192.168.174.134: icmp_seq=5 ttl=64 time=0.765 ms
^C
--- 192.168.174.134 ping statistics ---
5 packets transmitted, 5 received, 0% packet loss, time 96ms
rtt min/avg/max/mdev = 0.264/0.494/0.765/0.220 ms
midterm@server:~$ █
```

Connect to the SSH server (from the client machine). On the initial authentication challenge, a key will be provided. And then it will ask for the password. **Is this the server key or client key? What is it for? How does it work? Say 'yes' to accept key.** I believe this is the public server key. The key is used to authenticate the server to the host and add the server IP Address to the known authenticated devices. The key is configured by the administrator and verifies that both client and server have the same key.

```
midterm@Client:~$ ssh 192.168.174.136
The authenticity of host '192.168.174.136 (192.168.174.136)' can't be established.
ECDSA key fingerprint is SHA256:a8q7eYI0d9WyMvS+G8sG+Ze84d4EWTD5JbFEw8UtYiQ.
Are you sure you want to continue connecting (yes/no)? █
```

Now to confirm that we are working with stable versions of virtual machines, **confirm what versions of the OS each are running.**

VM1 OS version and codename: Cosmic Ubuntu 18.10
VM2 OS version and codename: Cosmic Ubuntu 18.10

```
 File Edit View Search Terminal Help
midterm@server:~$ sudo lsb_release -a
[sudo] password for midterm:
No LSB modules are available.
Distributor ID: Ubuntu
Description:    Ubuntu 18.10
Release:        18.10
Codename:       cosmic
midterm@server:~$ █
```
```
 File Edit View Search Terminal Help
midterm@Client:~$ sudo lsb_release -a
[sudo] password for midterm:
No LSB modules are available.
Distributor ID: Ubuntu
Description:    Ubuntu 18.10
Release:        18.10
Codename:       cosmic
midterm@Client:~$ █
```

There are a large number of configurable variables on a SSH server. We will be tackling a few important ones. In the field, reading man pages is a good skill, but knowing the top techniques for hardening an OS or a server running on a host is even more important.

_ Upgrading and Patching Systems
_ Cryptography
_ Disabling Unnecessary Services or Programs
_ Limiting Access
_ Data Confidentiality
_ Baseline Configurations

Investigate the server. There services running on this server that shouldn't be Try to connect on different ports/network services. There are 3 you are looking for. You could run a nmap or use some Linux commands. There are several quick ways. You can check the process list for software running that is software that shouldn't be there. And you could even open up a browser on the client machine and point to the server IP address. What do you see?

21/tcp open ftp, 80/tcp open http, telnet. When I point the to the IP Address of the server on a web browser, I get the home page of MSNBC News. I did finally see the Telnet service after using the dpkg – list | grep 'telnet' command. However, I did not show using the nmap scan as an open port.

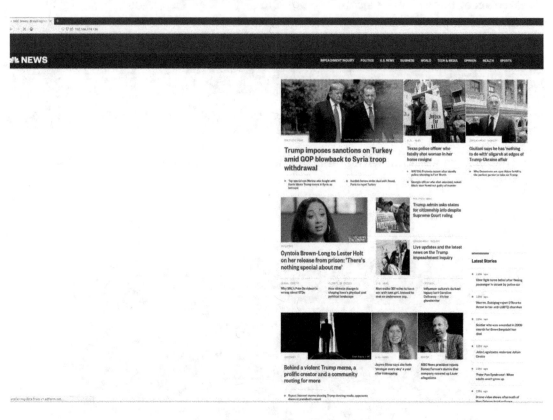

Bonus points: Look on the hamburger menu for the site, do you see anything strange? How many strange things can you find? Hint: there are 4. (This is bonus, don't spend too much time here). If the browser doesn't fully load, please let me know. My web browser pulled a MSNBC News website. On the righthand side of the menu the site has a link for, "click here I dare you", "Professor Deehring's Very Special Web Page for CTS240", and "Special Fake News Features."

In a production setting you could run a script or generate a fancy regex to see clear all services running on this machine. At this point there are 3 services to uninstall, ftp and http and telnet. They are vsftpd and apache2 software. **Remove these services and show proof they are removed.** Hint: the kill command only stops the service from running, it doesn't uninstall the software.

Now it's time to see if this system is patched and updated. (there are a few packages that need to be uninstalled.). **Remove these packages and show proof they are gone.**

```
midterm@server:~$ sudo apt-get upgrade
Reading package lists... Done
Building dependency tree
Reading state information... Done
Calculating upgrade... Done
The following packages were automatically installed and are no longer required:
  libncursesw5 libtinfo5
Use 'sudo apt autoremove' to remove them.
0 upgraded, 0 newly installed, 0 to remove and 0 not upgraded.
midterm@server:~$ sudo apt autoremove
Reading package lists... Done
Building dependency tree
Reading state information... Done
The following packages will be REMOVED:
  libncursesw5 libtinfo5
0 upgraded, 0 newly installed, 2 to remove and 0 not upgraded.
After this operation, 856 kB disk space will be freed.
Do you want to continue? [Y/n] Y
(Reading database ... 169006 files and directories currently installed.)
Removing libncursesw5:amd64 (6.1+20180210-4ubuntu1) ...
Removing libtinfo5:amd64 (6.1+20180210-4ubuntu1) ...
Processing triggers for libc-bin (2.28-0ubuntu1) ...
midterm@server:~$
```

Now that we have taken some steps to harden the server's operating system. Now let's harden the server itself. First things first, let's backup the configuration file, because if you break it....you need this file to get your server back up and running.

```
sudo cp /etc/ssh/sshd_config sshd_config.backup
```

```
midterm@Client:~$ ssh 192.168.174.136
midterm@192.168.174.136's password:
Welcome to Ubuntu 18.10 (GNU/Linux 4.18.0-25-generic x86_64)

 * Documentation:  https://help.ubuntu.com
 * Management:      https://landscape.canonical.com
 * Support:         https://ubuntu.com/advantage


0 packages can be updated.
0 updates are security updates.

Last login: Wed Feb 19 20:25:21 2020 from 192.168.174.134
midterm@server:~$ sudo cp /etc/ssh/sshd_config ssh_config.backup
[sudo] password for midterm:
midterm@server:~$
```

Next, we are going to disable password authentication and enable SSH keys. First, we are going to make some public key encryption keys. They come in pairs. Private and public. Run the following command to generate your keys on the **client machine**. Do not run this command `sudo`. It will ask you for a passphrase to protect the key. You can keep this blank, but I do not recommend that. A private SSH key with no passphrase protection can be used by anyone with possession of that key to access the server.

```
ssh-keygen
```

Show proof of your key pair ASCII art.

```
midterm@Client:~$ ssh-keygen
Generating public/private rsa key pair.
Enter file in which to save the key (/home/midterm/.ssh/id_rsa): scooper
Enter passphrase (empty for no passphrase):
Enter same passphrase again:
Your identification has been saved in scooper.
Your public key has been saved in scooper.pub.
The key fingerprint is:
SHA256:Xi9lC53mWQETnC8aBLlkdBslf88w+2SOePAWAATOxL8 midterm@ubuntu
The key's randomart image is:
+---[RSA 2048]----+
|      o==*o=o     |
|      +=..*oo     |
|      oo+. o.=    |
|      . o..+.B    |
|       S o+B.+ =  |
|      . .EB B B   |
|       . . * = o  |
|          . o     |
|                  |
+----[SHA256]-----+
```

Ssh-copy-id

Then you need to share your public key with the SSH server. Use the ssh-copy-id command to send you public key to the server. Make sure you are using the correct username and IP address.

```
ssh-copy-id midterm@192.168.1.1
```

Now try logging in. You may be asked for your passphrase.

```
ssh midterm@192.168.234.1
```

You may get a message back that looks similar too:

```
The authenticity of host '192.168.1.1 (192.168.1.1)' can't be established.
ECDSA key fingerprint is ff:fd:d5:f9:66:fe:73:84:e1:56:cf:d6:ff:ff.
Are you sure you want to continue connecting (yes/no)?
```

After you accept the fingerprint, you will be able to authenticate to the server with no additional challenge. This is what happens when you trust the server IP with the fingerprint it provides. The fingerprint will be checked every time the client machine connects, and as long as the IP matches the fingerprint, it will allow an instant connection. This is SSH server management use keypair authentication.

Show proof that your login did not require a password.

Now that the SSH server is using keys for authentication, you must go into the configuration file of the sever (sshd_config) and disable password authentication. Anytime you change a setting you need to restart the service. Test that you can still login.

Let's change the port number that the SSH server is listening/running on. We are going to change it to port 2223. Make this change, restart the server, and test it. Remember that when you want to force a port on a command line like ssh 1.2.3.4 you need to add the tac p. It looks like: ssh 1.2.3.4 -p 2223.

Show proof that the client can connect via SSH on port 2223.

```
# Change to yes if you don't trust ~/.ssh/known_hosts for
# HostbasedAuthentication
#IgnoreUserKnownHosts no
# Don't read the user's ~/.rhosts and ~/.shosts files
#IgnoreRhosts yes

# To disable tunneled clear text passwords, change to no here!
PasswordAuthentication no
#PermitEmptyPasswords no

# Change to yes to enable challenge-response passwords (beware issues with
# some PAM modules and threads)
ChallengeResponseAuthentication no

# Kerberos options
#KerberosAuthentication no
#KerberosOrLocalPasswd yes
#KerberosTicketCleanup yes
#KerberosGetAFSToken no

# GSSAPI options
#GSSAPIAuthentication no
#GSSAPICleanupCredentials yes
#GSSAPIStrictAcceptorCheck yes
```

```
midterm@server:~$ exit
logout
Connection to 192.168.174.136 closed.
midterm@Client:~$
midterm@Client:~$ ssh 192.168.174.136
^C
midterm@Client:~$ ssh 192.168.174.136
Welcome to Ubuntu 18.10 (GNU/Linux 4.1

 * Documentation:  https://help.ubuntu.com
 * Management:     https://landscape.canonical.com
 * Support:        https://ubuntu.com/advantage


0 packages can be updated.
0 updates are security updates.

Last login: Wed Feb 19 23:44:30 2020 from 192.168.174.134
midterm@server:~$
```

What other areas of the OS and server could you harden and why? Site your sources and for bonus points, harden this server further and provide documentation and proof that it is completed.

On the server, we can activate the firewall using the "sudo ufw allow 2223/tcp" command to add a rule. Using the "sudo ufw enable" command we activate the firewall.

```
midterm@server:~$ sudo ufw status
Status: inactive
midterm@server:~$ sudo ufw allow 2223/tcp
Rules updated
Rules updated (v6)
midterm@server:~$ sudo ufw enable
Command may disrupt existing ssh connections. Proceed with operation (y|n)? Y
Firewall is active and enabled on system startup
midterm@server:~$ sudo ufw status
Status: active

To                         Action      From
--                         ------      ----
2223/tcp                   ALLOW       Anywhere
2223/tcp (v6)              ALLOW       Anywhere (v6)

midterm@server:~$
```

We check the status of the firewall by using the "sudo ufw status" command. To disable the firewall, use "sudo ufw disable." Rules can also be written to allow or deny specific IP addresses (Not Shown).exit (Ubuntu 18.04 LTS Tutorials for Ubuntu Server and Desktop n.d.)

You are done!

Conclusion

While this lab setup ssh on your VM1 machine. the operation of ssh on the network with respect to routers is no different. When routers have telnet disabled and ssh enabled, the security profile of the network device is improved, and that is our goal.

Basic Endpoint Hardening:
GNU/Linux
By: Kevin John O. Hermosa

As a blue teamer it is invaluable to know the basics when it comes to securing computers may it be a humble endpoint or a high-performance server. So, I shall be focusing on the basic yet extremely essential hardening steps to perform on a GNU/Linux operating system and these steps are:

1. Entering a new root and user password.
2. Identify services that are listening on your GNU/Linux machine.
3. Disabling and stopping unneeded services.
4. Customizing the mirrors set for updating.
5. Keeping your GNU/Linux installation up to date.

Entering a new root and user password

It is imperative that a user immediately changes the default passwords set on the operating system because it is the most common entry point for hackers and it's actually the method that takes the least amount of skill and effort.

Also, it is important for you to know as a user that there is an account named "root" in every Linux operating system and it is the most powerful account in there and holds authority over the most sensitive parts of your OS so please, **never ever forget to set a password for "root"**.

So, let's go ahead and set a password for "root". Open up a terminal and enter "sudo passwd root". Please refer to the image below:

Successful changing of root and user passwords using passwd

You will be prompted for a new password so start typing it away! Please don't worry if nothing appears when you start typing the new password; it's actually capturing your keyboard input so type in the new password then press enter.

After that, you will be prompted to retype the new password for the sake of confirmation.

A successful change of password should show you "passwd: password updated successfully" just like what is shown in the image.

You probably noticed that asides from updating the root password, I also updated the password of another account called "liveuser". It happens to be the username of the default user account for the Linux distribution AKA distro (or flavor) that I am using; it varies from distro to distro i.e., the username is "mint" for Linux mint, "redcore" for Redcore Linux, and etc.

It is a good idea to change the default password for that user account as well because it is the default account used for the computer's login screen.

With that, I want you to know that it is good practice to change your passwords as frequently as every 3 to 6 months in order to maintain a strong cybersecurity posture. Better yet, use a password manager like KeePass and Passbolt in order to help you maintain strong passwords across your accounts.

Identify services that are listening on Linux

The next step in increasing the distro's security is to first identify services that are listening on your network as hackers actively scout for these and utilize vulnerabilities to exploit the listening program to take control of your computer. These services are programs ran on startup by default as part of your GNU/Linux distro installation. This guide will also include how to disable and stop services on distros using openrc and sysvinit as the initialization system.

Getting a list of these can be done by invoking the following command to the terminal:

```
$ sudo ss -ltpun
```

List of listening programs displayed by using ss

There are GNU/Linux distros that do not have the ss command by default so I'm gonna teach how to do the same thing using netstat.

```
$ sudo netstat -46lpn
```

List of listening programs displayed by using netstat

As you can see, there are many programs listening by default, and these usually come by default on many distros out there so I will be explaining what each are:

- **systemd-resolve** – a program responsible for performing DNS lookups which is needed when connecting to websites. This program is usually not needed because by default, the system will set a DNS server at /etc/resolv.conf after a DHCP query.
- **avahi-daemon** – a program that implements Apple's Zeroconf architecture. Usually not needed because there are simpler ways to interact with local machines in the network and I doubt Windows computers even have support for this by default.
- **cupsd** – a program responsible for communication with printers. You'll need this if you want to be printing documents on Linux but if not, it's safe to disable or remove it.
- **smbd** – a program made as part of the implementation of SAMBA in GNU/Linux which is responsible for network shares access and management. This is typically used in work environments but it's best to have this disabled or removed if it's not going to be used for work purposes because malware utilizes network shares to spread across a local network. And yes, malware exists in the world of Linux.
- **nomacs** – an image viewer program. Was included in the list because it was listening on localhost port 45454 as I was using it to review my screenshots. Thus, feel free to ignore this entry.

Do note that the list varies from distro to distro and at times there are even things that are ran on startup but are not even part of the list of services like Fedora's dleyna-renderer so you will have to perform additional research yourself in order to know what those programs/services do and disable it according to your use-cases.

Disabling and stopping unneeded services

Now let's proceed to disabling the services so they will no longer be run at startup.

```
$ sudo systemctl disable [service-name]
```

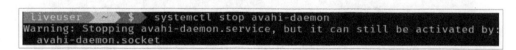

```
liveuser    ~    $    systemctl disable avahi-daemon
Removed /etc/systemd/system/dbus-org.freedesktop.Avahi.service.
Removed /etc/systemd/system/multi-user.target.wants/avahi-daemon.service.
Removed /etc/systemd/system/sockets.target.wants/avahi-daemon.socket.
```

Successful disablement of a service using systemctl

A successful disablement of a service should give you feedback that something was removed on the /etc/systemd/system/ directory.

After that, you should be all good on stopping said service using the same systemctl command.

```
$ sudo systemctl stop [service-name]
```

```
liveuser    ~    $    systemctl stop avahi-daemon
Warning: Stopping avahi-daemon.service, but it can still be activated by:
    avahi-daemon.socket
```

Successful stoppage of a service using systemctl

Getting that warning as shown in the image is normal as that's how avahi-daemon was designed. It simply means that the service will run again should a packet be received on the network port where the daemon's socket was listening. You may check a service's/socket's status by invoking:

```
$ systemctl status [name]
```

Status of avahi-daemon.socket; screenshot taken on Arch Linux-based SalientOS

Complete stoppage of this socket should be as simple as invoking:

```
$ sudo systemctl stop avahi-daemon.socket
```

You can now go ahead on disabling and stopping those unneeded services now that you know how to disable, stop, and query the status of a service.

Disablement and stoppage of various services in SalientOS

You may have noticed that some extra things were included in the disablement command like ntpd and nmb. Well apparently, some programs only start listening and appear on the list after connecting the computer running GNU/Linux to a network or internet connection so please do note that.

Another thing to note is the "org.cups.cupsd.service" where it was just "cupsd" in the list. I have no idea why the systemd service unit for cups is named like this but if you cannot find something then it's a good idea to view the full list of running services which can be done by by invoking $ systemctl or $ systemctl --list-units

Please do another query of listening programs after you have done the necessary disablement and stoppage.

There are no more listening programs listed because they were disabled and stopped

Once you have disabled and stopped all unneeded services then you should see an empty or a cleaner list with fewer entries on it where the lesser, the better.

Should you ever find yourself in trouble because you are using a GNU/Linux distro that is not using Systemd then fear not! I will be covering how to do the same things in a disro utilizing Openrc and Sysvinit as init.

Display all Openrc services and their respective runlevels:

```
$ rc-update show
```

Disablement of a service in Openrc:

```
$ sudo rc-update del [service-name]
```

157

Disablement of a service in Openrc that is in the boot runlevel:

```
$ sudo rc-update del [service-name] boot
```

Stoppage of a service in Openrc (2 ways):

```
$ sudo rc-service [service-name] stop
$ sudo rc-service [service-name] zap
```

Querying status of a service in Openrc:

```
$ rc-service [service-name] status
```

Checking all services in Sysvinit:

```
$ ls /etc/init.d/
```

Disablement of a service in Sysvinit (2 ways):

```
$ sudo chmod -x /etc/init.d/[service-name]
$ sudo chmod 644 /etc/init.d/[service-name]
```

Stoppage of a service in Sysvinit:

```
$ sudo /etc/init.d/[service-name] stop
```

Customizing the mirrors set for updating

The next big thing that you should be doing is modifying the mirrors configured for updating your GNU/Linux distro as these are usually limited according to the country that you specified during installation and most of these are HTTP-only mirrors which means that the connection is not encrypted and vulnerably to MITM attacks.

Many people these days are actually using either Debian-based distros or Arch-based distros so rest-assured that changing mirrors for those are included in this guide along with Fedora.

Let's start with Debian. The mirrors file/s are located at /etc/apt/sources.list.d/

```
Terminal - demo@mx1: ~
demo@mx1:~
$ ls /etc/apt/sources.list.d/
antix.list  debian.list  debian-stable-updates.list  mx.list  various.list
```

List of mirror files in the /etc/apt/sources.list.d/ directory

It looks more populated than your usual Debian-based distro because I am using MX Linux which is a Debian-based distro made and maintained by antiX and Mephis teams where they pull their personally maintained packages for this distro.

The main Debian mirrors file for this distro should be debian.list and debian-stable-updates.list and it appears that a seperate mirror list is being used for package updates.

Please take a look at the contents of both files:

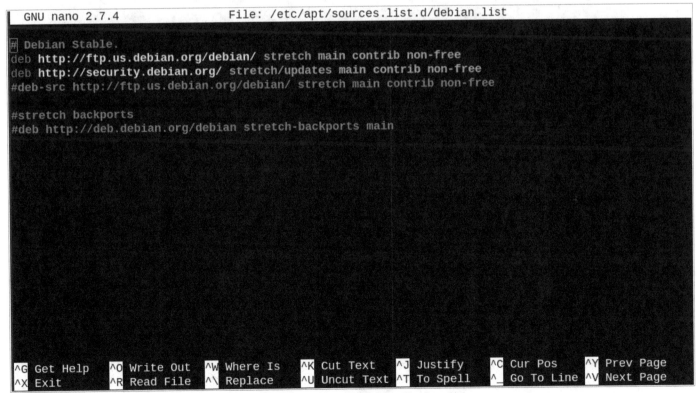

```
demo@mx1:~
$ sudo cat /etc/apt/sources.list.d/debian.list
# Debian Stable.
deb http://ftp.us.debian.org/debian/ stretch main contrib non-free
deb http://security.debian.org/ stretch/updates main contrib non-free
#deb-src http://ftp.us.debian.org/debian/ stretch main contrib non-free

#stretch backports
#deb http://deb.debian.org/debian stretch-backports main
demo@mx1:~
$ sudo cat /etc/apt/sources.list.d/debian-stable-updates.list
# Debian stretch Updates
deb http://ftp.us.debian.org/debian/ stretch-updates main contrib non-free
```

Contents of debian.list and debian-stable-updates.list displayed for reference

The main difference between these two files is that the first file includes security.debian.org as a mirror and that the second file is using the same mirror but explicitly indicates "stretch-updates" which means that the second file is strictly for getting package updates.

Do note that "stretch" is the name used to indicate to a particular version of Debian AKA Debian Stretch and this tells you that the particular version of the MX Linux that I am using is based on Debian Stretch.

The part about "main contrib non-free" specifies the sections of packages to be queried by for updating and installing packages/programs. "main" is where a large collection of free and open-source GNU/Linux packages are located, contrib is where various packages maintained by contributors are located, and nonfree is where various proprietary packages are located like the Steam game store, Skype, and etc.

So, for example, you erased the "non-free" inside the mirrors file then you will no longer be able to install Steam, Skype, etc. until you've written it back in there.

Now let's proceed to editing the the main Debian mirrors file. Please invoke the following command:

```
$ sudo nano /etc/apt/sources.list.d/debian.list
```

```
  GNU nano 2.7.4              File: /etc/apt/sources.list.d/debian.list

# Debian Stable.
deb http://ftp.us.debian.org/debian/ stretch main contrib non-free
deb http://security.debian.org/ stretch/updates main contrib non-free
#deb-src http://ftp.us.debian.org/debian/ stretch main contrib non-free

#stretch backports
#deb http://deb.debian.org/debian stretch-backports main




^G Get Help    ^O Write Out   ^W Where Is    ^K Cut Text    ^J Justify     ^C Cur Pos     ^Y Prev Page
^X Exit        ^R Read File   ^\ Replace     ^U Uncut Text  ^T To Spell    ^_ Go To Line  ^V Next Page
```

nano command being used to view debian.list for editing purposes

As you can see in the image above, the nano command is a terminal-based text editor where you can edit text-based files from the comfort of your terminal.

I shall be using mirror.aarnet.edu.au for the purpose of this guide because they are one of the best mirrors out there in terms of performance. We will then proceed to putting that mirror on this file.

Please go ahead and comment-out the default mirror set in debian.list by putting a hashtag AKA the number sign (#) before the line of text.

After that, you just go ahead and copy the default mirror's line of text then paste it just above that commented-out line.

Change the ftp.us.debian.org on the copy-pasted line and change it to mirror.aarnet.edu.au. Then add an s to http so it would become https.

Change the ftp.us.debian.org on the copy-pasted line and change it to mirror.aarnet.edu.au. Also, please change /debian/ to /pub/debian/ because the directory structure is different in aarnet's mirror.

Please refer to the image on the next page in order to see how it should look like after editing.

```
  GNU nano 2.7.4              File: /etc/apt/sources.list.d/debian.list

# Debian Stable.
deb https://mirror.aarnet.edu.au/pub/debian/ stretch main contrib non-free
#deb http://ftp.us.debian.org/debian/ stretch main contrib non-free
deb http://security.debian.org/ stretch/updates main contrib non-free
#deb-src http://ftp.us.debian.org/debian/ stretch main contrib non-free

#stretch backports
#deb http://deb.debian.org/debian stretch-backports main




                              [ Read 8 lines ]
^G Get Help    ^O Write Out   ^W Where Is    ^K Cut Text   ^J Justify    ^C Cur Pos    ^Y Prev Page
^X Exit        ^R Read File   ^\ Replace     ^U Uncut Text ^T To Spell   ^_ Go To Line ^V Next Page
```

debian.list after it was edited using nano

Once done with the editing, invoke CTRL+O to prepare for saving the file. The bottom of your terminal should look like the image below:

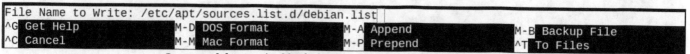

```
File Name to Write: /etc/apt/sources.list.d/debian.list
^G Get Help       M-D DOS Format      M-A Append       M-B Backup File
^C Cancel         M-M Mac Format      M-P Prepend      ^T To Files
```

Bottom of the terminal looks like this after pressing CTRL+O in nano

Press enter in order to save the file. An indicator below should appear which tells you how many lines were written into the file.

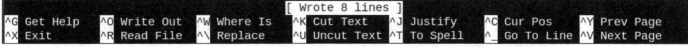

Bottom of the terminal shows this indicator upon pressing enter after CTRL+O in nano

Press CTRL+X to exit nano. Now go and do the same for debian-stable-updates.list and ensure that it will have "stretch-updates" beside it and NOT "stretch".

You're all set for Debian after that. Please proceed to the "Keeping your GNU/Linux machine up to date" section for details on how to update your distro which will now use the mirror that you specified.

Moving on, this time it's Arch-Linux's mirrors that we are changing to mirror.aarnet.edu.au.

Arch-Linux's mirrors are located at /etc/pacman.d/mirrorlist so likewise, edit with nano.

```
$ sudo nano /etc/pacman.d/mirrorlist
```

```
##
## Arch Linux repository mirrorlist
## Generated on 2018-10-21
##

## Worldwide
#Server = http://mirrors.evowise.com/archlinux/$repo/os/$arch
Server = http://mirror.rackspace.com/archlinux/$repo/os/$arch

## Australia
#Server = https://mirror.aarnet.edu.au/pub/archlinux/$repo/os/$arch
#Server = http://archlinux.mirror.digitalpacific.com.au/$repo/os/$arch
#Server = http://ftp.iinet.net.au/pub/archlinux/$repo/os/$arch
#Server = http://mirror.internode.on.net/pub/archlinux/$repo/os/$arch
#Server = http://archlinux.melbourneitmirror.net/$repo/os/$arch
#Server = http://ftp.swin.edu.au/archlinux/$repo/os/$arch

## Austria
#Server = http://mirror.digitalnova.at/archlinux/$repo/os/$arch
#Server = http://mirror.easyname.at/archlinux/$repo/os/$arch
#Server = http://mirror.reisenbauer.ee/archlinux/$repo/os/$arch
#Server = https://mirror.reisenbauer.ee/archlinux/$repo/os/$arch

## Bangladesh
#Server = http://mirror.xeonbd.com/archlinux/$repo/os/$arch
```

A look at the /etc/pacman.d/mirrorlist file

As you can see, the mirrorlist file is packed by a large list of mirrors but only one is actively being used because everything else is commented out except the mirror.rackspace.com line.

Thankfully, mirror.aarnet.edu.au is already included in this mirrorlist file so a simple commenting-out of rackspace mirror's line using a hashtag AKA the number sign (#) will do. Follow this up removing the hashtag on the left of mirror.aarnet.edu.au easily finishes the job of setting things up for your Arch-Linux distro.

If your mirrorlist file happens to not have included the https aarnet mirror, then please refer to the image on the format of writing it down to your mirrorlist file. Don't copy the # along with you or else it will be commented-out and will not be used.

Press CTRL+O then press enter. Press CTRL+X to exit nano just like how it was in the section for Debian mirrors.

You're all set for Arch after that. Please proceed to the "Keeping your GNU/Linux machine up to date" section for details on how to update your distro which will now use the mirror that you specified.

Lastly for this section is Fedora which is a distribution being maintained by people connected to RHEL or Red Hat Enterprise Linux. The packages of RHEL can be used in Fedora and Fedora uses DNF which is the upcoming successor of YUM that is still being used in RHEL as a package manager.

The mirror lists for Fedora are located at /etc/yum.repos.d/

```
[liveuser@localhost-live ~]$ ls /etc/yum.repos.d
fedora-cisco-openh264.repo      fedora-updates.repo
fedora-modular.repo             fedora-updates-testing-modular.repo
fedora.repo                     fedora-updates-testing.repo
fedora-updates-modular.repo
```

A look at /etc/yum.repos.d/ which is the directory of Fedora's mirror lists

There is a lot of stuff in there, but we will be disregarding the "testing" repo files because these are only used when you are doing testing on to help out in the development of the distro.

So, I was planning on editing these files using nano yet again, but it turns out that nano is not packaged along with this Fedora workstation distro that I got... not sure what's up with that.

In any case, I have confirmed that fedora comes with gedit which is a gui text editor so we can go ahead and use that:

```
$ sudo gedit /etc/yum.repos.d/fedora-modular.repo
```

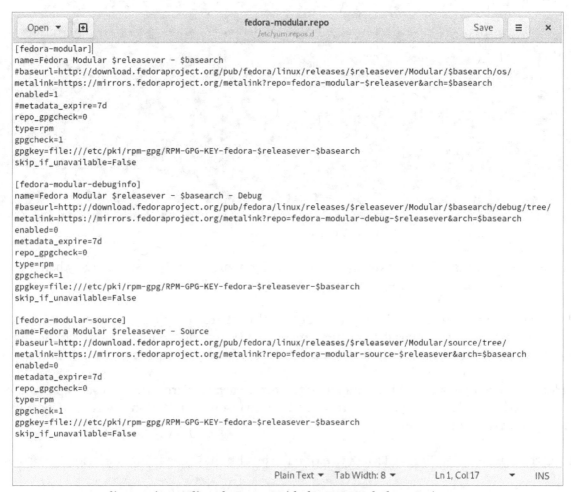

gedit – a gui text editor that comes with the GNOME desktop environment

That command should bring up a GUI-based text editor as shown in the image above.

Focus near the top and copy the "baseurl=http://download..." line. Paste it just above the same line. Comment-out the "metalink=https://mirrors..." line using a hashtag (#) at the beginning of the line.

Remove the hashtag on the baseurl line that you copied earlier then add an s to http for it to become https. Follow that up with changing "download.fedoraproject.org" into "mirror.aarnet.edu.au". Please refer to the image below on how the changes look like:

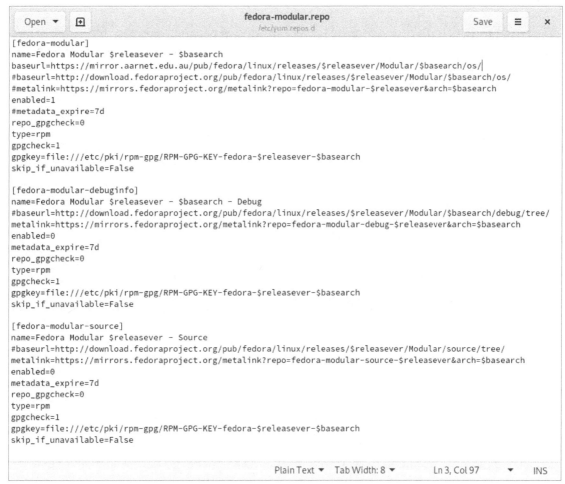

Reference to the changes done to fedora-modular.repo

Save the file after confirming your changes using the reference by pressing CTRL+S just like the usual notepad in Windows.

Repeat the steps for:

- fedora.repo
- fedora-updates.repo
- fedora-updates-modular.repo

One last thing about Fedora mirrors is the "enabled=1" parameter. This is the toggle for using the mirrors indicated above it and as you can see, there are three of these in fedora-modular.repo. That is because the repo file also contains mirror settings for debuginfo and the source repository which are definitely developer-level stuff and that is why they are set to "enabled=0" by default.

I want you to focus on the fedora-cisco-openh264.repo that is also located in /etc/yum.repos.d/ and the importance of this is that the repository is included as an option to install cisco's openh264 codec which is needed to play certain video file types like MP4 where the H.264 encoder is widely used.

Utilizing this is as simple as opening the file using gedit and changing "enabled=0" to "enabled=1" then installing it using dnf. Only thing is that I don't know the exact names of the packages to be installed using this repository, so I'll leave it as your little extra homework!

Now that we got those three outta the way let us proceed to actually updating the GNU/Linux distro!

Keeping your GNU/Linux installation up to date

Updating your GNU/Linux installation regularly is very important because package updates will tend to include bug-fixes or security updates to patch a vulnerability and likewise, stability improvements and the like.

So, for the final part of this guide, I shall be teaching you how to update a Debian-based distro, an Arch-based distro, and Fedora.

For Debian, it will be involving two commands:

```
$ sudo apt update
        and
$ sudo apt upgrade
        OR
$ sudo apt update && sudo apt upgrade
```

apt update will fetch the latest manifests from the repositories defined in the repository directory /etc/apt/sources.list.d/ while apt upgrade will update all your packages to the latest version. This is usually followed by a prompt to the user to get their confirmation to carry out the mass-update of all packages.

For Arch, it will involve only one command:

```
$ sudo pacman -Syu
```

Let me tell you about the parameters given to pacman:

-S is equivalent to "install" parameter of apt and dnf
-y will make pacman "download a fresh copy of the master package database from the server(s) defined in pacman.conf" as written in the manpages of pacman. Equivalent to "update" parameter of apt.
-u also invoked as --sysupgrade which will upgrade all out-of-date packages/packages with new versions.
-Syu combined is equivalent to "update" parameter of dnf and "update"+"upgrade" parameter of apt.

For Fedora, it also involves only one command:

```
$ sudo dnf update
```

This one command does the same thing as apt update && apt upgrade and will also show a prompt for confirmation to the user.

One last thing that I would like the readers to note is the fact that Debian-based distros and Fedora are not rolling releases, and this means that there is a fixed cycle of major releases where big updates are pushed to the distro which can only be carried out by a special parameter given to apt/dnf which will cause it to perform a distro-upgrade towards the new version. The good thing about Arch is that it's a rolling release and there is no need to perform a distro-upgrade because it does not use a major release cycle.

That's it for this writeup and I hope this will help the readers to become more familiar with the basic things to do on a Linux distro before settling down on it for daily use.

Resources

The screenshots are personally taken on my Artix Linux installation, live boot of MX Linux on my PC using a flash drive, and live boot of Fedora Workstation on my PC using a flash drive.

Special thanks to these amazing authors of programs and manpages:

nano authors

Made and maintained by GNU/Free Software Foundation
https://nano-editor.org/
https://savannah.gnu.org/bugs/?group=nano

openrc authors
"Roy Marples <roy@marples.name>"
"The OpenRC Team <openrc@gentoo.org>"
- Excerpt from the AUTHOR section of rc-update's manpage in GNU/Linux → RC-UPDATE(8)
The manual pages were originally written by the same author/s.
rc-update's manual page version date as of this writing is 13 January 2014

systemd authors
Systemd authors are not mentioned in its respective manpages but you should be able to know them by visiting Freedesktop.org.

sysvinit author
"Miquel van Smoorenburg <miquels@cistron.nl>"
- Excerpt from the copyright file found at /usr/share/doc/sysvinit-core/ of MX Linux
There are many varying authors and maintainers of sysvinit packages on each major distro like debian, arch, and gentoo which is too many to include in this book, but they are appropriately credited on each distro's respective sysvinit copyright/AUTHORS file.

apt authors
apt authors are not mentioned in its respective manpages, but you should be able to know them by visiting debian.org

pacman authors and maintainers
Current Maintainers:

- Allan McRae <allan@archLinux.org>
- Andrew Gregory <andrew.gregory.8@gmail.com>
- Dan McGee <dan@archLinux.org>
- Dave Reisner <dreisner@archLinux.org>
- Past major contributors:
- Judd Vinet <jvinet@zeroflux.org>
- Aurelien Foret <aurelien@archLinux.org>
- Aaron Griffin <aaron@archLinux.org>
- Xavier Chantry <shiningxc@gmail.com>
- Nagy Gabor **ngaba@bibl.u-szeged.hu**

Additional contributors can be found by using git shortlog -s on the pacman.git repository.
- Excerpt from the AUTHORS section of pacman's manpage in GNU/Linux → PACMAN(8)
pacman's manual page version date as of this writing is 2019-03-01

dnf authors
dnf authors are not mentioned in its respective manpages but you should be able to know them by visiting the project's homepage: https://github.com/rpm-software-management/dnf/

ThreatRESPONDER™ Platform

By: Jeremy Martin

The cybersecurity community is a small world inside a small world. You meet people, and it is not uncommon for your paths to cross again. I met the founder of NetSecurity, Inno Eroraha, at a Computer Forensics bootcamp about 15 years ago. A few years later, we worked on a penetration test together, and we have collaborated since.

Because of our working relationship, I was given the opportunity to test the ThreatResponder Platform when it was in Beta through the different version releases. ThreatResponder is a cloud-native endpoint threat detection and response (EDR) platform that adds threat prevention, hunting, analytics, intelligence, and forensics capabilities into the product. One of the things I like most about this solution is that the lightweight agent can be installed on almost any OS and allows you access to really dig into a target endpoint, regardless of its geolocation. Although the product is designed solely for DFIR, since I work with both DFIR and Penetration Testing/Red Teaming (two sides of the same coin), I did see some great potential on both sides on the first version. The product has only improved with more endpoint control in the management console. I believe ThreatResponder lives up to its claim of allowing DFIR and SOC analysts to perform a lot of security/forensics operations from a single pane of glass.

ThreatResponder's dashboards make both Incident Response and Threat Hunting very easy, especially when you are trying to verify a strange-looking process or a potential zero-day threat. You can drill down to view activities relating to a process such as parent/child process(es), registry/network activities, and threat score (derived from the platform's detection algorithms, machine learning, threat intelligence, and behaviors that leverage MITRE ATT&ACK). The report it generates on a process alone is massive. As a DFIR analyst, you should find the on-board Malyzer™ engine indispensable; this capability provides static and dynamic malware analyses with the click of a mouse, without the need of uploading suspicious binaries to third-party detonation chambers. A complete anatomy of a portable executable (PE) is rendered in seconds, showing capabilities of the potential malware being analyzed. This feature alone provides highly accurate results and saves the busy DFIR analyst days of detailed malware investigation.

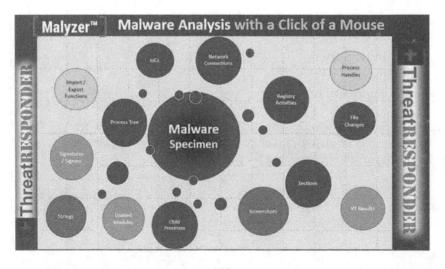

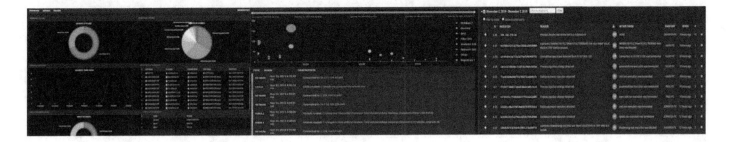

When you look under the hood, ThreatResponder leverages machine learning to automate a lot of the threat hunting operations. This helps save a lot of time and shows correlations that many analysts may miss. Running tools like Metasploit or CobaltStrike against a ThreatResponder protected endpoint, even leveraging the Veil Framework for evasion, will still get caught. Rootkits and shellcode alike can be found along with covert communication methods using encrypted tunnels. If you see the data before it makes the tunnel, it's usually still in plain text.

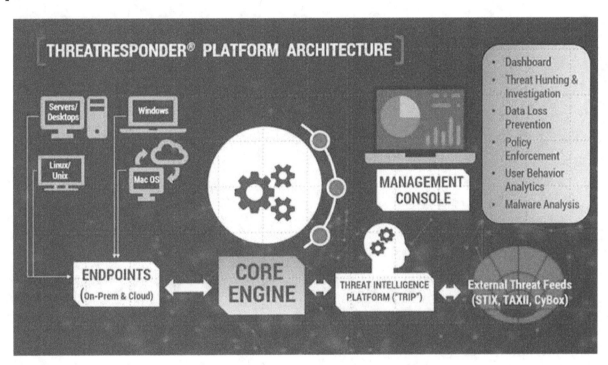

The platform also includes malicious document detection and prevention. If you have the need to investigate a malicious PDF or Office document, ThreatResponder prevents such execution and renders the embedded payload to provide context.

The team at NetSecurity has an extensive DFIR background, and it is nice to see the evidence collection capability added to this type of technology. This makes digital forensics MUCH easier with forensically-sound data capture. From here, you can analyze the information within the platform or offload it to another forensic solution.

For those of you who are in the malware analysis or reverse engineering fields, ThreatResponder Platform automates many of the basic processes, specifically static and dynamic analyses, and the ability to dump a process memory or "strings." There is no "easy button" in this field, but ThreatResponder is closer than what I have seen on the market without having to spend what you would on some of the bigger names.

With ThreatResponder being a cloud-based solution, you can hunt, investigate, remediate, contain, and manage the suspect system from anywhere in the world!

If you cannot tell, I REALLY like ThreatResponder

Cyber Secrets Contributors

Amy Martin, Editor
Daniel Traci, Editor/Design
Jeremy Martin, Editor/Author
Richard K. Medlin, Author
Frederico Ferreira, Author
Vishal M Belbase, Author
Mossaraf Zaman Khan, Author
Kevin John Hermosa, Author
LaShanda Edwards, Author
Carlyle Collins, Author
Nitin Sharma, Author
Ambadi MP, Author
Tajamul Sheeraz, Author
Steve "Butchy" Bartimote, Author

If you are interested in writing an article or walkthrough for Cyber Secrets or IWC Labs, please send an email to cir@InformationWarfareCenter.com

If you are interested in contributing to the CSI Linux project, please send an email to: conctribute@CSILinux.com

I wanted to take a moment to discuss some of the projects we are working on. They are a combination of commercial, community driven, & Open-Source projects.

 Cyber WAR (Weekly Awareness Report)

Everyone needs a good source for Threat Intelligence and the Cyber WAR is one resource that brings together over a dozen other data feeds into one place. It contains the latest news, tools, malware, and other security related information.

InformationWarfareCenter.com/CIR

CSI Linux (Community Linux Distro)

CSI Linux is a freely downloadable Linux distribution that focuses on Open-Source Intelligence (OSINT) investigation, traditional Digital Forensics, and Incident Response (DFIR), and Cover Communications with suspects and informants. This distribution was designed to help Law Enforcement with Online Investigations but has evolved and has been released to help anyone investigate both online and on the dark webs with relative security and peace of mind.

At the time of this publication, CSI Linux 2020.3 was released.

CSILinux.com

 **Cyber "Live Fire" Range (Linux Distro)**

This is a commercial environment designed for both Cyber Incident Response Teams (CIRT) and Penetration Testers alike. This product is a standalone bootable external drive that allows you to practice both DFIR and Pentesting on an isolated network, so you don't have to worry about organizational antivirus, IDP/IPS, and SIEMs lighting up like a Christmas tree, causing unneeded paperwork and investigations. This environment incorporates Kali and a list of vulnerable virtual machines to practice with. This is a great system for offline exercises to help prepare for Certifications like the Pentest+, Licensed Penetration Tester (LPT), and the OSCP.

 **CyberSec.TV**

We are building a site that pulls together Cyber Security videos from various sources to make great content easier to find.

Cyber Secrets

Cyber Secrets originally aired in 2013 and covers issues ranging from Anonymity on the Internet to Mobile Device forensics using Open-Source tools, to hacking. Most of the episodes are technical in nature. Technology is constantly changing, so some subjects may be revisited with new ways to do what needs to be done.

Just the Tip

Just the Tip is a video series that covers a specific challenge and solution within 2 minutes. These solutions range from tool usage to samples of code and contain everything you need to defeat the problems they cover.

Quick Tips

This is a small video series that discusses quick tips that covers syntax and other command line methods to make life easier

- CyberSec.TV
- Roku Channel: channelstore.roku.com/details/595145/cyber-secrets
- Amazon FireTV: amzn.to/3mpL1yU

 Active Facebook Community: Facebook.com/groups/cybersecrets

Information Warfare Center Publications

If you want to learn a little more about cybersecurity or are a seasoned professional looking for ways to hone your tradecraft? Are you interested in hacking? Do you do some form of Cyber Forensics or want to learn how or where to start? Whether you are specializing on dead box forensics, doing OSINT investigations, or working at a SOC, this publication series has something for you.

Cyber Secrets publications is a cybersecurity series that focuses on all levels and sides while having content for all skill levels of technology and security practitioners. There are articles focusing on SCADA/ICS, Dark Web, Advanced Persistent Threats (APT)s, OSINT, Reconnaissance, computer forensics, threat intelligence, hacking, exploit development, reverse engineering, and much more.

Other publications

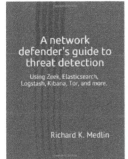

A network defender's guide to threat detection: Using Zeek, Elasticsearch, Logstash, Kibana, Tor, and more. This book covers the entire installation and setup of your own SOC in a Box with ZEEK IDS, Elasticstack, with visualizations in Kibana. amzn.to/2AZqBJW

IWC Labs: Encryption 101 – Cryptography Basics and Practical Usage is a great guide doe those just starting in the field or those that have been in for a while and want some extra ideas on tools to use. This book is also useful for those studying for cybersecurity certifications. amzn.to/30aseOr

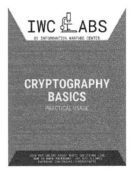

Are you getting into hacking or computer forensics and want some more hands-on practice with more tools and environments? Well, we have something that might just save you some time and money. This book walks you through building your own cyber range. amzn.to/306bTu0

This IWC Lab covers privilege escalation after exploitation. There are many ways to escalate privileges on both windows and Linux and we cover many of them including docker exploitation.

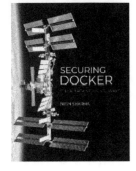

Containerization is increasing widely with the adoption of Docker for container workloads. It's always easy to spin a container and start working on it. But wait! Have you ever thought of the security of your container workloads? Did your Docker Container ecosystems can defend themselves against latest sophisticated attacks? Or you might be relying on legacy security systems to make them do the security work for you. If you are still thinking the same, you need to cope up with the existing solutions since container security concerns impose huge risks to the IT infrastructure... amzn.to/34KFDPq